A Reader's Guide to Literary Terms

KARL BECKSON AND ARTHUR GANZ

Farrar, Straus and Giroux
New York

A Reader's Guide to

LITERARY TERMS

A Dictionary

Copyright © 1960 by The Noonday Press
Library of Congress Catalog Card Number: 60-14127
Manufactured in the United States of America
by H. Wolff, New York
Designed by Marshall Lee
Eleventh printing, 1969

To Estelle
and
To J.G.

Acknowledgments

The authors wish to thank those listed below for permission to reprint certain works quoted in this volume:

George Allen & Unwin Ltd. for "The Curse," from *Poems and Translations* by J. M. Synge.

Doubleday & Co., Inc. for "The Short Night," from *An Introduction to Haiku* by Harold G. Henderson. Copyright © 1958 by Harold G. Henderson.

Grove Press, Inc. for "Oread," from *Selected Poems* by H.D. Copyright © 1957 by Norman Holmes Pearson.

Harcourt, Brace & Co. for passages from the Dudley Fitts and Robert Fitzgerald translation of Sophocles' *Antigone*.

The Macmillan Company for "A Glass of Beer," from *Collected Poems* by James Stephens.

Mrs. Mary Taylor for Geoffrey Taylor's "Cruel, Clever Cat."

Oxford University Press for "Peace" and "The Wreck of the Deutschland," from *Poems of Gerard Manley Hopkins.*

The Society of Authors as the literary representative of the Trustees of the Estate of the late A. E. Housman for "Infant Innocence."

Preface

Among the primary duties of the practitioners in any field is to originate (and then to refine) a body of terminology sufficiently esoteric to repel all but the bravest or the most foolhardy. Although the existence of this barrier to understanding may assure the professional a certain amount of happy privacy, it makes the way of the non-initiate extremely hard. In the case of literature, the way of even the initiate is fairly tortuous, for so extensive is the body of literary terms that the professional, as well as the student, sometimes finds himself at a loss.

There is, clearly, a need for a guide to these terms extensive enough for the teacher or writer yet clear enough for the student and the general reader. It is this need that we have tried to fill. We have chosen entries on the basis of their usefulness, including terms from such areas as poetry, criticism, fiction, and the drama, as well as discussions of movements in literary history. For the convenience of the user, we have placed at the back of the volume a Subject Index, which lists the terms most frequently encountered in a particular area.

K.B.
A.G.

Abbreviations

abbr. ...... abbreviated

ca. ...... about

cf. ...... compare with

e.g. ...... for example

i.e. ...... that is

q.v. ...... see this entry

qq.v. ...... see these entries

Prosodic symbols

⌣   either a short vowel or an unaccented syllable.

╱   an accented syllable

—   a long vowel

╲   a light or secondary stress

‖   a caesura, or pause.

╱   a virgule, which separates metrical feet.

A Reader's Guide to Literary Terms

A

ABECEDARIUS: See ACROSTIC.

ABSTRACT: 1. A summary of a book or document. 2. As opposed to *concrete*. A sentence can be described as abstract if it makes a general statement about a class of persons or objects ("Men are weak") or if its subject is an abstraction—that is, a quality considered apart from its object—such as *wealth, beauty,* or *deepness.* "Honesty is the best policy" is an abstract statement, but "Hotchkiss is a thief" is concrete. The latter statement refers to a particular object rather than to a general class of objects.

ACADEMIC DRAMA: See SCHOOL PLAYS.

ACATALECTIC: A term applied to verse which is metrically complete. If a verse lacks one or more unaccented syllables in its final foot, it is called *catalectic* (noun form, *catalexis*), or *truncated.* (A line from which the initial syllable or syllables are missing is called *headless.*) If a verse contains an extra syllable, it is called *hypercatalectic, hypermetrical, redundant,* or *extrametrical.* In the following quatrain by Blake, the first line is catalectic, the third acatalectic, and the second and fourth hypercatalectic:

> Whén Sĭr / Jóshŭa / Réynŏlds / díed
> Ăll Ná / tŭre wás / dĕgrád / ĕd;
> Thĕ Kíng / dropp'd ă téar / íntŏ / thĕ Quĕen's Éar,
> Ănd aĺl / hĭs Píc / tŭres Fád / ĕd.

ACCENT: The stress placed upon certain syllables in a line of verse. Stresses are determined by word, rhetorical, and metrical accent. *Word accent* refers to the natural stress pattern of the word itself, as in *cóndŭct,* the noun, or *cŏndúct,* the verb. *Rhetorical accent* is the stress put on a word because of its function or importance in the sentence, and *metrical accent* is the stress pattern established by the meter. When the metrical accent forces a change in the word accent, the phenomenon is called *wrenched accent.* This may be the result of simple ineptitude in the poet, but it is also a characteristic of both folk and literary ballads.

> This Hermit good lives in that wood
> Which slopes down to the sea.
> How loudly his sweet voice he rears!
>
> He loves to talk with marinéres
> That come from a far countrée.
>
> *Coleridge,* "The Rime of the Ancient Mariner"

See ICTUS, PRIMARY AND SECONDARY ACCENT, THESIS.

ACCENTUAL VERSE: See METER.

ACCIDENCE: That part of grammar concerned with the inflections, or changes in form, of words.

ACROSTIC: A poem in which letters of successive lines form a word or pattern. In a true acrostic, the initial letters form the word; in a mesostich, the middle letters do so, and in a telestich, it is the terminal letters. A cross acrostic forms the pattern with the first letter of the first line, the second letter of the second line, etc. If the pattern consists of the letters of the alphabet in order, the acrostic is called an *abecedarius,* as in the following, which is given in part:

> An Austrian army awfully array'd,
> Boldly by battery besieged Belgrade.
> Cossack commanders cannonading come
> Dealing destruction's devastating doom.
>
> *Alaric Watts*

ACT: One of the major divisions of a play. In Classical theory, a play is divided into five acts, but the number was reduced in the nineteenth century. Most modern plays employ three acts, although many have only two or eliminate act structure entirely and use only scene divisions.

ADAPTATION: The recasting of a work to fit another medium. Novels, for example, are frequently recast into screen plays.

AESTHETIC DISTANCE: For a work of art to make its effect as such, there must be at some level of the observer's apprehension an awareness of the formal unreality of art. Thus, the work of art is "distanced" from the beholder, who appreciates its aesthetic qualities but does not confuse it with reality. A knowing beholder may deplore the actions of a play's villain, but he does not rush onstage to succor the heroine. This necessary separation between the observer and the work is called "psychic" or, especially by the New Critics, "aesthetic distance."

AESTHETICISM: A term loosely applied to an English literary movement of the second half of the nineteenth century. The roots of the movement lay in the reverence for beauty instilled by Keats and the pre-Raphaelites. Oscar Wilde, the prophet of Aestheticism, taking his cue from his master, Walter Pater, preached that aesthetic considerations were absolutely independent of morality. The phrase *art for art's sake* was taken as the credo of the aesthetes, but was less enthusiastically received by such proper Victorians as Tennyson, who wrote:

> Art for Art's sake! Hail, truest lord of Hell!
> Hail Genius, Master of the Moral Will!
> "The filthiest of all paintings painted well
> Is mightier than the purest painted ill!"
> Yes, mightier than the purest painted well,
> So prone are we toward the broad way to Hell.

Although Wilde was the dominant figure of the movement, he was not entirely representative. The English Parnassians—Dobson, Lang, Gosse—were aesthetes much concerned with matters of form but were not belligerently amoral as Wilde was.

AESTHETICS: The science or study of the beautiful. There are two major approaches to aesthetics, the philosophical and the psychological. The philosophical approach has attempted by deductive reasoning to establish the nature of art and beauty, their

relations to truth and goodness, etc. The psychological approach
has emphasized the study of the process of creation in the artist
and of appreciation in the beholder.

AFFECTIVE FALLACY: In *The Verbal Icon,* W. K. Wimsatt, Jr., and
M. C. Beardsley have defined the Affective Fallacy as "a confusion between the poem and its *results* (what it *is* and what it
does) . . . . It begins by trying to derive the standard of criticism from the psychological effects of the poem and ends in
impressionism and relativism. . . . the poem itself, as an object
of specifically critical judgment, tends to disappear." Wimsatt
and Beardsley's work has been influential in reinforcing the New
Critics' concentration on actual texts rather than peripheral
matter. See INTENTIONAL FALLACY, NEW CRITICISM.

AGON: Greek: "a contest." That part of a Greek drama in which
two characters, each one aided by half the chorus, indulge in
verbal conflict.

ALAZON: The impostor or braggart of Greek comedy. The type
survives in the *Miles Gloriosus* of Plautus, in Molière's *Tar-
tuffe,* and other works.

ALEXANDRINE: 1. In French, a verse of twelve syllables containing
four (sometimes three) accents. It is used for elevated verse such
as that of the classical tragedies. 2. In English, an iambic hexameter verse is often called an alexandrine.

ALLEGORY: An extended narrative which carries a second meaning along with its surface story. Generally, the characters in an
allegory do not have individual psychologies but are incarna-
tions of abstract ideas and may bear such names as Lechery,
Pride, Meekness, etc. An allegory may be a prose narrative, such
as Bunyan's *Pilgrim's Progress,* a poem, such as Spenser's *Faerie
Queene,* or a play, such as *Everyman.*

ALLITERATION: The close repetition of consonant sounds, usually
at the beginnings of words; also called *head rhyme.*

> To sit in solemn silence in a dull, dark, dock,
> In a pestilential prison, with a life-long lock,
> Awaiting the sensation of a short, sharp, shock,
> From a cheap and chippy chopper on a big, black block!
>
> W. S. Gilbert, *The Mikado*

Anglo-Saxon verse was based on alliteration rather than rhyme.

ALLUSION: A reference, usually brief, to a presumably familiar person or thing. For example, the poem below contains, and depends upon, a reference to the phrase "in Abraham's bosom."

> Mary Ann has gone to rest
> Safe at last on Abraham's breast,
> Which may be nuts for Mary Ann,
> But is certainly rough on Abraham.
>
> *Anonymous*

ALTAR POEM: See CARMEN FIGURATUM.

AMBIGUITY: In *Seven Types of Ambiguity,* William Empson uses this word to refer not to carelessness that produces two or more meanings where a single one is intended but to the richness of poetic speech which can be brought about by "any verbal nuance, however slight, which gives room for alternative reactions to the same piece of language." Although Empson does not demand that his distinctions be regularly observed, for purposes of classification he groups his ambiguities into seven categories:

1. A word or syntax can be effective in several ways at once.
2. Two or more meanings may make up the single meaning of the writer.
3. In a pun two ideas can be given simultaneously.
4. Different meanings can combine to make clear a complicated state of mind in the writer.
5. An image or figure may lie halfway between two ideas.
6. The reader may be forced to invent interpretations because the things said are contradictory.
7. Two meanings may be contradictory and show a fundamental division in the author's mind.

Because of the pejorative connotations of *ambiguity,* other critics have suggested *multiple meaning* and *plurisignation* as alternate terms.

AMPHIBOLY (-E; -OGY; -OGISM): An ambiguity induced either by grammatical looseness (In the sentence "I stood by my friend crying," we do not know who cried) or by the double meanings of words (The sentence "A dark horse has won the triple

crown" may refer either to a rare achievement in horse racing
or to an obscure cardinal's election to the papacy). Prophecies
with double meanings, such as those made by the witches to
Macbeth, may also be called amphibolies.

AMPHIBRACH: A metrical foot of three syllables, consisting of one
long syllable flanked by two short ones or, in accentual poetry,
of one accented syllable flanked by two unaccented ones.

> Ĭ spráng tŏ / thĕ stírrŭp / ănd Jóris̆ / ănd hé
> I galloped, Dirck galloped, we galloped all three
> > *Browning,*
> > "How They Brought the Good News from Ghent to Aix"

AMPHIMAC: A metrical foot of three syllables, consisting of one
short syllable flanked by two long or, in accentual poetry, of one
unstressed syllable flanked by two stressed.

> Líve thy̆ lífe
> > Young and old,
> Like yon oak,
> > Bright in spring,
> Living gold.
> > *Tennyson,* "The Oak"

ANABASIS: Greek: "a going up." The rising of an action to its
climax.

ANACHRONISM: Something placed in an inappropriate period of
time. An anachronism may be unintentional, such as the clock
in *Julius Caesar,* or deliberate, such as Shaw's reference to the
Emperor in *Androcles and the Lion* as "The Defender of the
Faith."

ANACOLUTHON: A sentence which does not maintain a consistent
grammatical sequence. In the following sentence, which contains an example of the fabled dangling participle, the subject
is *water* when it should be *Hotchkiss:* "Going down for the third
time, the water closed over Hotchkiss' head."

ANACREONTIC VERSE: Verse in praise of wine, women, and Epi-
curean pleasures generally, after the manner of Anacreon, 6th
century B.C. Greek poet.

Leave off, fond hermit, leave thy vow,
 And fall again to drinking:
That beauty that won't sack allow,
 Is hardly worth thy thinking.
Dry love or small can never hold,
And without Bacchus Venus soon grows cold.

Dost think by turning anchorite,
 Or a dull small-beer sinner,
Thy cold embraces can invite,
 Or sprightless courtship win her?
No, 'tis Canary that inspires,
'Tis sack, like oil, gives flames to am'rous fires.
 Alexander Brome,
 "To His Friend That Had Vowed Small-Beer"

ANACRUSIS: An extra unaccented syllable or group of syllables at the beginning of a verse which regularly starts with an accented syllable, *e.g., To* in line four below:

Seamen three! What men be ye?
Gotham's three wise men we be.
Whither in your bowl so free?
To rake the moon from out the sea.
 Thomas Love Peacock, "Three Men of Gotham"

ANAGNORISIS: A term used by Aristotle in the *Poetics* to indicate the moment of recognition in which a character moves from ignorance to knowledge. The best type of recognition, Aristotle states, occurs at the same time as the reversal of the situation, or *peripeteia.* Thus, in Sophocles' *Oedipus Rex,* the anagnorisis involves Oedipus' discovery that he himself is the slayer of Laius; it is at that moment that the action of the play is reversed.

ANAGRAM: A word or name resulting from the transposition of letters. For example, the title of Samuel Butler's novel *Erewhon* is an anagram for the word *nowhere.*

ANALECTS: A group of short passages, usually collected from the works of one author.

ANALOGY: A resemblance between two different things, sometimes expressed as a simile.

'Tis with our judgments as our watches, none
Go just alike, yet each believes his own.

Pope, "An Essay on Criticism"

ANAPEST: A metrical foot consisting of two unstressed syllables followed by one stressed syllable. Except for the first foot of lines two and three, all the feet in the following stanza are anapests:

Oh, he flies / through the air / with the great / est of ease.
This daring young man on the flying trapeze.
His figure is handsome, all girls he can please,
And my love he purloined her away.

ANAPHORA: The repetition of an identical word or group of words in successive verses or clauses.

I gave her Cakes and I gave her Ale
   I gave her Sack and Sherry;
I kissed her once and I kissed her twice,
   And we were wondrous merry.

Anonymous

ANASTROPHE: The deliberate inversion of the common order of words. The first and fourth lines of the following stanza have normal word order while the second and third are examples of anastrophe:

He took his vorpal sword in hand;
   Long time the manxome foe he sought—
So rested he by the Tumtum tree,
   And stood awhile in thought.

Lewis Carroll, "Jabberwocky"

ANECDOTE: A brief narrative concerning a particular individual or incident.

ANNAL: A yearly record of historical events. Annals are less extensive in scope than chronicles.

ANNOTATION: A textual comment in a book. Annotations may range from a reader's penciled comments in the margins of a page to an editor's printed notes which clarify the meaning of the text.

ANTAGONIST: The major character in opposition to the hero or protagonist of a narrative or drama. In Melville's *Billy Budd* the antagonist is Claggart.

ANTEPENULT: The third syllable from the end of a word. The *nal* of *analogy* is the antepenult.

ANTHOLOGY: A collection of poetry or prose, sometimes divided into categories such as lyric verse, satiric verse, etc. *The Greek Anthology* is perhaps the most famous.

ANTICLIMAX: A descent from a comparatively noble or lofty tone to one noticeably less exalted. If the descent is sudden, the effect is often comic, as in this stanza by Crashaw describing the relationship between the tears of Mary Magdalene and Christ, the lamb:

> And now where e'er He strays,
> Among the Galilean mountains,
> Or more unwelcome ways,
> He's followed by two faithful fountains;
> Two walking baths; two weeping motions;
> Portable, & compendious oceans.
>
> "Saint Mary Magdalene, or the weeper"

ANTIMASQUE: See MASQUE.

ANTISTROPHE: The second of the stanzas which make up the triad of the Pindaric ode. See ODE.

ANTITHESIS: A rhetorical figure in which sharply opposing ideas are expressed within a balanced grammatical structure, as in the first line of this couplet by Pope:

> Worth makes the man, and want of it, the fellow;
> The rest is all but leather or prunella.
>
> "An Essay on Man."

ANTONYM: A word that means the opposite of another. *Heavy,* for example, is the opposite of *light, strong* of *weak,* etc.

APHAERESIS: The dropping of an initial letter, syllable, or sound, as in the development of the word *special* from *especial.*

APHORISM: A short, pithy statement of a truth or doctrine; similar to an apothegm or maxim. An example is Pope's "The proper study of mankind is man" ("An Essay on Man").

APOCOPE: The dropping of a final letter, syllable, or sound, as in the development of *curio* from *curiosity.*

APOCRYPHA: Writings of uncertain or unknown authorship. The term, applied to the Biblical *Apocrypha* (books in the Greek version of the Old Testament but not in the Hebrew Bible), is also used to designate literary works of doubtful authorship. Some scholars, for example, believe that the play *Pericles, Prince of Tyre* is apocryphal, that is, not Shakespeare's. See CANON.

APOLLONIAN—DIONYSIAN: In *The Birth of Tragedy,* Nietzsche used these terms to contrast reason and instinct, culture and primitive nature, etc. Nietzsche felt that these two elements were unified in Greek tragedy, in which the choral songs provided the Dionysian element and the dialogue the Apollonian. These terms have connotations similar to those associated with *Classicism—Romanticism* or Matthew Arnold's *Hellenism—Hebraism (q.v.).*

APOLOGUE: See FABLE.

APOLOGY, THE: Greek: "defense." A work written to defend the writer's ideas or to clarify a problem. Plato's *Apology,* in which Socrates defends himself before the governing body of Athens, is perhaps the most notable example. In English, Sir Philip Sidney's *Apologie for Poetrie* (1580) discusses poetical practice, while in *Apologia Pro Vita Sua* (1864), Newman defends some of his convictions.

APOTHEGM: See APHORISM.

APOSIOPESIS: An abrupt breaking off in the middle of a sentence without the completion of the idea, often under the stress of emotion. In the closet scene from *Hamlet,* the Prince, while raging against Claudius, is startled by the sudden entrance of the ghost:

> Hamlet: A murderer, and a villain;
> A slave that is not twentieth part the tithe
> Of your precedent lord; a vice of kings;
> A cut-purse of the empire and the rule,
> That from a shelf the precious diadem stole,
> And put it in his pocket!
> Queen: No more!
> Hamlet: A king of shreds and patches,—
>   *Enter Ghost*
> Save me, and hover o'er me with your wings,

> You heavenly guards! What would your gracious
> figure?

APOSTROPHE: A figure of speech in which a person not present or a personified abstraction is addressed. The heroine of Fielding's *Tom Thumb* is apostrophized thus:

> Oh! Huncamunca, Huncamunca, oh!
> Thy pouting breasts, like kettle drums of brass,
> Beat everlastingly loud alarms of joy;
> As bright as brass they are, and oh, as hard;
> Oh! Huncamunca, Huncamunca, oh!

More strictly, an apostrophe (Greek, "a turning away") is a digression in a speech, a turning away to address a judge or someone absent, and by extension a similar break in a poem.

APRON STAGE: The apron is that part of the stage which projects beyond the proscenium arch. Any stage which consists primarily or entirely of an apron and on which the action is not seen as framed within the proscenium may be called an apron stage. The Elizabethan theater, for which Shakespeare designed his plays, was built around such a stage.

ARCADIA: Though originally a mountainous district in the Peloponnesus, Arcadia symbolized in the pastoral verse of the Classical poets, *e.g.*, Virgil's *Eclogues,* the harmony and simplicity of an imagined Golden Age. Arcadia is populated by shepherds and shepherdesses who, removed from the complexities of actual life, both urban and rural, devote themselves to their flocks and their songs. The Renaissance saw the development of the Arcadian prose romance, of which the *Arcadia* of Sannazaro and that of Sir Philip Sydney are the most notable examples. See PASTORAL.

ARCHAISM: A word or phrase which is no longer used in actual speech. The use of archaisms has been a common device in poetry up to the twentieth century. The words *quoth, eftsoons,* and the spelling *dropt* were all archaic at the time these lines were written:

> He holds him with his skinny hand,
> "There was a ship," quoth he.

"Hold off! unhand me, grey-beard loon!"
Eftsoons his hand dropt he.

Coleridge, "The Rime of the Ancient Mariner"

ARCHETYPE: From the Greek *arché,* meaning "original" or "primitive," plus *typos,* "form." The term, employed by the psycho-
analyst C. G. Jung, has been used in the New Criticism (*q.v.*)
since the 1930's to characterize a pattern of plot or character
which evokes what Jung calls a "racial memory." Thus, the voyage in *The Rime of the Ancient Mariner* is an archetype of the
spiritual journey which all men experience, the Ancient Mariner
himself an archetype of the man who offends God. Such "primordial images," as Jung calls them, lie in the "collective unconscious," which is the repository of the experience of the race.
(See *Archetypal Patterns in Poetry* by Maud Bodkin.) See MYTH.

ARGUMENT: 1. A brief abstract or summary of the plot prefixed
to a literary work or to a section of it. Dryden's translation of
Virgil's *Aeneid,* for example, contains an "Argument" preceding each book of the poem.

   2. A division of a speech (*q.v.*).

ARSIS: See THESIS.

ART FOR ART'S SAKE: See AESTHETICISM

ASIDE: In the theater, a short passage spoken in an undertone or
directed to the audience. By theatrical convention, the aside is
presumed to be inaudible to other characters on the stage. This
device has rarely been used since the end of the nineteenth century, when it was prominent in melodrama.

ASSONANCE: The close repetition of similar vowel sounds, usually
in stressed syllables. Assonance is found in each line of the following quatrain:

Twinkle, twinkle, little star,
How I wonder what you are!
Up above the world so high,
Like a diamond in the sky.

Anonymous

ATMOSPHERE: The mood which is established by the totality of
the literary work. Foreshadowing, though related to atmosphere,
is primarily a plot device. In the first act of *Macbeth,* the pres-

ence of the three witches establishes the atmosphere of the play, which is dark and somber, but what they say is a foreshadowing of the evil which is later dramatized.

ATTITUDE: See TONE.

AUBADE: Called an *alba* in Provençal troubadour verse and a *Tagelied* in German, the aubade is a song sung by departing lovers at dawn. The most striking example of the genre in English occurs in Shakespeare's *Romeo and Juliet* when the lovers must part after their wedding night:

> Juliet: Wilt thou be gone? it is not yet near day:
> It was the nightingale and not the lark,
> That pierc'd the fearful hollow of thine ear;
> Nightly she sings on yon pomegranate tree:
> Believe me, love, it was the nightingale.
> Romeo: It was the lark, the herald of the morn,
> No nightingale: look, love, what envious streaks
> Do lace the severing clouds in yonder east:
> Night's candles are burnt out, and jocund day
> Stands tiptoe on the misty mountain tops.

AUTOBIOGRAPHY: The author of an autobiography presents a continuous narrative of the major events (and sometimes the minutiae) of his past. The autobiography differs from the diary or journal, which lacks continuity and is kept for the author's private purposes. (For examples, see *The Education of Henry Adams* and *The Autobiography of Lincoln Steffens.*) See CONFESSIONAL LITERATURE:

AVANT-GARDE: French: "vanguard." In literature, a term designating new writing that contains innovations in form or technique.

B

BALLAD: A narrative poem, usually simple and fairly short, originally designed to be sung. Ballads often begin abruptly, imply the previous action, utilize simple language, tell the story tersely through dialogue and described action, and make use of refrains. The folk ballad, which reached its height in England in the sixteenth and seventeenth centuries, was composed anonymously and handed down orally, often in several different versions. The literary ballad, consciously created by a poet in imitation of the folk ballad, makes use (sometimes with considerable freedom) of many of its devices and conventions. Coleridge's *Rime of the Ancient Mariner*, Keats' *La Belle Dame sans Merci*, and Wilde's *Ballad of Reading Gaol* are all literary ballads.

BALLADE: A fixed verse form derived from Old French poetry. In its most common form, the ballade consists of three stanzas and an envoy, a short concluding stanza often addressed to a person of importance. The meter is usually iambic or anapestic tetrameter, and the rhyme scheme is regularly *ababbcbC* in each of the octaves and *bcbC* in the envoy. (Capital letters represent lines repeated as refrains. Some eight-line ballades have double refrains, with the fourth line repeated in each octave and in the envoy thus: *bBcB*.) There is also a ten-line ballade, in which the rhyme scheme is *ababbccdcD* in the stanzas and *ccdcD* in the envoy. The double ballade contains six eight- or ten-line stanzas, still limited to three or four rhymes respectively, but often omits the envoy. In the *chant royal,* there are five eleven-line stanzas rhyming *ababccddedE* and an envoy rhyming *ddedE*. The *chant royal* is rare in English; the ballade in general tends to be used for light verse.

BALLAD STANZA: A quatrain of alternating tetrameter and trimeter lines rhyming *abcb:*

> Ben Battle was a soldier bold,
>   And used to war's alarms;
> But a cannonball took off his legs,
>   So he laid down his arms.
>
> *Thomas Hood,* "Faithless Nellie Gray"

BARBARISM: A mistake in the formation of a word, especially the mixing of elements from different languages. *Cablegram* is, in the eyes of the discriminating, a barbarism because it adds a Greek suffix to an English root. In a more general sense, any error in the form of a word, such as *speaked* for *spoke,* may be called a barbarism. See SOLECISM.

BARD: A word originally used to refer to an ancient Celtic order of minstrel-poets who composed and sang verses celebrating the achievements of chiefs and warriors; now a synonym for *poet*.

BAROQUE: Though the term *baroque* is used more frequently in discussing music and the visual arts, where it delineates specifically the period between Renaissance and Rococo, than in characterizing literature, where it is limited to stylistic matters, it is, if handled with discretion, a useful word. It suggests such characteristics of Baroque art as energy, lack of harmony, attraction to the ornate, etc. The term may, for instance, properly be applied to the poetry of Richard Crashaw.

BASIC ENGLISH: A language, formulated by C. K. Ogden and I. A. Richards in the 1920's from the elementary vocabulary of English, designed to clarify ideas by limiting discourse to a prescribed number of words.

BATHOS: 1. A sudden and ridiculous descent from the exalted to the ordinary, especially when a writer, striving for the noble or pathetic, achieves the ludicrous. The term *bathos* was first used in this sense by Alexander Pope in his essay *On Bathos, or, Of the Art of Sinking in Poetry*, a comic treatise inspired by Longinus' *On the Sublime*. *Bathos* and *anticlimax* are sometimes synonymous, but where anticlimax may be a deliberate device, bathos is always unintentional.

2. By extension, *bathos* has also come to signify sentimentality or excessive pathos.

BEAST EPIC: In the Middle Ages, a sequence of stories, the characters of which were animals who had human characteristics. Designed as allegory (*q.v.*), the beast epic satirized aspects of contemporary life, especially the court and the church.

The precise origin of the genre has been a subject of much speculation, but it is probably most indebted to Aesop's *Fables*, in particular, to the story of the sly fox and the sick lion, the fable which became the central episode in the first beast epic *Ecbasis captivi* (ca. 930), *The Prisoner's Escape*. Thereafter, the figure of the clever rogue called, in English, Reynard the Fox became a central character in the beast epic along with Chanticleer the Cock, Noble the Lion, Ysengrim the Wolf, and others. Interpreted allegorically, Reynard was seen as the Church, Noble as the King, and Ysengrim as the barons.

The most famous beast epic of the time was *Le Roman de*

Renard (twelfth century), in England, the genre became widely known when a Flemish version was translated and printed by Caxton in 1481. Earlier, however, Chaucer, in the "Nun's Priest's Tale" of the *Canterbury Tales,* had told the tale of Chauntecleer the cock and the fox as a separate story. In the Renaissance, Spenser's *Mother Hubberds Tale* continued the tradition of the beast epic, and in 1793 Goethe utilized the genre in his *Reineke Fuchs,* which contained political and social satire.

BEGINNING RHYME: Rhyme at the beginnings of lines, a device rarely used. (See Sidney Lanier's *The Symphony.*)

BELLES-LETTRES: Literally, "fine letters," the term has been used interchangeably with *literature,* though current usage restricts its meaning to lighter writings or to appreciative essays on the beauties of literature.

BESTIARY: A collection of descriptions of animals, some of them fabulous, *e.g.,* the unicorn. The actions of the animals are frequently presented and explained as an illustration of some point of Christian doctrine. This form was popular throughout the Middle Ages. See BEAST EPIC.

BIBLIOGRAPHY: A list of books or shorter works on a particular subject or a list of the works of a particular author or authors.

BILDUNGSROMAN: A term frequently used by German critics, *Bildungsroman* (*Bildung,* "formation"; *roman,* "novel") is a portrait of the youthful development of a central character. Examples are Dickens' *David Copperfield,* Mann's *The Magic Mountain,* and Samuel Butler's *The Way of All Flesh. Bildungsroman* is used interchangeably with *Erziehungsroman* (*Erziehung,* "upbringing" or "education"), a novel of initiation and education in life. See KUNSTLERROMAN.

BIOGRAPHY: An account of the life of a person. The modern biography which is based on careful research and which is relatively dispassionate in attitude is a comparatively recent form. Classical and medieval biographies were generally written to illustrate a thesis. In the typical saint's life, for example, the subject was reduced to an illustration of the qualities of a Christian saint. The Renaissance and the Reformation, however, produced a new emphasis on the individual, and by the time that Boswell wrote the life of Dr. Johnson, the development of the modern biography was substantially complete. The subjectivity of the Romantics, later reinforced by Freudian theory, has produced the biography which attempts to recreate the inner life of its subject. Recently, the techniques of the novel have begun to influence the writing of biography, as in the work of André Maurois.

BLANK VERSE: Although verse described as *blank* is, strictly, no more than unrhymed, the term is limited to unrhymed iambic pentameter. Blank verse was first used in English by Surrey in his translation of Virgil and first appeared in the drama in Sackville and Norton's *Gorboduc* (acted 1561), later becoming the standard verse form of the Elizabethan theater. It was chosen by Milton for *Paradise Lost* and has since been used more than any other form for serious verse in English.

BLUE FLOWER: A symbol of romantic longing, from Novalis' *Heinrich von Ofterdingen.*

BLURB: A brief description, usually enthusiastic, which appears on the dust jacket of a book and which recommends it to prospective readers.

BOASTING POEM: A poem in which the speaker boasts of his exploits in battle, common in oral literatures. The Old English epic *Beowulf* contains such poems.

BOMBAST: Originally referring to a stuffing made of cotton or horsehair to produce bulges that fashion demanded during the Elizabethan period in England, the term came to mean inflated language such as that sometimes employed by dramatists of the day, as in this passage from Marlowe's *Tamburlaine the Great:*

> Jove, viewing me in arms, looks pale and wan,
> Fearing my power should pull him from his throne.
> Where'er I come the Fatal Sisters sweat,
> And grisly Death, by running to and fro,
> To do their ceaseless homage to my sword.
> And here in Afric, where it seldom rains,
> Since I arriv'd with my triumphant host,
> Have swelling clouds, drawn from wide-gasping wounds,
> Been oft resolv'd in bloody purple showers,
> A meteor that might terrify the earth,
> And make it quake at every drop it drinks.

BOULEVARD DRAMA: Originally the body of plays produced in the late nineteenth century for the major theaters of Paris by such writers as Labiche and Halévy. The term is now applied to plays, usually comedies of some sophistication, designed primarily as commercial products. In the modern English theater, many of Noel Coward's plays are examples of boulevard drama.

BOURGEOIS DRAMA: A term widely used to describe the modern realistic drama dealing with the problems of middle-class characters.

BOUTS-RIMES: Sets of rhyme words unattached to verses. At various times since the seventeenth century, the making of impromptu verses to fit *bouts-rimés,* or preconceived rhyme words, has been a fashionable pastime.

BOWDLERIZE: Derived from Dr. Thomas Bowdler's expurgation of "offensive" passages from *The Family Shakespeare* (1818), which removed "whatever is unfit to be read by a gentleman in a company of ladies," the term now refers to the prudish expurgation of any supposed indecency.

BRAGGADOCIO: The braggart who is generally a coward at heart. A stock character in the drama and other literary forms. See MILES GLORIOSUS.

BROADSIDE: A sheet of paper, generally of large size, with printed matter on only one side. It is designed for distribution or posting.

BURLESQUE: A work designed to ridicule attitudes, style, or subject matter by either handling an elevated subject in a trivial manner or a low subject with mock dignity. Though burlesque embraces many types of satirical imitation, it is useful to distinguish it from parody, a closely related genre. Gilbert and Sullivan's *Patience* is not a parody, for it does not ridicule another work; it is, rather, a burlesque of the attitudes of Aestheticism. In the stanzas quoted below, Lewis Carroll is parodying the work of Southey:

> "You are old, Father William," the young man cried;
>   "The few locks which are left you are gray;
> You are hale, Father William,—a hearty old man:
>   Now tell me the reason, I pray."

"In the days of my youth," Father William replied,
"I remembered that youth would fly fast,
And abused not my health and my vigor at first,
That I never might need them at last.

> Southey, "The Old Man's Comforts
> and how he gained them"

"You are old, Father William," the young man said,
"And your hair has become very white,
And yet you incessantly stand on your head—
Do you think, at your age, it is right?"

"In my youth," Father William replied to his son,
I feared it might injure the brain;
But now that I'm perfectly sure I have none,
Why, I do it again and again."

> Carroll, "Father William"

Travesty, less subtle in technique than parody, is a broad or grotesque satiric imitation. For further distinctions and examples, see MOCK EPIC and PASTICHE.

BURLETTA: In the eighteenth- and nineteenth-century English theater, a short comic play with music. A considerable amount of music was essential to these productions in order to evade the law which limited legitimate drama to the patent theaters. A well-known nineteenth-century burletta was *Tom & Jerry! or Life in London,* produced at the Adelphi in 1821 and 1822.

BURNS STANZA: A six-line stanza, $aaa^4b^2a^4b^2$, named after the Scottish poet Robert Burns:

> Ha! whare ye gaun, ye crawlin' ferlie?
> Your impudence protects you sairly:
> I canna say but ye strunt rarely
>   Owre gauze an' lace;
> Though, faith! I fear ye dine but sparely
>   On sic a place.
>   "To a Louse"

The Burns stanza is a variant of the tail-rhyme stanza (*q.v.*).

BUSKIN: A half-boot covering for the foot and leg which reached to the calf; worn by actors in ancient Greek tragedy. Comic actors wore a low shoe or sock. "To put on buskins" consequently means to act or write tragedy.

C

CACOPHONY: Discordant or harsh sounds which are frequently introduced for poetic effect. Cacophony may perhaps be the result of difficulty of articulation, though the image presented also influences the readers. In these lines by Browning, the image of sudden flame combines abrupt rhythms and explosive consonants to produce a cacophonous effect:

> A tap at the pane, the quick sharp scratch
> And blue spurt of a lighted match.
>   "Meeting at Night"

CADENCE: The natural rhythm of language determined by its inherent alternation of stressed and unstressed syllables. When more precisely used in verse, the term *cadence* refers to the arrangement of the rhythms of speech into highly organized patterns. See FREE VERSE.

CAESURA (CESURA): A pause in a line of verse dictated not by metrics but by the natural rhythm of the language. There is usually a caesura in verses of ten syllables or more, and the handling of this pause to achieve rhythmical variety is a test of the poet's ability. Note Pope's skill in shifting the caesura in this passage:

> A little learning // is a dangerous thing;
> Drink deep, // or taste not the Pierian spring:
> There shallow draughts // intoxicate the brain,
> But drinking largely // sobers us again.
>   "An Essay on Criticism"

CANON: A body of writings established as authentic. Used particularly in reference to Biblical writings which have been received as authentic or authorized for the Christian Bible, the term is also used to designate an author's works which are accepted as genuine, such as Shakespeare's canon of thirty-seven plays. The term is likewise used by the Roman Catholic Church, which has a "Saints' Canon," a list of those who have been "canonized," *i.e.*, authorized by the Church.

CANSO: (Also *chanson*) In Provençal verse, a love lyric. See TROU-BADOUR.

CANTICUM: Parts of a Latin drama either sung or chanted. See DIVERBIUM.

CANTO: Italian: "song." A major section of a long poem. Dante's *Divine Comedy* and Byron's *Childe Harold,* for example, are divided into cantos.

CANZONE: A Provençal or Italian lyric, sometimes designed to be sung to music.

CAPA Y ESPADA: Spanish: "cloak and sword." The comedies of such sixteenth- and seventeenth-century Spanish playwrights as Lope de Vega and Calderón de la Barca, dealing with love and intrigue among the aristocracy.

CARICATURE: In literature, a character consisting of certain selected features exaggerated for comic effect. In Etherege's *The Man of Mode; or, Sir Fopling Flutter,* Sir Fopling, as the name suggests, is a caricature of the Restoration fop.

CARMEN FIGURATUM: Latin: "a shaped poem," the verses of which are so arranged that they form a design on the page. When the design is an object, such as a cross or an altar, it is usually the theme of the poem. Dylan Thomas' "Vision and Prayer" is such a poem, but the type is most common in the Renaissance, as exemplified in George Herbert's "The Altar":

> A broken ALTAR, Lord, thy servant reares,
> Made of a heart, and cemented with teares,
> Whose parts are thy hand did frame;
> No workman's tool hath touch'd the same.
> A H E A R T alone
> Is   such   a   stone
> Thy power doth cut,
> Wherefore each part
> Of my hard heart
> Meets in this frame,
> To praise thy name.
> That if I chance to hold my peace
> These stones to praise thee may not cease.
> O let thy blessed S A C R I F I C E be mine,
> And sanctifie this A L T A R to be thine.

CARPE DIEM: Latin: "seize the day." A theme characteristic of a considerable body of poetry, most of it lyric. A *carpe diem* poem advises the reader, or the person it addresses, to enjoy the pleasures of the moment before youth passes away.

> What is love? 'Tis not hereafter;
> Present mirth hath present laughter
>   What's to come is still unsure.
> In delay there lies no plenty;
> Then come kiss me, sweet and twenty,
> Youth's a stuff will not endure.
>   *Shakespeare, Twelfth Night*

CATACHRESIS: 1. The application of a word to something which it does not denote. Examples are the use of *individual* for *person* or *chronic* for *severe*. 2. Any strained or forced figure of speech. In Crashaw's "On our Crucified Lord Naked and Bloody," Christ's blood is referred to as a garment, his body a wardrobe:

> Th'have left thee naked Lord! O that they had!
> This Garment too I would they had deny'd.
> Thee with thyselfe they have too richly clad,
> Opening the purple wardrobe of thy side.
> O never could bee found garment too good
> For thee to weare, but these, of thine owne Blood.

CATALECTIC, CATALEXIS: See ACATALECTIC.

CATASTROPHE: The tragic conclusion of a play or narrative. In Sophocles' *Oedipus Rex,* the catastrophe is the scene in which, prior to self-exile, Oedipus appears with his eyes gouged out.

CATHARSIS: In Aristotle's *Poetics,* the purgation of the emotions of pity and fear aroused by the actions of the tragic hero. This concept has been the cause of considerable controversy since its appearance in the *Poetics,* where it is limited to this passage: "Tragedy through pity and fear effects a purgation of such emotions." No universally accepted explanation of the process has been made.

CAVALIER DRAMA: In the 1630's, Queen Henrietta Maria, wife of Charles I of England, extended royal patronage to the performance at court of a type of play now called Cavalier drama.

These plays, always decorous and solemn, drew their materials from Greek romances which were avidly read at court.

The background of the typical Cavalier play involves political and military conflict between two or three neighboring states. In the elaborate plot, crews of pirates either capture the central characters or rescue them from sinking ships. The ladies, always beautiful and virtuous, are in love with men who are always valiant and honorable. A lustful villain, a stock character in Cavalier drama, and numerous other impediments prevent the marriage which appears to be the natural course for the central figures. In time, however, all obstacles are removed; the play may therefore end in wedlock.

The florid dialogue, compounded of artifice and bombast, is in rhythmic prose, frequently arranged and printed to give the impression of blank verse. The most notable writers of this kind of drama were Thomas Killigrew and Sir John Suckling. With the Civil War and the ascendancy of Cromwell in the 1640's, Cavalier drama came to an end.

CAVALIER POETRY: The verse written by the courtiers of Charles I. The poems are generally graceful lyrics in praise of wine, women, song, and the King. Among the most distinguished of the Cavalier poets were Carew, Lovelace, and Suckling.

CELTIC RENAISSANCE: See IRISH LITERARY RENAISSANCE.

CELTIC TWILIGHT: A term used to suggest an atmosphere much admired by some Irish writers of the late nineteenth century who, interested in supplying Ireland with a romantic past, attempted to create in their work a dreamy, shadowy vision of Celtic myth and legend. In *The Wanderings of Oisin* (1889), for example, W. B. Yeats suggests remote, heroic times by means of legendary figures, many references to "dream" and "shadow," and a style characterized by such phrases as "dove-gray," and "pearl-pale." The poet of the Celtic Twilight is concerned with an unreal world, more beautiful than the real. A leader in the Irish Literary Renaissance (*q.v.*), Yeats called one of his books *The Celtic Twilight* (1893). James Joyce ridiculed the phenomenon in his phrase "cultic twalette."

CESURA: See CAESURA.

CHAIN VERSE: Verse in which the stanzas (occasionally lines) are linked by rhyme or various patterns of repetition. The villanelle (*q.v.*), is an example of chain verse.

CHANSON DE GESTE: French: "song of deeds." A French epic form describing the deeds of a historical or legendary hero. Many of the stories centered around Charlemagne and his knights. Some of the *chansons* dealt with battles against the Saracens while others told of rebellion and disloyalty among Charlemagne's nobles. Later, such romantic elements as giants, fairies, and loves between Christian knights and Saracen maidens were introduced. The form flourished between the eleventh and fourteenth centuries. There are about eighty surviving examples of the *chanson de geste,* of which the best-known is the *Chanson de Roland.*

CHANSONNIER: A collection in manuscript of Provençal troubadour poems.

CHANT ROYAL: See BALLADE.

CHANTEY (CHANTY, SHANTEY): A sailor's song sung while at work.

CHAPBOOK: A pamphlet hawked about the streets of London by peddlers or "chapmen," particularly from the sixteenth through the eighteenth centuries. These pamphlets contained such miscellaneous matters as ballads, romances, lives of notorious criminals, etc.

CHARACTER, THE: A literary genre, especially popular in the seventeenth and eighteenth centuries, deriving from the *Characters* of Theophrastus (died 278 B.C.). The character is a brief essay describing the virtues or vices of a particular social type, such as the fop, the country squire, etc.

CHAUCERIAN STANZA: See RHYME ROYAL.

CHIASMUS: A passage made up of two balanced parts which have their elements reversed, as in the line where Pope describes man, created to

> . . . flame lawless through the void,
> Destroying others, by himself destroy'd.
> > "An Essay on Man"

CHORIAMB(US): A foot of verse consisting of two stressed syllables flanking two unstressed, as in Swinburne's poem "Choriambics":

Swéet thĕ / kĭssĕs ŏf déath / sét ŏn thў líps,

cóldĕr ăre théy / thăn míne;
Colder surely than past kisses that love
poured for thy lips as wine.

In a choriambic line, the first foot is a trochee, the last foot an iamb.

CHORUS: The chorus, from which Greek drama developed, was originally a group of men who performed at religious festivals. Its importance diminished as the drama progressed. In Aeschylus, the chorus often takes part in the action; in Sophocles, it is a commentator, and in Euripides, the chorus is primarily a lyric element. The Romans took the chorus from the Greeks, and the Elizabethans imitated it from the Romans. The chorus, however, which has never been made an integral part of English drama, was sometimes reduced by the Elizabethans to a single figure, as in Shakespeare's *Henry V*. Choruses are rare in modern plays. When they appear, they may be either multiple, as in Eliot's *Murder in the Cathedral*, or single, as in Arthur Miller's *A View from the Bridge*.

CHRESTOMATHY: A collection of passages in prose or verse, especially one to be used in learning a language; loosely, an anthology.

CHRONICLE: A record of events in historical order. The medieval chronicles, which occasionally contained legendary material, were composed in either verse or prose. They were based on the local records of the annalists and listed rather than evaluated events.

CHRONICLE PLAY: A dramatization of material taken from the chronicle histories of England, the most widely used of which were those of Holinshed and Hall. Such plays were very popular in Elizabethan England. At first they were scenes loosely strung together, but they soon developed greater unity and, in such plays as Marlowe's *Edward II* and Shakespeare's *Henry IV*, (more appropriately called *history plays*), became subtle studies of character.

CIPHER: Writing which employs a secret method either by substitution or transposition of letters. In the *Journal to Stella,* Swift substitutes, among other things, "l" for "r":

> . . . zoo must cly Lele and Hele, and Hele aden. Must loo im- imitate pdfr, pay? Iss, and sola shall. And so leles fol ee rettle. Dood mollow.

Transcribed, this reads:

> ". . . you must cry There and Here, and Here again. Must you imitate Presto, pray? Yes, and so you shall. And so there's for your letter. Good morrow."

CLASSICAL: A word that has carried so many different meanings at different times that no single meaning can any longer be said to appertain to it, this term should be used with discretion. Orig- inally the *scriptor classicus* was one who wrote for the upper classes, as opposed to the *scriptor proletarius,* who wrote for the lower; soon, however, *classical* was applied to writing considered worthy of preservation and study; then the term referred simply to the literature of Greece and Rome; later it meant literature composed in imitation of the Graeco-Roman, and finally it was applied to literature which, though perhaps opposed to the ancient in concept and form, was worthy to be called *classical* because of the height of its achievement. In common use, the term *classical* is applied to literature which has at least some of these characteristics: balance, unity, proportion, restraint, and what Winckelmann called "noble simplicity and quiet gran- deur."

CLASSICISM: The principles held to be the bases of classical art. See above.

CLERIHEW: The invention of Edmund Clerihew Bentley, a cleri- hew contains two couplets which humorously characterize a per- son whose name is one of the rhymes. One of Bentley's original clerihews, inspired, according to G. K. Chesterton, by a chem- istry lecture, is as follows:

> Sir Humphrey Davy
> Abominated gravy.
> He lived in the odium
> Of having discovered sodium.

CLICHE: A timeworn expression which has lost its vitality and to some extent its original meaning. Several are included in the sentence below:

> Beckson and Ganz, *busy as bees,* are *working like dogs* to obtain *filthy lucre.*

Occasionally writers use clichés which are distorted for humorous effect, as in the case of *bated breath* in the poem below:

> Sally, having swallowed cheese,
> Directs down holes the scented breeze
> Enticing thus with baited breath
> Nice mice to an untimely death.
>
> *Geoffrey Taylor,* "Cruel Clever Cat"

CLIMAX: The moment in a play or story at which a crisis (*q.v.*) reaches its highest intensity and is resolved. The major climax may be preceded by several climaxes of lesser intensity. See FREYTAG'S PYRAMID, PLOT.

CLOAK AND SWORD PLAY: See CAPA Y ESPADA.

CLOSED HEROIC COUPLET: See HEROIC COUPLET.

CLOSET DRAMA: 1. A play written to be read rather than performed, *e.g.,* Byron's *Manfred.* 2. A play which, though intended to be performed, has survived as literature rather than as theater, *e.g.,* Shelley's *The Cenci.*

C. M.: The abbreviation for common measure, also called hymnal stanza (*q.v.*).

COLOPHON: 1. A publisher's emblem or trade-mark, usually found on the title page or at the end of a book. 2. Information about the writing or manufacture of a book given by the author or by the publisher. Formerly, such information was found at the end of a book but now often appears on the title page and its verso (*q.v.*).

COMEDIA ERUDATE: ("learned comedy"). In the Renaissance, the learned imitations of Classical comedies by such writers as Aretino, Ariosto, and Machiavelli, whose *Mandragola* is the best-known example. Such plays were largely concerned with reworking the complicated intrigues inherited from the Roman New Comedy (*q.v*).

COMEDIE LARMOYANTE: French: "tearful comedy." The sentimental comedy in eighteenth-century France. In response to the changing tastes of the age, a comedy developed, which aimed to produce not critical laughter but pleasurable tears. These were usually evoked by the misfortunes of a virtuous heroine. The *comédie larmoyante* is not much admired today, but it is part of the drama of private emotion, which has characterized much of the modern theater. Among the practitioners of this genre were Philippe Destouches and, especially, Nivelle de la Chausée.

COMEDY: Any literary work, but especially a play, less exalted and less serious than a tragedy, commonly having a happy ending. The term is flexible enough to include the satirical laughter of Aristophanes, the religious exaltation of Dante, and the near-tragedy of Chekov.

COMEDY OF HUMOURS: See HUMOURS.

COMEDY OF INTRIGUE: See INTRIGUE.

COMEDY OF MANNERS: A comedy concerned with the intrigues, regularly amorous, of witty and sophisticated members of an aristocratic society. The actions of those who oppose or ineptly imitate the manners of that society are the subjects of much raillery and laughter. Examples are the comedies of such Restoration playwrights as Etherege and Congreve.

COMIC RELIEF: A comic element inserted into a tragic or somber work, especially a play, to relieve its tension, widen its scope, or heighten by contrast the tragic emotion. See, for example, the drunken porter's speech in Shakespeare's *Macbeth*.

COMMEDIA DELL'ARTE: In medieval Italy, *arti* were groups of artisans or guilds. Thus, the *commedia dell'arte* was the comedy of the professional actors. These professional troupes, which came into prominence around the middle of the sixteenth century, worked primarily from skeletal scenarios which they filled out with dialogue and stage business, improvised in detail, though often rehearsed in essence. The companies consisted of about a dozen actors, who played rigidly typed roles such as Pantalone, the old man; Arlecchino, the lively clown; Il Capitano, the braggart soldier, etc. Masks and traditional costumes were worn by the clowns and old men. In the scenarios, most of which derived ultimately from Roman comedy, the young lovers, aided by their clever servants, outwitted their elders and attained money and happiness. The traditions of the *commedia dell'arte,* or masked comedy, were influential in the drama of the sixteenth and seventeenth centuries and, to some extent, survive today.

COMMON MEASURE: See HYMNAL STANZA.

COMMONPLACE BOOK: A notebook in which ideas and quotations are collected and grouped according to subject.

COMMON RHYTHM: See RUNNING RHYTHM.

COMMUNICATION, FALLACY OF: As defined by Allen Tate, the use of poetry to communicate ideas and feelings which should properly be conveyed by non-poetic discourse. Propaganda poetry, for example, arousing emotional states which are not directly related to the verse itself, relies on attitudes which are external to the aesthetic experience.

COMMUNICATION, HERESY OF: In the work of Cleanth Brooks, the mistaken belief that a poem is an ornament clothing an idea that the poet wishes to communicate. It is the total aesthetic experience of the poem which the reader should apprehend, not the "ideas" of the poem, for the poet, says Brooks, is not a "communicator." This attitude is notably expressed in Archibald MacLeish's "Ars Poetica":

> A Poem should not mean
> But be.

COMPARATIVE LINGUISTICS: See LINGUISTICS.

COMPENSATION: The method of adjusting for omitted unstressed syllables in a line of metrical verse. Though an omitted syllable may be compensated for in the succeeding line, it is usually added to a foot in the same line or its place is taken by a pause. In the following stanza by Tennyson, where all four lines are trimeter, the stresses on and pauses after the words of the first line compensate for the missing syllables:

> Break, break, break,
>   On thy cold gray stones, O sea!
> And I would that my tongue could utter
>   The thoughts that arise in me.

COMPLAINT: A lyric poem, common in the Renaissance, which bewails the misery of the speaker, who is often someone whose beloved is unresponsive or absent.

> O happy dames, that may embrace
>   The fruit of your delight,
> Help to bewail the woeful case
>   And eke the heavy plight
> Of me, that wonted to rejoice
> The fortune of my pleasant choice;
> Good ladies, help to fill my mourning voice.
>
> *Earl of Surrey*, "Complaint of the Absence of Her Lover Being Upon the Sea"

Occasionally, however, a complaint may be humorous, as in "The Complaint of Chaucer to His Empty Purse":

> To you, my purse, and to non other wight
> Compleyne I, for ye be my lady dere!
> I am sory, now that ye be light.

CONCEIT: A fanciful image, especially an elaborate or startling analogy. Petrarchan conceits are conventional comparisons imitated from the love sonnets of the Italian poet Petrarch. Such conceits were satirized by Shakespeare in the sonnet that begins, "My mistress' eyes are nothing like the sun;/Coral is far more red than her lips' red." The Metaphysical conceit, characteristic of Donne and other Metaphysical poets of the seventeenth century, is a comparison, often elaborate, extended, or startling, between objects which are apparently dissimilar. Donne, having noted a flea which has sucked blood both from himself and from his mistress, who is about to exterminate it, exclaims:

> Oh stay, three lives in one flea spare,
> Where we almost, yea, more than married are.
> This flea is you and I, and this
> Our marriage bed, and marriage temple is.
>
> "The Flea"

CONCORDANCE: An alphabetically organized index of words in a text (such as the Bible) or in the work of a major author. Thus, a concordance of the works of Shakespeare lists the words used in the plays as well as the places where they may be found.

CONCRETE UNIVERSAL: A term invented by W. K. Wimsatt (*The Verbal Icon*) to refer to the idea, common in the history of criticism, that the work of art unifies the particular and the general. Although from one point of view the work of art is the sum of its disparate details (analogous to the denotation of a word in the logical sense—see MEANING) and thus concrete, if the work is successful, says Wimsatt, these details coalesce into a totality, a "central abstraction" (analogous, as above, to connotation) which is the universal and which can be expressed only though the work.

CONFESSIONAL LITERATURE: A type of autobiography, confessional literature involves the revelation by an author of events or feelings which normally are discreetly concealed. The Romantic tendency to explore the depths, as well as the heights, of the soul has made the confession a characteristically, though not exclusively, Romantic form. For examples, see Jean Jacques Rousseau's *Confessions,* Thomas De Quincey's *Confessions of an English Opium-Eater,* George Moore's *Confessions of a Young Man.*

CONFIDANT (CONFIDANTE, fem.): A character in drama or fiction, a trusted friend to whom the protagonist reveals his most intimate feelings and intentions. Thus, Shakespeare uses Horatio, who has little effect on the plot, as a device to reveal Hamlet's plans to the audience. The device of the confidant eventually became so conventionalized that in the eighteenth century Sheridan made fun of it in *The Critic,* which contains the stage direction, "Enter Tilburina, stark mad in white satin, and her confidante, stark mad in white linen."

CONFLICT: In drama and fiction, the opposition of two forces or characters. Conflict may occur: 1) within one character (Macbeth's reverence for Duncan and his desire to kill him); 2) between a character and society (Jude, in Hardy's *Jude the Obscure,* cannot surmount the social barriers which prevent him from obtaining a university education); 3) between two characters, each of whom tries to impose his will on the other (in its simplest form, the hero and villain of melodrama).

CONNOTATION: The implications or suggestions which are evoked by a word. Connotations may be 1) highly individual, based on associations because of pleasant or unpleasant experiences in a person's life; 2) general, or culturally conditioned, as in the word *anarchist,* which commonly evokes a picture of a large black-bearded man holding a bomb. See DENOTATION, MEANING.

CONSISTENCY: The quality of internal coherence in the parts and in the tone of a literary work. Thus, a manipulation by the author to avoid the catastrophe in what appears to be a tragedy may be a violation of consistency in the work. The term may also be used to describe a character whose actions and speeches are in accord with his image as established by the author.

CONSONANCE: 1. The close repetition of identical consonant sounds before and after different vowels, such as "flip—flop," "feel—fill."

2. Some writers accept as consonance, the repetition of consonant sounds at the ends of words only, as in "east—west," or "hid—bed." Emily Dickinson uses consonance in place of rhyme in these quatrains:

'T was later when the summer went
Than when the cricket *came,*
And yet we knew that gentle clock
Meant nought but going *home.*

'T was sooner when the cricket went
Than when the winter *came,*
Yet that pathetic pendulum
Keeps esoteric *time.*

CONTRAST: The juxtaposition of images or ideas to heighten or clarify a situation. Dylan Thomas' line "I see the boys of summer in their ruin" suggests both youth and age, life and death.

CONVENTION: A generally accepted literary device or form. At a theatrical performance, for example, the audience accepts a set of conventions: As the curtain (itself a convention) goes up, the spectators see a three-walled room, but by another convention, the absence of the fourth wall is ignored. The action may be surrounded by obviously false scenery painted on a flat canvas, but this artificiality is also ignored. The arrangement of the furniture, all of which faces the audience, and the gestures and projected voices of the actors are dramatic conventions which, though not "true to life," are necessary to the presentation of the action. Consequently, if a character speaks in iambic pentameter verse, the audience is not startled by the unreality of his speech, for convention is a necessary device in all literature.

COPYRIGHT: Until the fifteenth century, when printing came into prominence, there was no need to provide for the protection of literary rights. However, when the pirating of works became a problem, rulers granted exclusive rights to printers' guilds, which then regulated the practices of their members.

The first English copyright law, in 1710, gave protection to the author for fourteen years, renewable once for a like number of years. This became the model for the earliest American copyright law (1790). The present law, enacted in 1891, grants an author exclusive rights for twenty-eight years, with a single renewal for a similar period. In addition to literary works, the law extends protection to maps, photographs, musical compositions, screenplays, textile designs, and works of art.

Today, most countries acknowledge the resolutions formulated at the Bern Convention (1887). Those which signed agreed that literary material copyrighted in one country would receive protection in the other countries which were parties to the agreement.

COUNTERPLOT: See SUBPLOT.

COUP DE THEATRE: A striking, unexpected, and theatrically effective turn of events in a play. An extraordinary *coup de théâtre* occurs in Act V, Scene vi, of Webster's *The White Devil,* when Flamineo, who has been shot by his sister, Vittoria, and his mistress, Zanche, finding that they do not intend to follow him in death, springs to his feet and exclaims: "Oh cunning devils! now I have tried your love,/And doubled all your reaches.—I am not wounded."

COUPLET: Two successive rhyming verses, usually of the same meter. The following stanza consists of a pair of couplets:

Lizzie Borden with an axe,
Hit her father forty whacks.

When she saw what she had done,
She hit her mother forty-one.
                                                    Anonymous

COURTESY BOOK: A type of conduct book popular in the Renaissance. It described the training and manner of life appropriate
to a gentleman, a man who was to be a soldier, an adviser to his
prince, and a gallant and accomplished courtier. The most
famous example of this genre is Castiglione's *The Courtier.*

COURTLY LOVE: A philosophy of love which exerted an important
influence on Medieval and Renaissance literature. The system
of courtly love—a compound of such elements as the fashions of
the Provençal troubadours, ideas drawn from Ovid, and the
medieval veneration of the Virgin Mary—was codified toward
the end of the twelfth century in the *Art of Courtly Love* of
Andreas Capellanus.

Courtly love was extra-marital and, as a result, secret. The
lover was expected to languish, become pale, and be given to
fits of sighing, trembling, and weeping. When accepted by his
lady, he vowed eternal faithfulness. Throughout, the lover was
subservient to his mistress and regarded her with an emotion
near veneration. In the work of Dante and other writers of the
dolce stil nuovo (q.v.), where courtly love takes on a Platonic and
idealistic character, the beloved does not inspire the lover to
chivalric deeds, as she had in earlier times, but leads him on to
a higher spiritual state. The influence of the Platonic school of
courtly love extended through Dante and Petrarch to the sonneteers of the English Renaissance. The earlier code of courtly
love, emphasizing the sensual, dominates the characters of
Chaucer's *Troilus and Criseyde.*

COWLEYAN ODE (IRREGULAR ODE): An ode *(q.v.)* in which the
stanzas, or verse paragraphs, are irregular in the rhyme scheme
and in the number and length of the lines. The type was established by Abraham Cowley (1618-1667) and has been widely used
since. Examples are Dryden's "Song for St. Cecilia's Day,"
Wordsworth's "Ode: Intimations of Immortality," Allen Tate's
"Ode to the Confederate Dead." See HORATIAN ODE.

CRADLE BOOKS: See INCUNABULA.

CRAFT CYCLE: See MIRACLE PLAY.

CRISIS: A brief period of time in a story or play when a conflict is intensified to the point where a resolution must occur. In the course of an action, there may be several crises, each of which precedes a climax (*q.v.*). In *Hamlet,* for example, a major crisis occurs during the play scene. The climax is reached when Claudius, having witnessed a representation of his own crime, rises from his chair, calls for lights, and rushes off.

CROSS ACROSTIC: See ACROSTIC.

CROWN OF SONNETS: A poem comprised of seven sonnets which are interlinked. The final line of each stanza is also the first line of the next. The last line of the seventh sonnet is also the first line of the opening sonnet. For an example, see Donne's "La Corona."

CURTAIN RAISER: A one-act play or other entertainment which is performed at the beginning of a program. In the late nineteenth and early twentieth centuries, curtain raisers served to entertain the audience while late-comers arrived; in this way, the main play of the evening could be presented without distraction.

CURTAL-SONNET: A term used by Gerard Manley Hopkins in the Preface to *Poems* (1876-1889) to describe a shortened form of the sonnet, which he invented. Instead of the traditional fourteen lines, he reduced the number to ten and a half, divided into two stanzas, one of six lines, the other of four, with a "half line tailpiece." In *Poems,* there are two curtal-sonnets, "Pied Beauty" and "Peace," which is given below:

When will you ever, Peace, wild wooddove, shy wings shut,
Your round me roaming end, and under be my boughs?
When, when, Peace, will you, Peace? I'll not play hypocrite
To own my heart: I yield you do come sometimes; but
That piecemeal peace is poor peace. What pure peace allows
Alarms of wars, the daunting wars, the death of it?

O surely, reaving Peace, my Lord should leave in lieu
Some good! And so he does leave Patience exquisite,
That plumes to Peace thereafter. And when Peace here does house
He comes with work to do, he does not come to coo,
   He comes to brood and sit.

D

DACTYL: A metrical foot consisting of three syllables, the first stressed, the other two unstressed.

Á wăs ăn / árchĕr, whŏ / shŏt ăt ă / frŏg;
B was a butcher, and had a great dog;
C was a captain, all covered with lace;
D was a drunkard, and had a red face.

Anonymous

DADAISM: Founded by Tristan Tzara in Zurich during World War I, Dadaism was a nihilistic movement in art and literature which protested against logic, restraint, social convention, and literature itself. (Though some Dadaists claimed that the word *dada* was selected arbitrarily, the term is also believed to have expressed what the members of the group wanted in literature and art—masculinity—instead of femininity, *dada* as opposed to *mama*.)

To demonstrate their contempt for civilization, they painted shocking pictures, wrote nonsensical poems, and arranged bizarre theatrical presentations in theaters and cabarets. One of its members, Marcel Duchamps, sent a toilet bowl to be exhibited at a sculpture show in Paris, but it was returned promptly. Hugo Ball, having composed a "sound poem," read it in a cabaret while dressed with blue cardboard on his legs, a movable scarlet collar, and a blue-and-white-striped top hat. It begins "gadji beri bimba/glandridi lauli lonni cadori," but becomes less clear as it proceeds.

Dadaism, flamboyant and self-conscious, spread to Germany, Holland, France, Italy, and Spain but waned shortly after the end of the war. By the early 1920's, André Breton was establishing Surrealism (*q.v.*), its successor.

DEBAT: One of the most popular literary forms of the twelfth and thirteenth centuries (it survived through the fifteenth century), the *débat* was a contest frequently involving a question of theology, politics, morality, courtly matters, or love. After the *débat* had been argued by two personifications or abstractions, it ended in a decision arrived at by a judge.

DECADENCE: In its most general sense, the term *decadence* refers to any period in art or literature which is in decline as contrasted with a former age of excellence, as, for example, the "silver age" of Latin literature (Tacitus, Martial, Lucan, etc.) as opposed to the preceding "golden age" (Virgil, Horace, Ovid, etc.)

More specifically, *Decadence* designates a literary movement originating in nineteenth-century France which emphasized the autonomy of art, the hostility of the artist to bourgeois society, the superiority of artifice to nature, and the quest for new sensations. The young decadents of the time venerated Baudelaire's *Les Fleurs du mal* (*The Flowers of Evil*) and trumpeted Gautier's dictum that art should be independent of moral and social concerns. Self-consciously and flamboyantly, they published, briefly, *Le Décadent* (1886), the journal of the movement.

In Huysmans' novel *À Rebours*, which Arthur Symons called "the breviary of the movement," Des Esseintes, its central character, typifies the decadent who is affected by the *maladie fin de siècle* ("end-of-the-century illness"), which Symons characterized as "the unreason of the soul," the result of spiritual confusion. Abnormal in his tastes and behavior, Des Esseintes, with his bizarre curiosity, seeks to replace the natural with the unnatural in his search for new experiences.

In England, George Moore, announcing himself in *Confessions of a Young Man* (1888) as "feminine, morbid, perverse," wrote what was perhaps the first English "manifesto" proclaiming Decadence, which thereafter came to be identified with Aestheticism (*q.v.*). Later, Arthur Symons, in "The Decadent Movement in Literature" (1893), referred to the literature of the movement as "a new and beautiful and interesting disease." Much of the English Decadence, though perhaps diseased, was deliberately posed and designed to be startling. Among the representative figures are Oscar Wilde, Ernest Dowson, and Aubrey Beardsley.

DECASYLLABIC VERSE: Lines consisting of ten syllables.

> Say what strange motive, Goddess! could compell
> A well bred Lord t'assault a gentle Belle?

O say what stranger cause, yet unexplored,
Could make a gentle Belle reject a Lord?

Pope, "The Rape of the Lock"

DECORUM: In Classical and Renaissance criticism, the idea that each of the elements of a work should fit appropriately into the whole and, especially, that the style of a passage should be suitable to the occasion and the character. Thus, a king should speak, not like an ordinary man, but in a grand and kingly manner. In Books I and II of *Paradise Lost,* for example, the fallen angels do not address each other colloquially but in a high, rhetorical style suitable to the great occasion with which they are concerned.

DENOTATION: The thing or situation to which a word refers, exclusive of attitudes or feelings which the writer or speaker may have; a word's most literal and limited meaning. Thus, the denotation of *elephant* is a large five-toed mammal with an extraordinary proboscis and long tusks of ivory. If the word, however, suggests to the listener or reader *clumsiness* or *remarkable memory,* it has acquired connotations (*q.v.*). See MEANING.

DENOUEMENT: French: "unknotting." The events following the major climax of a plot. Sometimes, however, *dénouement* designates only a final scene in which mysteries are unraveled and misunderstandings set straight. The *dénouement* of Shakespeare's *Midsummer Night's Dream* consists of the final rearrangement of the lovers and their subsequent marriages. In Shaw's *Major Barbara,* the "unknotting" occurs in Act III, in which Barbara finds a new faith to replace that which Undershaft had destroyed at the end of Act II, the climax of the play.

DESCRIPTION: In a literary work, description, by presenting details of time, place, character, and social setting, creates the "world" in which the story moves. Whereas novelists in the past have exhaustively described environment as though distinct from character, many writers since the late nineteenth century have conceived of social setting as virtually inseparable from character. More recently, writers under the influence of psychoanalytic theory have utilized the stream of consciousness, a technique for depicting the fragmentary conscious and semi-conscious thoughts of their characters.

DESCRIPTIVE LINGUISTICS: See LINGUISTICS.

DETECTIVE STORY: A narrative in which a mystery, frequently involving murder, is unraveled by a detective. First established as a distinct literary form by Poe in "Murders in the Rue Morgue" (1841), the detective story generally contains at least some of the following conventions: the seemingly perfect crime; the dull-wittedness of the police; the detective's confidant, who lacks his associate's brilliance but who always asks questions which clarify the situation; the suspect who appears guilty from the circumstantial evidence but who is later proved innocent; the sensational *dénouement*, in which the detective explains in minute detail who killed whom and how. The method of discovery, is, of course, deductive, for it is generally axiomatic that the sleuth should not be in possession of clues of which the reader is unaware. By ingenious plotting, the writer of the detective story invites his reader to match wits with the central character as both uncover clues leading to the culprit. By extension, many literary works, such as *Oedipus Rex* and *Hamlet* may also be called "detective stories," since the hero in both plays seeks to unravel a mystery involving a murder. Some modern detective stories have ceased to be strict puzzles; instead, they emphasize the psychological implications of a crime or the violent adventures of the protagonist.

DEUS EX MACHINA: Latin: "god out of the machine." In Greek drama, the use of a god lowered by a mechanism of some sort onto the stage to rescue the hero or untangle the plot. Euripides uses this device in half of his extant plays while Aeschylus and Sophocles avoid it in most of theirs. In the *Poetics*, Aristotle, condemning the use of the *deus ex machina*, argues that the *dénouement* of the plot must grow from the action itself. By extension, the term refers to any artificial device for the easy resolution of all difficulties. Serious modern writers avoid the *deus ex machina*, though it has sometimes been used in comedy. Brecht and Weill employ the device at the conclusion of the *Three-Penny Opera* in the form of a proclamation by Queen Victoria which saves Mac the Knife from hanging.

DEUTERAGONIST: The second actor in Greek drama, added by Aeschylus, often synonymous with *antagonist*, although the deuteragonist could, when necessary, assume more than one role. In subsequent usage, the term has been applied to the character of second importance, such as Claudius in *Hamlet*. See PROTAGONIST and TRITAGONIST.

DIALOGUE: 1. The speeches of characters in a narrative or a play, especially the latter. In earlier literature, the dialogue of at least the principal characters made no pretense of being like the actual conversation of men. It was elaborate, deliberately heightened, usually in verse. Realistic dialogue was limited to comic characters or to those on a comparatively low social level. In modern plays, however, the dialogue is usually designed to imitate ordinary speech, although when examined closely, it will regularly be found to be far more selective and highly organized. Modern novelists, relishing the directness and immediacy of dialogue, have made it prominent in their works till, in the stream-of-consciousness novel (*q.v.*), they have produced a form made up almost entirely of the dialogue of the mind with itself.

2. A literary genre in which characters discourse at length on a given topic. See Dryden's "Essay on Dramatic Poesy" and Wilde's "The Critic as Artist," as well as the Socratic dialogues of Plato.

DIBRACH: See PYRRHIC.

DICTION: The choice and arrangement of words in a literary work. Diction varies according to the ends a writer wishes to achieve. The kind of diction will, consequently, be decided by the nature of the literary form, the subject, and the style of the day. Thus, the ornate, balanced rhetoric of much eighteenth-century prose, considered elegant in its time, is deemed inappropriate in modern writing. Dr. Johnson's opening lines in his "Life of Dryden" may serve as an example of the diction which we now admire but rarely imitate:

> Of the great poet whose life I am about to delineate, the curiosity which his reputation must excite, will require a display more ample than can now be given. His contemporaries, however they reverenced his genius, left his life unwritten; and nothing, therefore, can be known beyond what casual mention and uncertain tradition have supplied.

Attempting to bring loftiness and distinction to his subject, Johnson here utilizes a diction suitable for his end. In a recent biography of the young Johnson, a modern scholar, James L. Clifford, uses homely diction in the opening lines of *Young Sam Johnson* to achieve a direct and forceful beginning:

> "Sept. 7, 1709, I was born at Lichfield." Samuel Johnson's pen scratched across the paper. In the drab quarters just above the ground floor of No. 1 Inner Temple Lane, he was beginning an account of his own early years. At intervals he made half whistling sounds and soft clucking noises with his tongue, or talked to himself in a low voice.

DIDACTIC: When the primary aim of a work of literature is to expound some moral, political, or other teaching, it is called *didactic*. Ever since Plato banished the poets from his republic, the relation between literature and doctrine has been a point of contention in a continuing dispute about the nature and function of art. If literature is a unique form of discourse and the function of the writer is different from that of the politician on the platform or the clergyman in the pulpit, then the didactic element may be considered irrelevant or intrusive and *didacticism* a derogatory word. On the other hand, many remarkable literary works—Dante's *Divine Comedy,* for example, or Milton's *Paradise Lost*—are didactic, at least in intent. The didactic element in these works, however, does not dominate them; it forms only a part of the aesthetic experience. Pending settlement of the dispute, this term may be most appropriately used to describe a work rather than to judge it. See MORAL.

DIGEST: 1. A publication devoted exclusively or primarily to abridgments of books or articles which have previously appeared elsewhere. 2. The abridgment itself.

DIMETER: A verse of two metrical feet. The third and fourth lines of a limerick are regularly dimeter, as below:

> There once was a sculptor named Phidias,
> Who did things that were perfectly hideous.
>
>   He carved Aph / rodite,
>
>   Without an / y nightie,
> Which shocked the overfastidious.

DIPODY: Two metrical feet considered as a unit. The use of the dipody as a unit of measure (an iambic trimeter, for instance, would consist of six iambs or three dipodies) is not usually characteristic of English prosody.

DIRGE: A lyrical poem or song of lament originally composed in commemoration of the dead and chanted in Roman funeral processions or banquets. Similar in intent, the Greek threnody and monody are also dirges, the latter sung by one person. In Shakespeare's *The Tempest,* the dirge appears as a poignant mournful lyric when Ariel sings of Ferdinand's lost father:

> Full fathom five thy father lies;
>   Of his bones are coral made:
> Those are pearls that were his eyes:
>   Nothing of him that doth fade
> But doth suffer a sea-change
>   Into something rich and strange.
>   Sea-nymphs hourly ring his knell:
> Hark! now I hear them,—ding-dong, bell.

DISSOCIATION OF SENSIBILITY: In his essay "The Metaphysical Poets," T. S. Eliot complained that the intermingling of thought and feeling characteristic of the Metaphysical poets had been lost, especially through the influence of Milton and Dryden, who lacked this integration of sensibility. Where Donne had produced feeling impregnated with thought, Eliot said, Tennyson and Browning produced only ruminations. As examples of modern poets who had successfully avoided the "dissociation of sensibility," Eliot mentioned the late nineteenth-century French poets Tristan Corbière and Jules Laforgue, who had an admitted influence on his own work.

DISSONANCE: 1. The juxtaposition of harsh or jarring sounds or rhythmical patterns; a synonym for *cacophony* (*q.v.*).

2. The close repetition of consonant sounds; a synonym for *consonance.*

3. The juxtaposition of closely related but not identical vowel sounds in one or more lines, as in the various "o" and "a" sounds in this stanza:

> In a coign of the cliff between lowland and highland,
> At the sea-down's edge between windward and lee,
> Walled round with rocks as an inland island,
> The ghost of a garden fronts the sea.
>
> *Swinburne,* "A Forsaken Garden"

Since definitions 1. and 2. already have appropriate synonyms, the word *dissonance* may best be limited to the sense of definition 3.

DISTICH: A couplet, particularly that used in Greek and Latin elegiac verse.

DISTRIBUTED STRESS: See HOVERING ACCENT.

DITHYRAMB: 1 Originally a Greek choral song, probably sung at the sacrifice to Dionysus. The meters were varied, the tone vehement and passionate. Aristotle says that tragedy was, in origin, associated with the dithyramb. 2. Any poem of dithyrambic character.

DIVERBIUM: In Latin drama, dialogue verse which is spoken. See CANTICUM.

DOGGEREL: Rough, crudely written verse. It is usually humorous, though sometimes unintentionally so. The humor is intended in this passage from Samuel Butler's doggerel epic, *Hudibras:*

> When civil fury first grew high,
> And men fell out, they knew not why;
> When hard words, jealousies, and fears,
> Set folks together by the ears,
> And made them fight, like mad or drunk.
> For Dame Religion as for Punk;
> Whose honesty they all durst swear for,
> Tho' not a man of them knew wherefore
> When Gospel-Trumpeter, surrounded
> With long-ear'd rout, to battle sounded,
> And pulpit, drum ecclesiastick,
> Was beat with fist, instead of a stick;
> Then did Sir Knight abandon dwelling,
> And out he rode a colonelling.

DOLCE STIL NUOVO: Italian: "sweet new style." Though Dante uses this phrase in the "Purgatorio" of the *Divine Comedy*

(Canto XXIV, line 57), to characterize his style and that of certain of his predecessors, particularly Guido Guinicelli, it indicated an attitude toward women and earthly love rather than a literary "style." In the poetry of Guinicelli, the idea is advanced that the essential quality of the "gentle heart" is love, kindled by God. The woman, embodying God's beauty and truth, arouses in the gentle heart that love which has its source in God. As the "lover" revolves about the woman, she leads him to Divine Love and Truth by purifying his earthly desires so that he may achieve saintliness. In short, the beauty of the woman's body, the physical manifestation of the beauty of her soul, becomes the vehicle for her lover's union with God. By combining earthly and divine love, the *stilnovist* poets established a new set of poetic attitudes under the animus of Christianity. The roots of this doctrine lay in troubadour verse and song which were designed for courtly or aristocratic audiences. Dante's *Divine Comedy* is an example, in epic form, of the *dolce stil nuovo*. A survival of the "style" appears later in Spenser's *Faerie Queene*.

DOMESTIC TRAGEDY: A serious play, generally realistic in style, with its protagonist drawn from the lower or middle classes and its action concerned with personal or domestic matters rather than high politics. The term has been applied to such plays as Lillo's *The London Merchant* or Hebbel's *Maria Magdalena* and even to the plays of Ibsen and other modern dramatists, but it is often limited to the Elizabethan domestic tragedy, which includes such plays as *Arden of Feversham, A Warning for Fair Women,* and *A Woman Killed with Kindness.*

DOUBLE RHYME: See FEMININE RHYME.

DRAMA: In the most general sense, any work designed to be represented on a stage by actors. More strictly, however, a drama is a serious play (though it may end either happily or unhappily) dealing with a problem of importance but not aiming at tragic exaltation. This usage of the term originated in mid-eighteenth century France, when Diderot and later Beaumarchais adopted the word *drame* to describe their plays of middle-class life. In modern usage, however, the term *drama* is frequently extended to all serious plays. For some of the major types of plays, see the following entries: CHRONICLE PLAY, COMEDY, COMEDY OF MANNERS,

HIGH COMEDY, MIRACLE PLAY, MORALITY PLAY, MYSTERY PLAY, THESIS PLAY, TRAGEDY, WELL-MADE PLAY.

DRAMA OF IDEAS: See THESIS PLAY.

DRAMA OF SENSIBILITY: See SENTIMENTAL COMEDY.

DRAMATIC IRONY: See IRONY.

DRAMATIC LYRIC: See DRAMATIC MONOLOGUE.

DRAMATIC MONOLOGUE: A poem consisting of the words of a single character who reveals in his speech his own nature and the dramatic situation. Unlike the stage soliloquy, in which place and time have been previously established and during which the character is alone, the dramatic monologue itself reveals place, time, and the identities of the characters. Called a *dramatic lyric* by Browning, who brought the form to its highest development, the dramatic monologue discloses the psychology of the speaker at a significant moment. Though Browning entitles one of his poems "Soliloquy of the Spanish Cloister," it is, in reality, a dramatic monologue, a striking example of the speed with which he establishes character and situation:

> Gr-r-r—there you go, my heart's abhorrence!
> Water your damned flower-pots, do!
> If hate killed men, Brother Lawrence,
> God's blood, would not mine kill you!

DRAMATIC PROVERB: See PROVERBE DRAMATIQUE.

DRAMATIS PERSONAE: The characters in the play. Frequently a list of the characters, with an indication of their relationships, is printed at the beginning of the play.

DRAMATURGY: The composition of plays. The term is sometimes used to include the acting as well as the writing of drama.

DREAM ALLEGORY: A type of medieval poem in which the major portion involves a dream of allegorical significance. *The Romance of the Rose,* a widely read French dream allegory of the thirteenth century, established some of the conventions of the form: the idyllic garden in which the dreamer finds himself; the characters with such allegorical names as Fear, Chastity, Hypocrisy, etc.; physical struggles representing spiritual and moral conflicts.

Widely influential, the poem provided a model for other dream allegories of the time. Chaucer, for example, wrote four: *The Book of the Duchess, The House of Fame, The Parliament of Fowls,* and the "Prologue" of *The Legend of Good Women.* A contemporary of his, William Langland, used the form for *Piers Plowman.*

DROLL: A short, comic piece, often coupled with dancing, performed most often at fairs during the Commonwealth (1649-1660) in England. Since the government had closed the theaters and forbidden full-length plays, the performances of drolls, often comic scenes extracted from earlier plays, were among the few ways of evading the Puritan edicts.

DUODECIMO: Latin: "twelfth." (Abbr. 12mo or 12°) The size of a book (about 5 × 7½ inches) derived from printing on sheets which are folded into twelve leaves or twenty-four pages. See FOLIO.

DUOLOGUE: A conversation between two characters in a play or story. See DIALOGUE.

DUPLE METER OR RHYTHM: One with two syllables to the metrical foot.

E

ECHO VERSE: 1. A line and an "echo" which repeats the final syllables with a change in meaning. 2. A poem made up of such lines.

> Shepherd: Echo, I ween, will in the woods reply,
>   And quaintly answer questions: shall I try?
>   Echo: Try.
>
> What must we do our passion to express?
>   Press.
> How shall I please her, who ne'er loved before?
>   Be Fore.
> What most moves women when we them address?
>   A dress.
> Say, what can keep her chaste whom I adore?
>   A door.
>   *Jonathan Swift,* from "A Gentle Echo on
>   Woman"

ECLOGUE: From Greek: "selection." Originally a short poem or a section of a longer one. Later, the term was applied to the bucolic or pastoral poems of Virgil. In the Renaissance it came to designate any verse dialogue on pastoral themes, such as Spenser's *Shepheardes Calendar*. By the eighteenth century, when town eclogues appeared, the term referred simply to the form. In such modern poems as Frost's "Build Soil" and Mac-Neice's "Eclogue from Iceland," as well as Auden's "Age of Anxiety," the eclogue has openly become a vehicle for the poet's political and social ideas.

EDITION: The total number of copies of a work printed from a single set of type. If, following a first edition, changes are made in the original setting-up of type, the book is printed as a second edition. The term *impression*, though related to *edition*, refers to the total number of copies printed at one time while the type or plates are in the press. Thus, an edition may go to several impressions, or printings, before a second edition is published. The term *issue*, lacking a precise meaning, generally refers to a form of a book in which new material has been added to the original printing or a new arrangement adopted. Frequently, however, the term *re-issue* may refer to the reprinting of a book with no changes. Sometimes different paper may be used for an impression; an inexpensive book may be printed on cheap paper while a de luxe "issue" may also appear. The term *issue* here merely refers to the different paper used.

In older books, the terms *impression* and *edition* are virtually inseparable, since type was broken up after a first printing. In an extended use of the term *edition*, a reference to the "one-volume edition" of Chaucer's works edited by F. N. Robinson indicates its format; the "Robinson edition" of Chaucer, on the other hand, indicates any printed form of the text as edited by Robinson.

EGLOGUE: See ECLOGUE.

ELEGIAC COUPLET: See ELEGIAC METER.

ELEGIAC METER: The meter used in Greek and Roman prosody for the elegiac couplet, a dactylic hexameter followed by a dactylic pentameter or a hexameter in which the unaccented parts of the third and sixth feet have been dropped. The elegiac coup let, which was Greek in origin, was widely used by Catullus and other Latin poets.

ELEGY: In Greek and Roman literature, any poem using the elegiac couplet (*q.v.*), often on such subjects as love and war as well as death. Since the sixteenth century, however, the term has designated a dignified poem mourning the death of an individual (Auden's "In Memory of W. B. Yeats") or of all men (Gray's "Elegy Written in a Country Churchyard"). A specific subtype is the pastoral elegy, originated by the Sicilian Greek poets Theocritus, Bion, and Moschus, and exemplified in English by such poems as Milton's "Lycidas" and Shelley's "Adonais." The poet and his subjects are spoken of as shepherds or goatherds, and the setting is the Classical pastoral world. The nymphs, shepherds, and other inhabitants of this world join in mourning, but the poem usually ends peacefully or even joyfully.

ELISION: In verse, the slurring or omission of an unstressed syllable so that the line may conform to the metrical pattern, as in the second and fourth lines of this quatrain by Michael Drayton:

> Calling to mind since first my love begun,
> Th'incertain times oft varying in their course,
> How things still unexpectedly have run,
> As't please the Fates, by their resistless force . . .

When one of two adjacent vowels is omitted, as in the second line above, the phenomenon is called *synalepha,* though the term *elision* is sometimes restricted to this sense. See SYNCOPE.

EMBLEM: See EMBLEM BOOK.

EMBLEM BOOK: A book of symbolic pictures called *emblems,* each of which is accompanied by a motto and occasionally by exposition. Popular in the later Middle Ages and the Renaissance, the emblem book was moral and didactic. William Blake revived the form in *The Gates of Paradise* (1793).

EMENDATION: The alteration of a text where it appears to be corrupt.

EMOTIVE LANGUAGE: Language designed to evoke or express emotional reactions towards its subject, as opposed to referential language—such as the language of science—designed to carry only denotative meanings. The distinction between emotive and referential language was stressed by C. K. Ogden and I. A. Richards in *The Meaning of Meaning* (1923).

ENCOMIASTIC VERSE: Poems which praise or glorify people, objects, or abstract ideas. In his odes, Pindar, for example, praises the winners of the Olympic games, and Wordsworth in his "Ode to Duty" glorifies the notion of duty.

END RHYME: See RHYME.

END-STOPPED LINE: One in which a grammatical pause—such as the end of a phrase, clause, or sentence—coincides with the end of the line. Most eighteenth century verse, such as this passage from Pope, was end-stopped:

> Meanwhile, declining from the noon of day,
> The sun obliquely shoots his burning ray;
> The hungry Judges soon the sentence sign,
> And wretches hang that jurymen may dine.
>
> "The Rape of the Lock"

ENGLISH SONNET: See SHAKESPEAREAN SONNET.

ENJAMBEMENT: See RUN-ON LINE.

ENTR'ACTE: A brief performance, usually musical, to entertain the audience between the acts of a drama.

ENVOY (ENVOI): From French: "a sending on the way." A concluding stanza, shorter than the preceding ones. See BALLADE.

EPATER LE BOURGEOIS: See PHILISTINE.

EPIC: An extended narrative poem, exalted in style and heroic in theme. Early or "primary" epics, such as the *Iliad*, the *Odyssey*, and the Anglo-Saxon *Beowulf*, are written versions, often anonymous, of the oral legends of a tribe or nation. "Literary" epics, such as Virgil's *Aeneid*, are later imitations of early epics. The term *epic* is also applied to a number of poems—Dante's *Divine Comedy*, Tasso's *Gerusaleme Liberata*, and Spenser's *Faerie Queen*, for example—which do not observe all of the conventions established by Homer.

These conventions, only some of which can be mentioned here, are followed by writers of epic with varying degrees of strictness. The poet begins by announcing his theme, invoking the aid of a muse, and asking her an epic question, with the reply to which the story begins. He then launches his action *in medias res,* in the middle of things. (The preceding events are narrated at some appropriate point later on.) This action concerns a hero, a man of stature and significance; Odysseus, for example, is King of Ithaca, and Aeneas is the founder of the Roman Empire. In the course of the story, the hero performs many notable deeds, one of which is to descend into the underworld. The major characters are catalogued and described, many of them having dignified set speeches which reveal their characters. There are usually great battles in which the gods themselves, who are regularly involved in epic stories, take part. Finally, the epic poet adopts a style, dignified, elaborate and exalted, suitable to his theme.

Byron satirizes the epic apparatus in the following stanza from *Don Juan:*

> My poem's epic, and is meant to be
>   Divided in twelve books; each book containing,
> With love, and war, a heavy gale at sea,
>   A list of ships, and captains, and kings reigning,
> New characters; the episodes are three:
>   A panoramic view of hell's in training,
> After the style of Virgil and of Homer,
> So that my name of Epic's no misnomer.

EPIC (*or* HOMERIC) SIMILE: An extended simile in which one or both of the objects compared are elaborately described. This device is regular in epic poetry but appears in other types as well.

> Thus Satan talking to his nearest mate
> With head uplift above the wave, and eyes
> That sparkling blazed; his other parts besides
> Prone on the flood, extended long and large
> Lay floating many a rood, in bulk as huge
> As whom the fables name of monstrous size,
> Titanian, or Earth-born, that warred on Jove,
> Briareas or Typhon, whom the den
> By ancient Tarsus held, or that sea-beast
> Leviathan, which God of all his works
> Created hugest that swim the ocean stream:
> Him haply slumbering on the Norway foam

The pilot of some small night-foundered skiff,
Deeming some island, oft, as seamen tell,
With fixëd anchor in his scaly rind
Moors by his side under lee, while night
Invests the sea, and wishëd morn delays:
So stretched out huge in length the Arch-Fiend lay
Chained on the burning lake . . .

Milton, Paradise Lost

EPIGRAM: A short usually witty statement, graceful in style and ingenious in thought.

Man is a rational animal who always loses his temper when he is called upon to act in accordance with the dictates of reason.

Oscar Wilde, "The Critic as Artist"

Originally referring to an inscription on a monument, the term came to be associated with short satirical poems, such as those of Martial (first century A.D.). In English literature, such poets as Jonson, Herrick, and Byron have carried on the epigrammatic tradition.

EPILOGUE: 1. The final section of a speech (*q.v.*) also called the *peroration*. 2. The conclusion of a fable where the moral is pointed out. 3. A speech by an actor at the end of a play in which the indulgence of the critics and the applause of the audience is requested.

EPIPHANY: A term used by James Joyce in *Stephen Hero* to refer to "a sudden spiritual manifestation" which an object or action achieves as a result of the observer's apprehension of its significance. Sometimes, when observing a trivial incident or listening to a fragment of conversation, Stephen perceives it as a symbol of a spiritual state; the action achieves an epiphany ("a showing forth") as a result of his awareness of its meaning. In the novel, Stephen plans to gather such epiphanies. In Joyce's *Portrait of the Artist as a Young Man,* a rewrite of the uncompleted *Stephen Hero,* a number of these "insights" appear; one is described in the following passage:

. . . he felt that the augury he had sought in the wheeling darting birds and in the pale space of sky above him had come forth from his heart like a bird from a turret quietly and swiftly. Symbol of departure or loneliness?

EPISODE: An incident within a longer narrative, sometimes closely related to the plot, sometimes a digression.

EPISTLE: 1. A verse letter. This form has been used by many English poets, such as Johnson, Burns, Shelley, Byron, and Donne, whose "To the Countesse of Bedford" is an example:

> Madame,
> Reason is our Soules left hand, Faith her right,
> By these wee reach divinity, that's you;
> Their loves, who have the blessing of your light,
> Grew from their reason, mine from faire faith grew.

2. From the Renaissance through the eighteenth century, dedications of books and poems were usually cast in the form of a letter, and the word *epistle* sometimes carried the sense of preface.

EPISTOLARY NOVEL: A narrative in the form of letters. Popular in the eighteenth century, the epistolary device was notably successful in Samuel Richardson's *Pamela* (1740) and *Clarissa Harlowe* (1747-48). The form enabled Richardson to conveniently reveal his heroine's private thoughts and feelings while advancing the plot. The reader, in the role of literary voyeur, could then see the shifting points of view without the intrusion of the author. The artificiality of the method, however, soon led to the demise of the genre as a popular form, though later writers have employed its technique from time to time.

EPITAPH: Originally referring to an inscription in verse on a tombstone, the term has also been used to designate a poem or a part of a long poem which expresses respect, and occasionally disrespect, for the dead. (See the Epitaph from Gray's "Elegy Written in a Country Churchyard.") Some epitaphs are humorous in intent:

> Here lie I, Martin Elginbrodde:
> Have mercy on my soul, Lord God,
> As I wad do, were I Lord God,
> And ye were Martin Elginbrodde.
>   *Anonymous*

EPITHALAMI (ON) (UM): Greek: "upon the bridal chamber." A song or poem, solemn or ribald, written to celebrate a marriage. In Biblical literature, the *Song of Solomon* is a notable example, while in English, the classic nuptial song is Spenser's "Epithalamion":

> And thou, great Juno! which with awful might
> The laws of wedlock still dost patronize;
> And the religion of the faith first plight
> With sacred rites hast taught to solemnize;
> And eek for comfort often called art
> Of women in their smart;
> Eternally bind thou this lovely band,
> And all thy blessings unto us impart.

EPITHET: An adjective or other term used to characterize a person or thing, as in Ethelred *the Unready* or Jack *the Ripper*. Homer tended to link certain adjectives and nouns which are called *Homeric epithets:* swift-footed Achilles; rosy-fingered dawn; Odysseus, sacker of cities.

EPODE: Greek: "additional song." 1. A poem in which a long verse is followed by a shorter one, as in the *Epodes* of Horace. 2. A section of the Pindaric ode. See ODE.

EQUIVALENCE: In quantitative verse (*q.v.*), the rule that two short syllables equal one long. See SUBSTITUTION.

ERZIEHUNGSROMAN: See BILDUNGSROMAN.

ESSAY: A short composition which is usually in prose (Pope's "An Essay on Man" and "An Essay on Criticism" are exceptions) and which discusses, either formally or informally, one or more topics. Such essays as those in the *Characters* (*q.v.*) of Theophrastus or in the *Meditations* of Marcus Aurelius were well-known in the ancient world, but the term *essai* ("attempt") was first applied to the form by Montaigne when he published a volume of informal pieces in 1580. Seventeen years later, Francis Bacon used the English word *essay* to describe his brief philosophic discourses. Montaigne, intimate, informal, and graceful, and Bacon, dogmatic, formal, and expository, illustrate the range of the essay. With the development of periodicals, the essay became a popular form, and such writers as Addison, Steele, Lamb, Hazlitt, Pater, and Beerbohm made it their major concern.

EUPHONY: Agreeable sounds which are perhaps as much the result of ease of articulation and a sequence of attractive images as of the inherently pleasing nature of the sounds, as in the following lines from Tennyson's "Lotus-Eaters":

> Dark faces pale against that rosy flame,
> The mild-eyed melancholy Lotus-eaters came.

EUPHUISM: The convoluted and highly colored style which takes its name from John Lyly's prose romance *Euphues*, published in 1579. The style, with its heavy alliteration, elaborate antitheses, and extended comparisons, was condemned by some and imitated by others, but it helped to demonstrate the capabilities of English prose as an instrument of expression:

> You see what love is, begon with griefe, continued with sorrowe, ended with death. A paine full of pleasure, a joye replenished with misery, a Heaven, a Hell, a God, a Divell, and what not, that either hath in it solace or sorrowe? Where the days are spent in thoughts, the nights in dreames, both in daunger, either beguylying us of that we had, or promising us that we had not. Full of jealousie without cause, and voyde of feare when there is a cause: and so many inconveniences hanging upon it, as to recken them all were infinite, and to taste but one of them, intollerable.

EXEGESIS: An explanation or interpretation, especially of the Bible. In literature, an exegesis is an analysis and, it is presumed, a clarification of a difficult text.

EXEMPLUM: A story told to illustrate a moral point. The telling of exempla was a common practice of preachers in the Middle Ages, and from the sermon the form passed into literature. In Chaucer's *Canterbury Tales*, the "Pardoner's Tale" and the "Nun's Priest's Tale" are both exempla. Unlike the parable (*q.v.*), the exemplum was usually presumed to be true and the moral placed at the beginning rather than at the end.

EXISTENTIALISM: Though existentialism has been called a philosophical "school," the existentialists themselves differ markedly in doctrine and attitude. Since World War II, there have been two major developments of existentialist thinking. One, Christian existentialism, influenced by Kierkegaard, has stressed the idea that in God man may find freedom from tension, for in

Him the finite and infinite are one. Some of the leading exponents of this general orientation are Karl Barth, Paul Tillich, and Gabriel Marcel. Karl Jaspers, though a believer in some transcendent reality in the universe, does not accept the restrictions of any formal theology. The other major development is attributable to Jean-Paul Sartre and Martin Heidegger, who posit the idea that man is alone in a godless universe; in this atheistic philosophy, man has no reality if he unthinkingly follows social law or convention. Suffering anguish and despair in his loneliness, he may, nevertheless, become what he wishes by the exercise of free will.

Both groups of existentialists, however, hold certain elements in common: the concern with man's being; the feeling that reason is insufficient to understand the mysteries of the universe; the awareness that anguish is a universal phenomenon; and the idea that morality has validity only when there is positive participation.

As a basis for literary expression, existentialism has provided an orientation for such writers as Albert Camus, Simone de Beauvoir, and others, as well as for Sartre himself. Many of the existentialist writers look to Dostoevsky and Kafka, often considered analogous in their philosophical outlook, for literary inspiration.

EXODOS: See GREEK TRAGEDY, STRUCTURE OF.

EXORDIUM: See SPEECH, DIVISIONS OF A.

EXPERIMENTAL NOVEL: See NATURALISM.

EXPLICATION DE TEXTE: A detailed analysis of a passage of prose or verse. In the *explication*, as practiced in the study of French literature, where it is one of the basic pedagogic devices, the student is presented with a scene from a play, a passage of prose, a short poem, or a section from a long one. The writing is then analyzed in detail, with consideration being given both to the style and the significance of the content. In English, the term *explication* denotes any detailed explanation of a text.

EXPOSITION: That part of a play in which the audience is given the background information which it needs to know. Shakespeare, like many dramatists before him, sometimes begins with a section of undisguised exposition, as in *Richard III* and

Henry V, but, as in *Hamlet* and *Othello,* he can also introduce expository material with great subtlety. In a modern realistic drama the exposition presents a particularly difficult problem, for the playwright often finds himself with a great deal of information which must somehow be conveyed with an appearance of ease and naturalness. The maid and butler of nineteenth-century drama, who began the play by discussing the affairs of their employers, eventually became such familiar stage figures as to be, in later times, objects of satire. (See the beginning of Thornton Wilder's *The Skin of Our Teeth.*) Ibsen, a master of exposition, developed the technique of gradually revealing the past as the play developed. The exposition remains one of the tests of a playwright's technical skill.

EXPRESSIONISM: A term which, though it can be defined with some exactness in the history of painting, has been so widely applied in literature as to be, like the word *Romanticism,* devoid of any precise or single meaning. In painting, it refers to a movement begun in Germany around 1905 in which a group of painters, among them Kokoschka, Kandinsky, and Klee, rejected the imitation of external reality in order to try to express the inner self or some essential vision of the world. But in literature, there is no agreed-upon chronology or school of writers. The flowering castle of Strindberg's *Dream Play* has been called an expressionistic device, as has the fragmentary construction of Eliot's *The Waste Land* and the symbolic metamorphoses of the characters of Joyce's *Finnegans Wake.* In fact, almost any of the deliberate distortions of reality in modern literature could, with some justification, be considered examples of Expressionism. This is a word which should be used with discretion.

EXPRESSIVE FORM, FALLACY OF: The idea, held to be fallacious by such New Critics as R. P. Blackmur and Yvor Winters, that sufficiently intense feeling on the part of the poet will regularly produce adequate expression in the poem. This dependence upon inspiration, Blackmur says, deprives the poet of any external criteria, which are necessary if he is to know whether his work functions effectively for his readers.

EXTENSION: See MEANING.

EXTRA-METRICAL VERSE: See ACATALECTIC.

EXTRAVAGANZA: In nineteenth-century English drama, a fairy tale or other fanciful subject in an elaborate production with song and dance. In current usage, the term refers to a theatrical presentation, usually musical, characterized by exuberant staging, elaborate costumes, and a notable irregularity of form. The Ziegfeld Follies is a well-known example of the extravaganza.

EYE RHYME: Rhyme which is apparent to the eye but not to the ear, usually the result of a change in pronunciation. In the first and third lines of the following quatrain by the seventeenth-century poet William Habington, the words *spread* and *read* constitute an eye rhyme:

> My soul her wings doth spread
> And heavenward flies,
> Th'Almighty's Mysteries to read
> In the large volumes of the skies.
> "Nox Nocti Indicat Scientam (David)"

F

FABLE: A brief narrative, in either verse or prose, which illustrates some moral truth. The characters are often animals, as in the fables attributed to the Greek slave Aesop, but are not invariably so. Animal fables are sometimes distinguished by being called *apologues,* but this term is also used as a general synonym for *fable*. For recent examples of this form, see James Thurber's *Fables for Our Time* and George Orwell's extended political fable, *Animal Farm.*

FABLIAU: A type of short verse tale popular in the Middle Ages. The *fabliaux* were comic, often ribald, accounts of middle-class life, satirizing such things as the sanctity of the clergy, the chastity of women, etc. Although the form is primarily French, there are examples, such as Chaucer's "Miller's Tale" in the *Canterbury Tales,* in English.

FALLING ACTION: The part of a play following the climax. See DENOUEMENT, FREYTAG'S PYRAMID.

FALLING RHYTHM: One in which the stress comes on the first syllable of the metrical foot:

Georgie Porgie, pudding and pie,
Kissed the girls and made them cry;
When the boys came out to play,
Georgie Porgie ran away.
                                        Anonymous

See RISING RHYTHM.

FANCY: Up to the Romantic period, *fancy* and *imagination* were largely synonymous, though Dryden suggested that imagination was the more significant of the two qualities. But the Romantic critics, particularly Wordsworth and Coleridge, make a distinction between them. Fancy, they said, was a relatively superficial matter of memory and association, the ability to correlate images into metaphor. Imagination, however, was creative and unifying. The poet who possessed this power, which was in some way allied to the creative power of the universe, could perceive new things which had not been seen before. Coleridge illustrated the distinction by describing Milton's mind as imaginative and Cowley's as fanciful.

FARCE: From Latin: *farcire,* "to stuff." Originally any insertion in the church liturgy. Later, farces were the comic scenes interpolated in the early liturgical plays. The word now refers to any play which evokes laughter by such devices of low comedy as physical buffoonery, rough wit, the creation of ridiculous situations, and which is little concerned with subtlety of characterization or probability of plot. Shakespeare's *Comedy of Errors* is almost entirely farcical, but many plays which are not farces, such as *Twelfth Night,* contain farcical elements, *e.g.,* the mock duel between Viola and Sir Andrew.

FEELING: See FOUR MEANINGS OF A POEM.

FEMININE ENDING: An extra unstressed syllable at the end of a verse, as in the second and fourth lines of the following quat-rain:

Sigh no more, ladies, sigh no more,
    Men were deceivers ever,
One foot in sea and one on shore,
    To one thing constant never.
                    William Shakespeare, from *Much Ado About Nothing*

FEMININE RHYME: A rhyme extending over two or more syllables (usually an accented syllable followed by one or more unaccented). It may be called *double rhyme* if it includes two syllables and *triple rhyme* if it includes three. (By some critics, however, the term *feminine rhyme,* though used synonymously with *double rhyme,* is not extended to *triple rhyme.*) Although they are used in all types of poetry, feminine rhymes are especially common in humorous verse. In this poem by John Millington Synge, all the rhymes except those of the concluding couplet are feminine:

The Curse
(To a Sister of an Enemy of the Author's
Who Disapproved of "The Playboy")

Lord, confound this surly sister,
Blight her brow and blotch and blister,
Cramp her larynx, lung and liver,
In her guts a galling give her.

Let her live to earn her dinners
In Mountjoy with seedy sinners:
Lord, this judgment quickly bring,
And I'm your servant, J. M. Synge.

FIGURATIVE LANGUAGE: Language which makes use of certain devices called *figures of speech,* most of which are techniques for comparing dissimilar objects, to achieve effects beyond the range of literal language. These devices are by no means limited to poetry; everyone uses them to add color and intensity to his speech. If someone says, "Hotchkiss is as blind as a bat," he is using figurative language. To be precise, he is using the device called *simile (q.v.)* to compare Hotchkiss' eyesight with that of a bat, but he does not intend the comparison to be taken literally. He does not mean that the unfortunate Hotchkiss is nearly blind, but only that he is unobservant. In ordinary speech, these devices are casually employed (the expression "beyond the range" in the first sentence of this paragraph is a metaphor, but most of us grasp its meaning without recognizing it as such), but the poet uses them not only as ornament but also to express ideas which can be expressed in no other way. Thus, Shakespeare's phrase, "bare ruined choirs, where late the sweet birds sang," contains complexities of association beyond the power of literal language to delineate. For a discussion of some of the major figures, see HYPERBOLE, METAPHOR, METONYMY, PERSONIFICATION, SYNECDOCHE.

FIGURE OF SPEECH: Any of the devices of figurative language. See above.

FIN DE SIECLE: See DECADENCE.

FLASHBACK: A scene inserted into a film, novel, story, or play, showing events which happened at an earlier time. The device is particularly useful in the film. In *Citizen Kane,* for example, Orson Welles employed it with great skill, but it is also effective in literature. See Thornton Wilder's *The Bridge of San Luis Rey* for its use in the novel.

FLAT AND ROUND CHARACTERS: Terms used by E. M. Forster in *Aspects of the Novel* (1927) to designate different types of characterization. A flat character is one centering about a single idea or quality. Lacking any complexity, it never surprises. The flat character, Forster states, is sometimes called a "type" or "caricature," for it can be summed up in one sentence. An advantage of flat characters is that they are immediately recognizable. To the writer, they are convenient, for he may move them about without concerning himself with their development. To the reader, they are easy to remember later. A flat character may be delightful in comedy but dull if he is the central character in tragedy, for complexity is necessary to move our deepest feelings. By creating flat characters which have depth, if not complexity, a writer such as Dickens may achieve vividness and size. An inept writer, on the other hand, may attempt to make his flat characters round and produce, instead, unconvincing portraits.

A round character must, according to Forster, be capable of surprising a reader in a convincing manner. Complexity of characterization, moreover, must be accompanied by an organization of traits or qualities. Forster believes that though Jane Austen's characters, which are usually round, are smaller than Dickens' flat characters, they are more highly organized. He concludes by saying that serious work often requires a combination of flat and round characters, for the intermingling of both types reflects life as we view it.

FOLIO: 1. Latin: "a leaf." (Abbr. F.) A book made by folding the original printer's sheet once to make two leaves or four pages. In general, a folio is a very large book, but in modern publishing, the dimensions of a printer's sheet vary considerably and the term does not designate a precise size. In addition, this subject is complicated by the fact that some publishers use such terms as *folio, quarto, octavo,* and *duodecimo (qq. v.)* as arbitrary designations of size regardless of the number of leaves to the sheet.

2. In Shakespearean criticism, the term *folios* refers to the collections of his plays published in folio editions some years after his death. The First Folio, one of four, appeared in 1623. The quartos are the editions of separate plays published during and after Shakespeare's lifetime. The texts of a single play often vary widely among the quartos and folios.

FOLK DRAMA: 1. Plays on folk themes produced by amateurs at popular festivals and religious celebrations. In medieval England, these plays concerned such characters as Robin Hood and St. George. The body of medieval liturgical drama (*q.v.*), though derived from a highly developed theology, is considered by some as a part of folk drama.

2. Plays written by sophisticated literary craftsmen on folk themes. Such plays are usually performed not by or for the "folk" but by professional actors before a literate, urban audience. Much of the drama of the Irish Literary Renaissance (*q.v.*), such as the plays of John Millington Synge and Lady Gregory, are folk plays of this sort, as are the peasant plays of Pirandello and Garcia Lorca.

FOLKLORE: The songs, stories, myths, and proverbs of a people or "folk" as handed down by word of mouth. Some scholars also consider such things as traditional ceremonies, architectural forms, and agricultural techniques to be parts of folklore. Since the publication of Percy's *Reliques of Ancient English Poetry* in 1765, the study of folklore has developed steadily. The art of

the "folk" has influenced such disparate figures as Sir Walter
Scott and D.H. Lawrence.

FOLK TALE: A traditional story handed down, in either written
or oral form. This term covers a variety of material from primitive myths to fairy tales, or *Märchen*, to such literary works as
the stories of Hans Christian Anderson. Folk tales had long been
recorded in such collections as the *Thousand and One Nights*
and the *Gesta Romanorum*, but since the collection of the German philologists Wilhelm and Jacob Grimm early in the nineteenth century, the nature and distribution of the folk tale has
been extensively studied.

FOOT: A group of syllables forming a metrical unit. Most of the
feet recognized in English verse contain one accented and one
or two unaccented syllables. The most commonly used feet are
as follows:

Iamb(us): ‿╱   Anapest: ‿‿╱
Trochee: ╱‿   Dactyl: ╱‿‿
        Spondee: ╱╱

See the individual listings of these terms for further discussion
and examples. See also, AMPHIBRACH, AMPHIMAC, CHORIAMB,
DIBRACH, METER.

FORESHADOWING: See ATMOSPHERE.

FORM: 1. A fixed metrical arrangement, such as the sonnet form,
the ballade form, etc.

2. The essential structure of a work of art. *Form* is sometimes
contrasted with *content* (the terms *expression* and *thought* are
often substituted) as if the two were separable entities. We speak
of the poet as having "something to say" and saying it in, for
example, the sonnet form, as if this form were a decoration in-
scribed on the outside of the thought. But this artificial separation of form and content is misleading, for it implies that the
poet's business is to *say* things rather than to *make* things. A poet
makes a poem out of words, which inevitably carry various meanings, but it is only when the complex structure of meanings expresses a particular unity that it achieves aesthetic form. Taken
in this sense, form is more than an external scheme; it is, rather,
the total structural integration of the work itself. The form of a

successful work of art is, as Coleridge said, shaped from within, not imposed from without.

FORMAT: The physical make-up of a book. See FOLIO.

FOUR LEVELS OF MEANING: In a letter to his patron Can Grande della Scala, Dante explained the way in which *The Divine Comedy* should be read. The reader, he said, should be aware of four levels of meaning: 1) *the literal or historical,* that which actually occurs; 2) *the moral meaning;* 3) *the allegorical,* the symbolic significance which pertains to mankind; and 4) *the anagogical,* the spiritual or mystical meaning stating an eternal truth. Dante adds that all except the first level may be called "allegorical."

The technique of the four-fold interpretation was widespread in medieval criticism. Cassian (ca. 400) was perhaps the first to interpret the Scriptures according to the levels which Dante later refers to. In his *Moralia on the Book of Job,* Pope Gregory I likewise demonstrated how this device of exegesis could be employed. Later, secular poetry was also subjected to this method.

FOUR MEANINGS OF A POEM: In *Practical Criticism* (1929), I. A. Richards, discussing the total meaning of a communication, particularly poetry, outlines four different meanings: 1) *Sense:* what is said, or the "items" referred to by a writer; 2) *Feeling:* the emotional attitudes which he has towards these items; 3) *Tone:* the writer's attitude toward his audience. (The use of language is determined by the writer's "recognition" of his relation to his readers.); 4) *Intention:* the writer's purpose, whether conscious or unconscious—the effect he tries to achieve. A scientist writing a treatise, for example, puts the sense first, subordinates his feeling, establishes his tone by following academic convention, and clearly states his intention. In verse, however, the poet makes statements which function as vehicles for the expression of feelings and attitudes. The perceptive reader, Richards suggests, must be prepared to apprehend the interplay of the four meanings which together comprise the total meaning of the poem.

FOURTEENER: A line of fourteen syllables, usually seven iambs. Though once popular—Chapman's translation of the *Iliad* is in this meter—it has seldom been used in recent verse.

FRAME STORY: See STORY WITHIN A STORY.

FREE VERSE: Called *vers libre* by the French, free verse lacks regular meter and line length, relying upon the natural speech rhythms of the language, the cadences which result from the alternation of stressed and unstressed syllables. Though free verse has had its vogue particularly in this century, it was employed by French poets of the nineteenth century trying to free themselves from the metrical regularity of the alexandrine (*q.v.*) and by English and American poets seeking greater liberty in verse structure. Earlier, free verse had been used in the King James translation of the Bible, particularly in the *Song of Solomon* and the *Psalms*. Whitman's *Leaves of Grass* is, perhaps, the most notable example of the organization of speech patterns into verse cadences:

> A child said *What is the grass?* fetching it
> to me with full hands,
> How could I answer the child? I do not know
> what it is anymore than he.
> I guess it must be the flag of my disposition, out
> of hopeful green stuff woven.

FRENCH FORMS: Certain elaborate metrical forms which originated in Provençal troubadour verse and which were later imported into English. They were much used by the Victorians for light verse. For individual definitions and examples, see BALLADE, RONDEAU, RONDEL, SESTINA, VILLANELLE, VIRELAY.

FREYTAG'S PYRAMID: In his *Die Technik des Dramas* (1863) the German critic Gustav Freytag described the structure of the typical five-act play in terms of rising action, climax, and falling action, as illustrated in the diagram below. This pattern has been widely used, though it is not appropriate to all plays.

a. Introduction
a¹. Inciting moment
b. Rise (rising action)
c. Climax
d. Fall (falling action)
e. Catastrophe

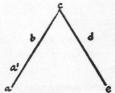

FUSTIAN: Referring to thick cotton cloth, the term *fustian* has also come to mean bombastic or pompously ornate language. In "Epistle to Dr. Arbuthnot," Pope makes reference to a writer

. . . whose fustian's so sublimely bad,
It is not poetry, but prose run mad.

G

GATHERING: The group of leaves in a book cut from a single printer's sheet. See FOLIO.

GENIUS AND TALENT: As we use the word today, *genius* designates an extraordinary, innate intellectual capacity, especially for imaginative creation or for original speculation or invention. It is often contrasted with *talent,* a lesser order of ability or artistic gift.

Originally, a genius was a spirit (in this sense, we now use *genii* as the plural and usually *jinn* or *jinni* as the singular), then one of the two spirits—good and bad—supposed to attend on every man. By extension, it became a person's natural bent or inclination and then his capacity or quality of mind. By the late eighteenth century, it designated a man's inborn ability as contrasted with a skill which could be acquired. Probably reinforced by the original sense of *genius* as spirit, the word took on its modern connotations of transcendent power in the Romantic period. In this sense, it was much used in Germany, where the epoch of the *Sturm und Drang* (*q.v.*) is sometimes called the *Genie-periode,* but the usage seems to have originated in England. In an autobiographical sketch, Thomas De Quincey wrote, "Talent and genius . . . are not merely different, they are in polar opposition to each other. Talent is intellectual power of every kind, which acts and manifests itself . . . through the will and the active forces. Genius . . . is that much rarer species of intellectual power which is derived from the genial nature— from the spirit of suffering and enjoying—from the spirit of pleasure and pain . . . It is a function of the passive nature."

GENRE: 1. A literary type or class. Works are sometimes classified by subject—thus *carpe diem* poems (*q.v.*) may be said to consti-

tute a genre—but the more usual classification is by form and
treatment. Some of the recognized genres are epic, tragedy, comedy, lyric, etc. From the Renaissance through the eighteenth
century, the various genres were rigorously distinguished and
were governed by sets of rules which a writer was expected to
follow. Recently, however, criticism has become less directly prescriptive and less concerned with distinctions among the genres,
though they are still considered useful.

2. A "genre painting" is one which takes its subject from ordinary life rather than mythology or history. By analogy, a literary
work which portrays ordinary people or scenes may be called a
"genre piece."

GEORGIAN POETRY: The poetry which appeared in a group of five
Georgian anthologies edited by Edward Marsh and published
between 1912 and 1922. The diction of these poems was, for the
most part, the traditional one of nineteenth-century poetry, and
their subject was nature in its more gentle aspects. The anthologies presented the work of such poets as Edmund Blunden,
John Masefield, Walter de la Mare, Rupert Brooke, and D. H.
Lawrence.

GEORGIC: A poem about rustic life, especially the *Georgics* of
Virgil.

GESTA: Deeds or tales of adventure, as in the fourteenth century
Gest Historiale of the Destruction of Troy. One of the most
famous medieval collections of tales was the *Gesta Romanorum*
(*Deeds of the Romans*). See CHANSON DE GESTE.

GLOSS: 1. Originally a marginal or interlinear explanation of a
difficult word or phrase. Many Greek manuscripts, when copied,
were given Latin glosses. E.K.'s gloss to Spenser's *Shepheardes
Calender* contains general comment on the poem as well as explanations of difficult words. Coleridge's gloss to *The Rime of
the Ancient Mariner* consists of marginal paragraphs which
sometimes summarize the story.

2. A deliberately misleading interpretation.

GNOMIC VERSE: Verse made up of or largely characterized by
gnomes, or aphorisms. Gnomic verse has been common since
early Greek poetry. There are many ancient and medievai collections of gnomes, and they appear in innumerable works from

Homer to *Beowulf*. Among the best-known gnomic verses in English are the following:

He that is in the battle slain
Will never rise to fight again:
But he that fights and runs away
Will live to fight another day.

Anonymous

GOLIARDIC VERSE: Verse, primarily Latin, of the twelfth and thirteenth centuries attributed to the Goliards, or wandering scholars. Much of it was ribald and satiric, devoted to the praise of love and wine. The most notable collection of such verse is the famous *Carmina Burana,* a thirteenth-century songbook originally in the Benedictbeuern Monastery in Bavaria.

GONGORISM: An intricate and affected style, so called from the work of the Spanish poet Luis de Gongora y Argote (1561-1627). In an effort to add polish to the language of his day, Gongora began introducing new words coined from Greek, Latin, and Italian, along with puns, paradoxes, conceits, and inversions of word order. Because this controversial style was designed to appeal to the cultivated, it was also called *cultismo* or *culteranismo*. See MARINISM.

GOTHIC NOVEL: A type of romance popular in the late eighteenth and early nineteenth centuries. The form was inaugurated by Horace Walpole's *Castle of Otranto* (1764), whose popularity attracted many imitations, among the best known of which were Ann Radcliffe's *The Mysteries of Udolfo* and Matthew Lewis' *The Monk*. These stories, usually set in medieval castles complete with secret passageways, mysterious dungeons, peripatetic ghosts, and much gloom and supernatural paraphernalia, were thrillers designed to evoke genteel shudders, although Mary Shelley's *Frankenstein* (1817), one of the most original of the Gothic novels, had a more serious purpose. The influence of this genre extended to such works as Coleridge's "Christabel," the novels of the Brontës, the mysteries of Edgar Allan Poe, and the writings of innumerable imitators.

GRAND GUIGNOL: See GUIGNOL.

GRAVEYARD SCHOOL OF POETRY: A group of English poets of the

mid-eighteenth century who, unlike the contemporary Neo-
Classicists, cultivated the mysterious and the melancholy. The
members of this group, which included Thomas Parnell, Robert
Blair, and Edward Young, were much attracted to death and
gloomy scenery, anticipating some of the melancholy of the Romantics. The most famous of the "Graveyard" poems is Gray's
"Elegy Written in a Country Churchyard."

GREEK TRAGEDY, STRUCTURE OF: In general, the structure of Greek
tragedy is as follows: 1) *Prologus* or *Prologue:* the introductory
scene, containing either a monologue or dialogue which is devoted to exposition, though portrayal of character is often important. (In Sophocles' *Oedipus Rex*, the first scene finds Oedipus and a priest in a conversation which both presents the
problem of the play and characterizes its hero.) 2) *Parodos:* the
entrance of the chorus which, in song, usually presents further
exposition or foreshadows the tragedy of the play; 3) *Episodes:*
frequently four or five which contain the action of the play.
Episodes are separated by choral odes, or *stasimons.* In some
plays, part of an episode may be a *Kommos,* a lamentation involving actors and chorus. 4) *Exodos:* the final section following
the last ode sung and danced by the chorus. In this part, two
characteristic features recur in Greek tragedy: the messenger's
speech—though sometimes occurring in earlier sections of the
play—and the *deus ex machina* (*q.v.*). (In *Oedipus Rex* a messenger reports Jocasta's suicide and Oedipus blinds himself.)
The device of the *deus ex machina* is characteristic only of the
plays of Euripides.

GRUB STREET: Once the name of a London Street (now Milton
Street) much inhabited by indigent writers whose hack work
resulted in their earning no more than a meager living. Since
many critics found even this result insufficient justification for
their scribblings, the term *Grub Street* has come to be applied
to any inept commercial writing.

GUIGNOL: Originally a puppet character created in Lyons around
the end of the eighteenth century, the witty and audacious Guignol achieved great popularity. He was brought from Lyons to
Paris, where he gave his name to a theater, the Grand Guignol,
which eventually came to produce plays, performed by live

actors, dealing with the horrifying and the macabre. The term *Grand Guignol* is now applied to any such play.

H

HAGIOGRAPHY: The writing or study of saints' lives, widespread in the Middle Ages.

HAGIOLOGY: See HAGIOGRAPHY.

HAIKU (HOKKU): Consisting of seventeen syllables in three lines (5,7,5), the *haiku* is the shortest form in Japanese poetry. Complete in itself, it frequently expresses delicate emotion or presents an image. The Imagists (*q.v.*), inspired by Ezra Pound, attempted to achieve the effects of the form by concentrating on the image, though they did not attempt to imitate the verse structure. The following *haiku* by Taniguchi Buson (1715-83) is characteristic of this genre:

> The short night is through:
> on the hairy caterpillar,
> little beads of dew.
>> Translated by *Harold G. Henderson*

HALF RHYME: See RHYME.

HAMARTIA: Greek: "error." An error in judgment, whether through ignorance or moral fault. Aristotle, discussing the tragic hero, states that he should be a man "not pre-eminently virtuous and just, whose misfortune, however, is brought upon him not by vice and depravity but by some error." Oedipus' error is two-fold: the slaying of his father is the result of impetuousness; the marrying of his mother the result of ignorance.

HARANGUE: A speech, frequently addressed to a crowd, to urge a person or persons to action or to influence attitudes by appealing to the emotions rather than to reason. In Shakespeare's *Julius Caesar,* Antony's speech to the citizens of Rome over Caesar's body is perhaps the most notable instance of the harangue in dramatic literature.

HEADLESS LINE: See ACATALECTIC.

HEAD RHYME: See ALLITERATION.

HEBRAISM—HELLENISM: In Chapter IV of *Culture and Anarchy,* Matthew Arnold characterized the two governing forces in man by the words *Hebraism* and *Hellenism:* "The uppermost idea with Hellenism," he wrote, "is to see things as they really are; the uppermost idea with Hebraism is conduct and obedience." Arnold described the essence of Hellenism as "spontaneity of consciousness" and that of Hebraism as "strictness of conscience." He maintained that both these forces were necessary for a full life but that in England Hebraism had been emphasized at the expense of Hellenism and that a corrective emphasis on culture was in order. Since Arnold's day, these terms have been widely used in social and literary criticism.

HEMISTICH: A half-line of verse, frequently on one side of a caesura (*q.v.*).

HENDECASYLLABIC VERSE: A verse of eleven syllables.

HEPTAMETER: A line of verse consisting of seven metrical feet, as in Robert Southwell's "The Burning Babe":

As Ĭ / ĭn hóar / y̆ wín / tĕr's níght / stŏod shí / vĕring ín / thĕ
    snow,
Surprised I was with sudden heat which made my heart to glow;
And lifting up a fearful eye to view what fire was near,
A pretty babe, all burning bright, did in the air appear . . .

HEPTASTICH: A stanza of seven lines.

HERO—HEROINE: The most important characters, male and fe- male respectively, in a literary work. As technical terms in criti- cism, these words do not necessarily suggest that a character possesses either prowess or virtue. He may be a cowardly rogue, but because he is the central character, he is the "hero."

HEROIC COUPLET: A pair of rhymed iambic pentameter lines. The heroic couplet first appeared in English in the verse of Chaucer (*e.g.,* "She was a worthy womman al hir lyve:/Housbondes at chirche dore she hadde fyve") and has, though varying in popu- larity, remained in continuous use. In the Neo-Classic writers, for whom the heroic couplet was the dominant form, there is usually a pause at the end of the first line and the termination of a syntactical unit at the end of the second. Such a unit is called a *closed heroic couplet*. The most skillful exponent of this form was Alexander Pope, who used it almost exclusively:

> One science only will one genius fit;
> So vast is art, so narrow human wit:
> Not only bounded to peculiar arts,
> But oft in those confined to single parts.
>
> "An Essay on Criticism"

HEROIC DRAMA: A type of play popular for a time in Restoration England. Usually written in heroic couplets (*q.v.*), it was regularly serious, though it might have a happy ending. In a typical heroic drama, a conflict between love and honor was the motivating force. The hero, a paragon of the amorous and military virtues, is forced to choose between the demands of duty and those of love. He may, for example, as commander of his country's army, be forced to conquer the empire ruled by his inamorata's father. The heroine's rival is usually a passionate princess of dubious virtue; the hero's rival may be the villain or his closest friend. The fates of empires regularly hang upon the whims of these improbable personages. Seasoned with bombast, larded with spectacle, and served up by such writers as Dryden, Howard, and Otway, these plays pleased the Restoration palate for a while, but their excesses began to cloy; finally, ridicule, such as that of Buckingham's satirical play, *The Rehearsal*, destroyed such taste for them as remained.

HEROIC QUATRAIN (or STANZA): A stanza composed of two heroic couplets (*q.v.*).

HEXAMETER: 1. A line of six metrical feet, as in the last line of this stanza from Shelley's "To a Skylark":

> Hail to thee, blithe Spirit!
>   Bird thou never wert,
> That from Heaven, or near it,
>   Pourest thy full heart
>
> In pro / fuse strains / of un / premed / ita / ted art.

2. In the classical hexameter, which was the line used for the epic and some other poetry, the first four feet were either

dactylic or spondaic, the fifth was dactylic, the sixth spondaic (*qq.v.*).

HEXASTICH: A stanza of six lines.

HIATUS: A pause or break caused by the occurrence of two vowel sounds unseparated by a consonant in successive words or syllables, as in *coöperate*. Its "repair" by the running together of the two vowels is called *elision* (*q.v.*).

HIGH COMEDY: A term broadly applied to satiric comedy whose appeal is primarily intellectual. There are no precise criteria for distinguishing high from low comedy, but where the latter achieves its effect with jokes and buffoonery, high comedy works with intellect and wit. In general, it is graceful, witty, and urbane. George Meredith wrote: "The laughter of comedy is impersonal and of unrivaled politeness, nearer a smile—often no more than a smile. It laughs through the mind, for the mind directs it . . . The test of true comedy is that it shall awaken thoughtful laughter." (*The Idea of Comedy and the Uses of the Comic Spirit.*) High comedy avoids the excesses of sentimental comedy, but it includes the comedy of manners (*qq.v.*). Although this term is usually used to describe plays such as those of Congreve and Molière, it can be extended to other literary works such as Pope's *Rape of the Lock*.

HIGHER CRITICISM: 1. The study of the antecedents, genesis, and historical surroundings of a work as distinguished from Lower Criticism, which concerns itself with the establishment of a correct text by such means as restitution, emendation, etc. Through consideration of the historical and philosophical aspects of texts, especially the Greek and Roman classics and the Scriptures, the Higher Criticism attempts to interpret a writer's meaning and to delineate the intellectual and cultural climate of a historical period. As a discipline, this critical technique originated in Germany, especially at the University of Göttingen in the latter part of the eighteenth century.

2. When the term *Higher Criticism* is limited to Biblical studies, it then denotes the application of the scientific method, particularly modern historical techniques, to the study of the Scriptures. The books of the Bible, considered as human documents rather than as divine revelations, are studied to determine

the time and place of their composition, their authorship, and their relations to each other and to their cultural and historical backgrounds.

HISTORICAL LINGUISTICS: See LINGUISTICS.

HISTORICAL NOVEL: A narrative which utilizes history to present an imaginative reconstruction of events, using either fictional or historical personages or both. While considerable latitude is permitted to the historical novelist, he generally attempts, sometimes aided by considerable research, to recreate, with some accuracy, the pageantry and drama of the events he deals with. Scott's novels, for example, combine the adventure generally associated wth the historical novel with events and characters drawn from history. A modern example of this genre is Thornton Wilder's *Ides of March,* which deals with Caesar and his time.

HISTORIC PRESENT: The use of the present tense to describe past events. Note the shift from the vivid present tense to the past in the middle of this passage of the player's speech from *Hamlet:*

> Anon, he finds him
> Striking too short at Greeks; his antique sword,
> Rebellious to his arm, lies where it falls,
> Repugnant to command. Unequal match'd,
> Pyrrhus at Priam drives; in rage strikes wide;
> But with the whiff and wind of his fell sword
> The unnerved father falls. Then senseless Ilium,
> Seeming to feel this blow, with flaming top
> Stoops to his base, and with a hideous crash
> Takes prisoner Pyrrhus' ear: for lo! his sword
> Which was declining on the milky head
> Of reverend Priam, seem'd i' the air to stick:
> So, as a painted tyrant, Pyrrhus stood,
> And like a neutral to his will and matter,
> Did nothing.

HISTORY PLAY: See CHRONICLE PLAY.

HOKKU: See HAIKU.

HOLOGRAPH: A document, such as the original manuscript of a literary work, wholly written by the author. The holographs of many early works, such as Shakespeare's plays, are lost and so are unavailable for study. Many modern holographs, however, such as the partial holograph of Oscar Wilde's *The Importance of Being Earnest,* now in the Arents Collection of the New York Public Library, enable scholars to study the development of a literary work.

HOMERIC EPITHET: See EPITHET.

HOMERIC SIMILE: See SIMILE.

HOMILY: 1. A sermon addressed to a congregation. 2. A work which admonishes its readers and urges them to adopt moral attitudes.

HORATIAN ODE: An ode (*q.v.*), such as Keats' "Ode to a Nightingale," in which each stanza follows the same metrical pattern, so called after the Roman poet Horace. Note the pattern in the opening stanzas of Marvell's "An Horation Ode upon Cromwell's Return from Ireland":

> The forward youth that would appear
> Must now forsake his muses dear,
> Nor in the shadows sing
> His numbers languishing:
>
> 'Tis time to leave the books in dust,
> And oil the unused armor's rust,
> Removing from the wall
> The corselet of the hall.

HORNBOOK: A primer which was popular in England between the sixteenth and eighteenth centuries. Consisting of a single sheet of paper or vellum mounted on wood, on which were printed the alphabet, the Lord's Prayer, and Roman numerals, the hornbook derived its name from the protective covering of horn over the sheet. The term is used by Thomas Dekker in his *Gull's Hornbook,* a witty pamphlet for the young men about town of early seventeenth-century London.

HOVERING ACCENT: Occurs when it is difficult to determine which of two consecutive syllables in a verse is to be stressed. This phenomenon, also called *distributed stress,* may result from the poet's clumsiness, but it may also be introduced intentionally to achieve certain effects. In "The Lotus-Eaters," Tennyson uses hovering accent to evoke a mood of languorous ease:

There is sweet music here that softer falls
Than petals from blown roses on the grass
Or night-dews on still waters between walls
Of shadowy granite, in a gleaming pass.

HUBRIS (HYBRIS): Greek: "insolence," "pride." The emotion in the Greek tragic hero which leads him to ignore warnings from the gods or to transgress against their moral codes. By extension, the term is applied to tragic pride in the heroes of later dramas. In Sophocles' *Antigone,* Tiresias, the blind prophet, having told Creon of the foreboding signs of death, attempts to persuade him that he has mistakenly condemned Antigone:

> O my son!
> These are no trifles! Think: all men make mistakes,
> But a good man yields when he knows his course is wrong,
> And repairs the evil. The only crime is pride.

Rejecting Tiresias' warnings, Creon must endure not only Antigone's death but also the self-inflicted deaths of his wife and son. At the conclusion of the play, the leader of the chorus, addressing the audience, cautions against the danger of *hubris:*

> There is no happiness where there is no wisdom;
> No wisdom but in submission to the gods.
> Big words are always punished,
> And proud men in old age learn to be wise.
>
> Translated by *Dudley Fitts* and *Robert Fitzgerald*

HUDIBRASTIC VERSE: Octosyllabic couplets consisting of iambic tetrameter verses—in the manner of Samuel Butler's *Hudibras.* For an example, see DOGGEREL.

HUMANISM: In its most general sense, humanism is the philosophy which emphasizes the achievement of an admirable human life on earth rather than the preparation for a blissful life hereafter. The word derives from the Renaissance humanists, or students of the *litterae humaniores,* the works of the ancient poets, philosophers, rhetoricians and historians. The discoveries of the Renaissance, coupled with the decline of medieval scholasticism, led to the study of the Greek and Latin writers. The humanists, attracted by the Classical view of man as the center of the universe, a creature possessed of dignity, reason, and creative capacity, wished to create a civilization in which educated men could live a life of morality and reason. Such men as Marsilio Ficino and Pico della Mirandola were instrumental in disseminating these ideals.

Within the mainstream of humanism were some who, like Erasmus, retained their allegiance to the traditional religious institutions and others who, like Montaigne, became skeptics and even atheists. Most of the humanists remained Christians, but they placed little emphasis on the sinful nature of man and the desirability of monastic withdrawal. Whatever their divergencies, they were bound together by their reverence for the Classical ideals.

This reverence for the Classical past had a variety of consequences in literature. It produced the imitation of Classical styles and genres and the rigid codification of "rules" supposed to have been followed by the ancients, who were held up as the models of perfection. Literature was polished and enriched by what it learned from the Greek and Latin authors but sometimes hindered in its own development by the attempt to conform to its revered models. In the Neo-Classicism (*q.v.*) of the eighteenth century, this admiration of Classical literature reached its height. The emulation of the ancient writers is no longer a dominant force in literature, but humanistic ideals are still influential in modern thought.

HUMOR: The most general of the terms denoting the laughable. Originally, humor had no connection with laughter, but was a term in medieval medicine. The humours (we retain the British spelling for this sense) were the four bodily fluids, any excess of which distorted the personality. By extension, the term came to mean "disposition" or "mood," then "whim," "fancy," or "personal eccentricity." Finally, something "humorous" was something which made people laugh.

Just what it is that makes us laugh, however, though it has been the subject of much investigation, is still disputed. Aristotle said that the subject of comedy was some defect or ugliness which was not great enough to cause pain. His remark suggests that laughter was directed at some person when he was placed in an inferior position. This idea was developed by Thomas Hobbes, the seventeenth-century British philosopher, who said that "those grimaces called laughter" were the result of self-delight or "sudden glory." Hobbes' leading modern disciple, Anthony Ludovici, replaced "self-glory" with the phrase "superior adaptation," but did not alter Hobbes' primary ideas. The modern French philosopher Henri Bergson, who saw laughter as a weapon which the *élan vital* used to chastise social rigidities, must be placed in the Hobbesian camp. Kant, Schopenhauer, and Herbert Spencer are the most renowned names to be associated with the incongruity theory, the idea that perception of an incongruity, causing our expectations to be disappointed, is the source of our laughter. Spencer advanced the notion that the laughter at the culmination of a joke was a release of energy gathered for a larger purpose. Freud accepted part of this but suggested that the release of suppressed sexual or aggressive tendencies from the control of the psychic censor was the key element in laughter. Research and debate on the sources of humor still continue.

The word *humor* is sometimes limited to gentle and sympathetic laughter and contrasted with *wit* (*q.v.*), which evokes intellectual and derisive laughter.

HUMOURS: During the Middle Ages and the Renaissance, this term referred to the four fluids of the human body: blood, phlegm, yellow bile, and black bile. According to the theory of the time, physical diseases as well as mental and moral temperaments were the result of the relationship of one humour to another. Since the humours released vapors which rose to the brain, an imbalance would result in the dominance of one humour, affecting the behavior of the person accordingly. Thus, a person's physical, mental and moral condition was determined by the state of his humours. When they were in balance, an ideal temperament prevailed. But an excess of one of the bodily fluids resulted in the following behavior:

Excess	Type of Personality	Traits
Blood	Sanguine	kindly, joyful, amorous
Phlegm	Phlegmatic	cowardly, unresponsive, lacking intellectual vitality
Yellow Bile	Choleric	obstinate, vengeful, impatient, easily aroused to anger
Black Bile	Melancholic	excessively contemplative, brooding, affected, gluttonous, satiric.

By the beginning of the seventeenth century, the term *humour* meant "mood" or "peculiarity." In the drama, the humours came to be used by writers who designed types based on the theory of the imbalance of the bodily fluids. The comedy of humours, consequently, depicted "humourous" characters whose behavior was determined by a single trait or humour. Ben Jonson utilized the theory of the humours in his comedies, of which *Every Man in His Humour* (1598) is typical. The first play to be written according to a theory of personality, it contains many characters with names suggesting their controlling trait: Brainworm, Downright, Wellbred, Formal. In his "Induction" to the play, Jonson presents his view of the "humourous" character:

> Some one peculiar quality
> Doth so possess a man, that it doth draw
> All his affects, his spirits, and his powers,
> In their confluctions, all to run one way.

Other Elizabethans were influenced by this physiological theory of personality. In Shakespeare's plays, the humours appear with some frequency. The melancholy Jacques in *As You Like It,* for example, describes his own sadness by using the characteristic vocabulary of the theory of humours:

> I have neither the scholar's melancholy, which is emulation; nor the musician's, which is fantastical; nor the courtier's, which is proud; nor the soldier's, which is ambitious; nor the lawyer's, which is politic; nor the lady's, which is nice; nor the lover's, which is all these: but it is a melancholy of mine own, compounded of many

simples, extracted from many objects, and indeed the sundry contemplation of my travels, which, by often rumination, wraps me in a most humorous sadness.

HYBRIS: See HUBRIS.

HYMN: Greek: *hymnos,* a song praising heroes or the gods. In religious practice, any songs in praise of God, except psalms, may be called *hymns.* By extension, a literary hymn is any song of praise, either serious, as Shelley's "Hymn to Intellectual Beauty," or humorous, as Ben Jonson's "Hymn to Comus," which begins:

> Room! room! make room for the bouncing belly,
> First father of sauce and deviser of jelly;
> Prime master of arts, and giver of wit,
> That found out that excellent engine the spit.

HYMNAL STANZA: Duplicates the ballad stanza ($a^4b^3c^4b^3$) but retains the exact rhymes and undeviating iambic meter found in the hymnal; also called *common measure.* The hymnal stanza sometimes rhymes *abab.*

HYPERBOLE: A figure of speech in which emphasis is achieved by deliberate exaggeration. Like many such figures, it appears in ordinary speech as well as in verse. Such common expressions as "I wouldn't give him the time of day," or "They were packed in the subway like sardines," are examples of hyperbole. Andrew Marvell, in one of the most remarkable hyperboles in English verse, describes the way in which he would adore his mistress had he but time:

> My vegetable love should grow
> Vaster than empires, and more slow,
> An hundred years should go to praise
> Thine eyes, and on thy forehead gaze:
> Two hundred to adore each breast:
> But thirty thousand to the rest;
> An age at least to every part,
> And the last age should show your heart.
> For, lady, you deserve this state,
> Nor would I love at lower rate.
>
> "To His Coy Mistress"

HYPERCATALECTIC: See ACATALECTIC.

HYPERMETRICAL: See ACATALECTIC.

HYPOCORISM: A diminutive or "pet" name, such as Bobby for Robert. Hypocoristic language is that which makes extensive use of endearing terms or euphemistic expressions.

HYSTERON-PROTERON: A figure of speech in which the element which should logically come at the end is put at the beginning. Such a figure may result from the writer's clumsiness or from his desire to achieve a particular rhetorical effect, as in this passage from Matt. xxvi:26: "And as they were eating, Jesus took the bread, and blessed it, and brake it, and gave it to the disciples, and said, *Take, eat; this is my body.*"

I

IAMB(US): A foot of verse consisting of an unstressed syllable followed by a stressed. The following quatrain is in regular iambic meter:

> The Gríz / zly Béar / is húge / and wíld;
> He has devoured the infant child.
> The infant child is not aware
> It has been eaten by the bear.
>   *A. E. Housman,* "Infant Innocence"

ICON: The delineation of some person or object, usually through figurative language, as in this stanza by Thomas Lodge:

> Her neck like to a stately tower
>   Where Love himself imprison'd lies,
> To watch for glances every hour
>   From her divine and sacred eyes:
>   Heigh ho, fair Rosaline!
> Her paps are centers of delight,
>   Her breasts are orbs of heavenly frame,
> Where Nature moulds the dew of light
>   To feed perfection with the same:
>   Heigh ho, would she were mine!
>   "Rosaline"

ICTUS: The stress placed on certain syllables in a line of verse. When a poet wishes to mark the ictus, he usually uses the sign (ʹ) as Gerard Manley Hopkins does in "Spring and Fall," where his stress pattern is not always the one which the reader would normally adopt:

> Márgarét, are you gríeving
> Over Goldengrove unleaving?
>
> Leáves, líke the things of man, you
> With your fresh thoughts care for, can you?
>
> Ah! ás the heart grows older
> It will come to such sights colder
> By and by, nor spare a sigh
> Though worlds of wanwood leafmeal lie.

IDEAL SPECTATOR: 1. The "ordinary" observer or reader to whom the playwright addresses his work. Sometimes this observer is synonymous with the "average man" who, in theory at least, approaches a work simply and without literary preconceptions.

2. The character in the play who expresses or seems to share the attitudes and emotions of the playwright or of the majority of the audience. The *raisonneur* (*q.v.*), who acts as the author's spokesman, and the chorus of Greek tragedy often fulfill this function.

IDENTICAL RHYME: See RHYME.

IDYLL: A short lyrical poem depicting rural or pastoral life. Such verse frequently contains conventional, idealized descriptions of the simple life of the shepherd. Begun by Theocritus and followed by many Classical poets, such as Virgil, poetry of this kind has been called *pastoral* or *bucolic*. However, the pastoral idyll differs from the pastoral elegy in that it avoids a mournful tone. In the Classical writers, the idyll and the eclogue contained similar material, though in the Renaissance and in modern times, the latter is often used for social and political satire. The Renaissance lyricists, in imitation of their Classical models, carried on the tradition of the idyll by writing of the tranquillity of nature, the drowsiness of contented sheep, and the joyousness of

gamboling swains. Perhaps the most famous of these idylls is
Marlowe's "The Passionate Shepherd to his Love":

> Come live with me and be my love,
> And we will all the pleasures prove,
> That hills and valleys, dales and fields,
> Or woods or steepy mountain yields
>
> There we will sit upon the rocks,
> And see the shepherds feed their flocks,
> By shallow rivers to whose falls
> Melodious birds sing madrigals.
>
> And I will make thee beds of roses
> With a thousand fragrant posies,
> A cap of flowers, and a kirtle
> Embroidered all with leaves of myrtle;
>
> . . . .
> The shepherd swains shall dance and sing
> For thy delight each May morning:
> If these delights thy mind may move,
> Then live with me and be my love.

Later writers, tiring of the artificiality of the pastoral idyll,
attempted to bring other material to the form. Wordsworth, in
"The Solitary Reaper," retains the country scene but portrays a
working girl in the fields:

> Behold her, single in the field,
> Yon solitary Highland Lass!
> Reaping and singing by herself;
> Stop here, or gently pass!
> Alone she cuts and binds the grain,
> And sings a melancholy strain;
> O listen! for the vale profound
> Is overflowing with sound.

The idea of work, foreign to the Classical idyll, and the note of
melancholy mark a departure from the conventions of the form.
In Tennyson's *Idylls of the King*, the pastoral element is
omitted; instead, tales of a heroic king portray an age of chivalry,

just as the pastoral idyll presents an ideal existence removed from the complexities of civilization.

ILLUSION: A quality of belief which is evoked by every successful narrative or drama. No matter how intensely a story or play moves a reader, it is never "real" in the way that the actions of his own life are. If, however, the work produces an illusion of reality, he can, by the process which Coleridge called "a willing suspension of disbelief," accept the work as aesthetically valid. For the most part, the maintenance of illusion is one of the writer's primary tasks, but he may, on occasion, deliberately break the illusion to achieve certain effects. The novelist who stops his story to address the reader in his own person or the playwright who has his actors address the audience directly sacrifices illusion to gain some other end. For an example, see the speeches of the knights immediately after the murder of Becket in T. S. Eliot's *Murder in the Cathedral*.

ILLUSION OF THE FIRST TIME: The impression of spontaneity given by a successful actor. Although he has rehearsed his role many times and may have played it for weeks, months, or even years, to be believable, the actor must appear to be saying his lines for the first time under the emotional impetus of the dramatic situation.

IMAGERY: In general, the term *imagery* refers to the use of language to represent descriptively things, actions, or even abstract ideas. This word, however, has been so widely used by recent critics that it cannot be said to have a single agreed-upon meaning. In its most common use, *imagery* suggests visual pictures, though many critics insist that words denoting other sensory experiences are, properly speaking, images. Frequently, a writer combines both visual and non-visual images, as in Poe's "The Haunted Palace":

> Along the ramparts plumed and pallid
> A wingèd odour went away.

An example of an auditory image occurs in Coleridge's *Rime of the Ancient Mariner*. Though instruments are referred to, it is the sound, which is compared to that of all instruments, that the reader "hears":

> And now 'twas like all instruments,
> Now like a lonely flute;
> And now it is an angel's song,
> That makes the heavens be mute.

To express abstract ideas, imaginative writers turn to figures of speech, such as metaphors and similes, to give vividness and immediacy to their thought. In Shakespeare's Sonnet LX, for example, the ideas of time and the inevitability of death are visualized in the images of the opening lines:

> Like as the waves make towards the pebbled shore,
> So do our minutes hasten to their end.

Similarly, an abstract idea personified may be presented in an image, as in Keats' "To Autumn":

> Who hath not seen thee oft amid thy store?
> Sometimes whoever seeks abroad may find
> Thee sitting careless on a granary floor,
> Thy hair soft-lifted by the winnowing wind . . .

At a certain point in our use of the term *image,* we refer not to a single picture but to an abstraction or condensation of a series of pictures. Thus, we speak of the image of autumn in Keats' poem as a symbol for the writer's feelings about the nature of time and its passage. All symbols, in fact, are apprehended through specific images, such as the white whale in *Moby Dick.* In its furthest extension, the term *image* becomes synonymous with *idea* or *vision,* as when we speak of the "Paradiso" in Dante's *Divine Comedy* as the author's image of salvation and bliss. In short, imagery serves as the vehicle for the imaginative thought, the aesthetic experience, which the writer attempts to communicate.

IMAGINATION: See FANCY.

IMAGISM: The theory and practice of a group of poets who, between 1909 and 1917 in England and America, believed that the precise image was central in verse. Under the leadership of Ezra Pound, who edited the first imagist anthology *Des Imagistes* (1914), such poets as H.D. (Hilda Doolittle), John Gould Fletcher, F. S. Flint, and Richard Aldington, attempted to discard what Pound called the loose and sentimental poetry of the nineteenth century. Amy Lowell, who displaced Pound as "leader," edited *Some Imagist Poets* (1915), which contained a manifesto proclaiming the ideals of what was to be called "amygism": Poetry should 1) employ the language of common speech; 2) create new rhythms; 3) have absolute freedom in subject matter; 4) present precise images with "hardness" and clarity. Pound thought that H.D.'s "Oread" was a "perfect" imagist poem:

> Whirl up, sea—
> Whirl your point pines;
> Splash your great pines
> On our rocks,
> Hurl your green over us,
> Cover us with your pools of fir.

IMITATION: In our time, imitation is in poor repute, suggesting the second hand and derivative rather than the original and creative. These pejorative associations are part of our inheritance from Romantic criticism, but to earlier periods such associations were unknown. For most of literary history, in fact, imitation has been not only a respectable practice by which apprentice writers learned their craft but also the way in which later writers sought to achieve the excellence which had been attained by the ancients.

Plato, it is true, attacked the poets for imitating the appearances of nature and ignoring the absolutes, but Aristotle defended them as imitators not of the external or incidental but of the universal, as opposed to the historians, who dealt with particulars. In Rome, such writers as Cicero, Quintilian, and Horace, advocated that young writers steep themselves in the traditions of their Greek predecessors in order to develop their own skills. In no sense was the imitation of earlier poets regarded as plagiarism by the Romans or by their medieval and Renaissance successors.

Some critics advocated the strict imitation of earlier models, but the commonest idea was that since the proper rules for the imitation of nature had been discovered by the writers of an-

tiquity, their practices should be followed. Pope expresses this
view in the eighteenth century in "An Essay on Criticism":

> Those RULES of old discovered, not devised,
> Are Nature still, but Nature methodized;
> Nature, like liberty, is but restrained
> By the same laws which first herself ordained
>   Hear how learned Greece her useful rules indites,
> When to repress, and when indulge our flights:
> High on Parnassus' top her sons she showed,
> And pointed out those arduous paths they trod;
> Held from afar, aloft, th'immortal prize,
> And urged the rest by equal steps to rise.
> Just precepts thus from great examples given
> She drew from them what they derived from Heaven.

As the Neo-Classic period developed into the Romantic, in
which the poet's originality was stressed, the pejorative connotations of the word *imitation* became more prominent. In our
day, the word is largely absent from the vocabulary of criticism
or is limited to the Aristotelian sense, in which it is largely
synonymous with *mimesis* (*q.v.*).

IMPRESSION: See EDITION.

IMPRESSIONISM: In general, literary practice which emphasizes not
objective reality as it is, but rather the impressions the author or
character derives from it. The term comes from the school of
mid-nineteenth century French painting which was in reaction
to the academic style of the day. Such painters as Monet and
Renoir concerned themselves with the effects of light, sometimes
rendering several paintings of the same object or scene to
demonstrate that "objective reality" was different to the viewer
at different times of day. Developing a technique by which
objects were seen, not as solids but as fragments of color which
the spectator's eye unified, the impressionists, as they called
themselves, made the act of perception the key for the understanding of the structure of reality. The basic premise involved
was that "truth" lay in the mental processes, not in the precise
representation of external reality.

The literary use of the term *impressionism* is, however, far less
precise. Many of the French Symbolist poets have, at one time or

another, been called impressionists. In England, Walter Pater, concerned with aesthetic matters, used the term *impression* in *The Renaissance* (1873) to indicate that the critic must first examine his own reactions in judging a work of art. The verse of such aesthetes as Lord Alfred Douglas, Oscar Wilde, and Arthur Symons abounds in poems entitled "Impression" to suggest their indebtedness to the French impressionists and to indicate that they were painting word pictures. Symons felt that the impressionist in verse should record his sensitivity to experience, not the experience itself; he should "express the inexpressible." In Wilde's *Impression du Matin,* perhaps influenced by Whistler's paintings, the impressionist technique is apparent in the subjectivity of description and the suggestiveness of the colors:

> The Thames nocturne of blue and gold
>   Changed to a Harmony in grey:
>   A barge with ochre-coloured hay
> Dropt from the wharf: and chill and cold

> The yellow fog came creeping down
>   The bridges, till the houses' walls
>   Seemed changed to shadows and St. Paul's
> Loomed like a bubble o'er the town.
>   . . . .
> . . . one pale woman all alone,
>   The daylight kissing her wan hair,
>   Loitered beneath the gas lamps' flare,
> With lips of flame and heart of stone.

In the modern novel, *impressionism* frequently refers to the technique of centering on the mental life of the chief character rather than on the reality around him. Such writers as Proust, Joyce, and Virginia Woolf dwell on their characters' memories, associations, and inner emotional reactions. In the *Portrait of the Artist as a Young Man,* for example, Joyce presents Stephen Dedalus' unarticulated feelings, but comparatively little of his physical surroundings is described. Stephen's environment is consequently shadowy, almost "unreal" to the reader, but his inner life is vivid. See STREAM OF CONSCIOUSNESS.

IMPRESSIONISTIC CRITICISM: That in which the critic is concerned not with analysis, biography, or abstract questions of aesthetics, but with presenting, often in carefully wrought language, his own experience or "impression" of the work of art. Anatole France described such criticism as "the adventures of a soul among masterpieces."

In the preface to *The Renaissance,* Walter Pater, one of the most distinguished impressionistic critics, speaks of the necessity of knowing fully one's own impression: "Our education becomes complete," he wrote, "in proportion as our susceptibility to these impressions increases in depth and variety. And the function of the aesthetic critic is to distinguish, analyze, and separate from its adjuncts, the virtue by which a picture, a landscape, a fair personality in life or in a book, produces this special impression of beauty or pleasure, to indicate what the source of that impression is, and under what conditions it is experienced." In *The Renaissance* itself, Pater produced a series of essays which typify impressionistic criticism in their sensitivity, their evocative and elaborate style, and their ignoring of intellectual analysis. Probably no passage is more renowned than his description of Leonardo's *La Giaconda:*

> She is older than the rocks among which she sits; like the vampire she has been dead many times, and learned the secrets of the grave; and has been a diver in deep seas, and keeps this fallen day about her; and trafficked for strange webs with Eastern merchants; and, as Leda, was the mother of Helen of Troy, and, as Saint Anne, the mother of Mary; and all this has been to her but as the sound of lyres and flutes.

Among other writers who have produced notable examples of impressionistic criticism are Oscar Wilde, George Moore, Arthur Symons, and perhaps the finest critic of the group, Virginia Woolf.

IMPRINT: 1. The name of the publisher, place, and date of publication, usually placed at the bottom of the title page.

2. The printer's name on any printed matter; in a book, usually at the back.

INCREMENTAL REPETITION: A term coined by Francis B. Gummere

(*The Popular Ballad,* 1907) to describe one of the important structural devices of the ballad form. Incremental repetition refers not to the use of refrains but to the repetition of succeeding stanzas with increments, changes in certain key words to indicate a development of the situation. One of the commonest accompaniments to this device is the question and answer formula, as in this passage from the ballad "Edward":

> "Why dois your brand sae drap wi bluid,
> > Edward, Edward
> Why dois your brand sae drap wi bluid,
> > And why sae sad gang ye O?"
> "O I hae killed my hauke sae guid,
> > Mither, mither,
> O I hae killed my hauke sae guid,
> > And I had nae mair bot hee O."

> "Your haukis bluid was nevir sae reid,
> > Edward, Edward,
> Your haukis bluid was nevir sae reid,
> > My deir son I tell thee O."
> "O I hae killed my reid-roan steid,
> > Mither, mither,
> O I hae killed my reid-roan steid,
> > That erst was sae fair and frie O."

INCUNABULA: Latin: "swaddling clothes." Books printed before the year 1501 are referred to as *incunabula,* or *cradle books*. Many of the estimated eight million *incunabula* survive and are deposited in libraries or sought after by collectors. Some of them are remarkable examples of workmanship, resembling medieval manuscripts in size and ornamentation. In the United States, there are considerable collections of *incunabula* in the Library of Congress in Washington, the Morgan Library in New York, and Huntington Library in California.

INDUCTION: An archaic word for *introduction* or *prologue*. As used in the sixteenth century, the induction sometimes served as the "frame" for the work. In Shakespeare's *Taming of the Shrew,* for example, the opening scene, marked "Induction," precedes Act I. In it, Christopher Sly, a drunken tinker, is made to believe that he is a lord. For his amusement, a play is performed—*The Taming of the Shrew*. The *Mirror for Magistrates* (1563), however, has for an "Induction" a long poem which describes, in the manner of Virgil and Dante, a descent into Hell. There the shades of historic personages are encountered; following this "Induction," each shade tells of the tragic circumstances which led to his fall.

INFLECTION: 1. A change in the form of a word to mark a change in its grammatical function. The change is usually an addition to the stem from which various forms of the word are made. In English, a language which does not make extensive use of this element, the noun, for example, usually has only one inflection, the "s" added to the stem to form the plural and the possessive (the possessive apostrophe is a printer's device, comparatively recent in date). In Latin, on the other hand, a regular noun of the first declension has seven inflectional forms.

2. The term *inflection* is also used to designate vocal changes in pitch.

INKHORN TERM: In Elizabethan times, a phrase applied contemptuously to learned words newly coined or brought into English from other languages, especially Latin but also Greek, French, Italian, and Spanish. Thomas Wilson, whose *Arte of Rhetorique* (1553) was reprinted several times during the century, wrote, "Among all other lessons this should first be learned, that we never affect any straunge ynkhorne termes, but to speake as is commonly received." As a sample of what he opposed, he adduced a letter to the Lord Chancellor supposed to have been written by a Lincolnshire man requesting a benefice. The first sentence will illustrate Wilson's point: "Pondering, *expending*, and *revoluting* with my selfe, your *ingent affabilitie*, and *ingenious capacity* for *mundane* affaires: I cannot but *celebrate* and *extol* your *magnifical dexteritie* above all other." The italicized words are those unfamiliar in Wilson's day, but it should be noted that several of them have since become accepted in the language.

IN MEDIAS RES: See EPIC.

INSCAPE AND INSTRESS: In the work of Gerard Manley Hopkins, the term *inscape* refers to the "individually-distinctive" inner structure. or underlying pattern, of a thing. The essence, or inscape, of an object may be perceived, Hopkins believes, through the senses in a moment of illumination. This experience is possible because the instress, or force, ultimately divine, which determines the inscape and holds it together, impresses the inner design upon the mind. Thus, writing about a bluebell, Hopkins states: "I know the beauty of our Lord by it."

INSPIRATION: Writers, attempting to account for the sources of their own creativity, have sometimes resorted to the term *inspiration,* which suggests supra-human origins. (The Latin *inspirare,* meaning "to breathe into," implies the infusion of divine power; the Greeks thought of the soul as a "breath.") In older literature, the writer's direct appeal to a god or a muse was traditional, though it is sometimes difficult to determine whether the device was a literary convention or an earnest appeal for aid. In the *Iliad* and *Odyssey,* for example, Homer repeatedly invokes the muse to give him the creative energy to tell his tale.

Convinced that poets were possessed by divine forces which drove them mad, Plato said in the *Ion* that the epic and lyric poets uttered all their beautiful poems not through art but through divine inspiration. A poet, he said, is only capable of poetry when he is inspired by the gods and "out of his mind"— when there is no reason in him. Influenced by Plato, Aristotle wrote in the *Poetics* that poetry implied either a happy gift of nature or a strain of madness. In the latter, the poet is "lifted out of himself," a phrase suggesting the power of the gods.

In the Renaissance, the Classical view of the poet's madness was popularly believed. Indeed, Plato's discussion of inspiration in the *Ion* was referred to as *de furore poetica,* "concerning poetic madness." In Shakespeare's *Midsummer Night's Dream,* this idea finds expression in the speech in which Theseus, with some levity, suggests the relationship of "divine power" and creativity:

The lunatic, the lover, and the poet,
Are of imagination all compact:
One sees more devils than vast hell can hold,
That is the madman; the lover, all as frantic.

Sees Helen's beauty in a brow of Egypt:
The poet's eye, in a fine frenzy rolling,
Doth glance from heaven to earth, from earth to heaven;
And, as imagination bodies forth
The forms of things unknown, the poet's pen
Turns them to shapes, and gives to airy nothing
A local habitation and a name.

Later, Milton, substituting the divine light of Christan inspiration for the pagan notion of poetic frenzy, wrote in *Reason in Church Government* that the poet needs the assistance of the "eternal Spirit . . . who sends out his seraphim with the hallowed fire of his altar."

Modern psychoanalytical theory suggests that inspiration, or creativity, has its source in the unconscious, which is the wellspring of repressed emotions craving expression. Adopting this notion, the surrealists have theorized that art which is the true image of the creator's soul should be wrought without the interference and control of reason. In short, some surrealists, at least, have permitted themselves to be possessed by that modern "muse," the force of the unconscious. But whether from the id or from the gods, the source of a poet's gift is still called his *inspiration*.

INSTRESS: See INSCAPE AND INSTRESS.

INTENSION: See FOUR MEANINGS OF A POEM.

INTENTIONAL FALLACY: In "An Essay on Criticism," Alexander Pope suggested that the critic should "In every work regard the writer's End,/Since none can compass more than they intend." Many modern critics, however, regard a poem as a public document, complete in itself, and the writer's intention, if he had one other than the invariable intention of writing a poem, an external irrelevance. The error of judging a work by the author's success or failure in achieving his intention these critics call the *intentional fallacy*. In *The Verbal Icon,* W. K. Wimsatt, Jr., and Monroe C. Beardsley wrote, "The poem is not the critic's own and not the author's (it is detached from the author at birth and goes about the world beyond his power to intend about it or control it). The poem belongs to the public . . . What is said about the poem [such as the poet's statement of intention] is subject to the same scrutiny as any statement in linguistics or in the general science of psychology." Wimsatt and Beardsley find the source of the intentional fallacy in Romantic subjectivism, in the concern for the artist's psyche rather than his art.

Certain of the New Critics (*e.g.,* J. C. Ransom and Cleanth Brooks) recognize a "total intention," by which they refer to the total meaning or organization of a work. See AFFECTIVE FALLACY, NEW CRITICISM.

INTERIOR MONOLOGUE: See STREAM OF CONSCIOUSNESS.

INTERLUDE: A type of short play, often a farce, popular in fifteenth and sixteenth-century England. The English interlude resembles such continental works as the anonymous French farce *Pierre Patelin* and the comedies of the German mastersinger Hans Sachs. Designed to be played as the entertainment, or part of the entertainment, at the banquets of the aristocracy, the interludes might be serious and moralistic, like Medwall's *Fulgens and Lucres,* but were more likely to be rough and farcical, like Heywood's *The Foure PP.* This play, by the master of the singing boys of St. Paul's Cathedral, is simply a lying contest held by a palmer, a pardoner, a pothecary, and a peddler and won by the palmer, who stuns his companions by announcing that in all his travels he has never seen a woman out of patience. Other interludes by Heywood are *The Play of the Wether* and *A Mery Play betwene Johan Johan, the Husbande, Tyb, his Wyfe, and Syr Johan, the Preest.*

The term *interlude* is sometimes applied to comic episodes in the medieval drama, such as the scene in Mak's house in the Towneley, *Second Shepherds' Play.*

INTERNAL RHYME: Occurs within a single verse. It may serve several functions: giving pleasure in itself, pointing up the rhythmical structure, or, as in this example from Gilbert and Sullivan's *Iolanthe,* breaking a long line into shorter units:

> When you're lying *awake* with a dismal head*ache,* and repose is taboo'd by anxiety,
> I conceive you may *use* any language you *choose* to indulge in, without impropriety;
> For your brain is on *fire*—the bedclothes con*spire* of usual slumber to plunder you:

First your counterpane *goes,* and uncovers your *toes,* and your
sheet slips demurely from under you.
Then the blanketing *tickles*—you feel like mixed *pickles*—so ter-
ribly sharp is the pricking,
And you're hot, and you're *cross,* and you tumble and *toss* till
there's nothing twixt you and the ticking.

See LEONINE RHYME.

INTRIGUE: The incidents which make up the plot of a play. Although the word *intrigue* may properly be used to refer to any
plot in the drama, it is most likely to be applied to one which
is elaborate and especially to one in which the schemes of one or
more of the characters provide the motivating force. Such in-
tricately plotted works as Congreve's *Love for Love* and *The
Way of the World* are sometimes called *comedies of intrigue.*

INTRODUCTION: 1. Usually an essay, though sometimes a poem,
which precedes a literary work. The function of the introduction
is frequently to state the author's intention and acquaint the
reader with some of the material to be found in the work. The
term *prolegomena* (sing. *prolegomenon* is rare) designates a
series of preliminary remarks on the subject of the book.

2. The first part of a speech. See SPEECH, DIVISIONS OF A.

INVECTIVE: An attack, on a person or idea, using abusive language
to ridicule or denounce. James Stephens' "A Glass of Beer" is a
particularly good example:

The lanky hank of a she in the inn over there
Nearly killed me for asking the loan of a glass of beer;
May the devil grip the whey-faced slut by the hair,
And beat bad manners out of her skin for a year.

That parboiled ape, with the toughest jaw you will see
On virtue's path, and a voice that would rasp the dead,
Come roaring and raging the minute she looked at me,
And threw me out of the house on the back of my head!

If I asked her master he'd give me a cask a day;
But she, with the beer at hand, not a gill would arrange!
May she marry a ghost and bear him a kitten, and may
The High King of Glory permit her to get the mange.

INVENTION: In the modern period, an inventive writer is one whose work is marked by originality, either in form or material. At first, however, invention, the *inventio* of Classical and medieval rhetoric, referred to the finding of an orator's arguments. By extension, it came to mean the original finding and arranging of material for any literary work. In Renaissance and Neo-Classical criticism, *invention* was a word used widely but without any agreed-upon denotation. Generally, it was a synonym for such words as *wit* or *imagination,* and to say of a writer that he possessed invention was merely to say that he had literary ability. The word is little used in Romantic and post-Romantic criticism.

INVERTED ACCENT, FOOT, STRESS: See SUBSTITUTION.

INVOCATION: An appeal, usually directed to Calliope, the muse of epic poetry, in which the poet asks for divine assistance at the beginning of an epic or other long work. The invocation remained a literary convention through the Renaissance and Neo-Classic periods. At the beginning of *Paradise Lost* occurs the most famous invocation in English, but Milton appeals not to Calliope but to Urania, who is officially the muse of astronomy but is here converted into a holy spirit:

> Sing, Heavenly Muse, that on the secret top
> Of Oreb, or of Sinai, didst inspire
> That Shepherd, who first taught the chosen seed,
> In the beginning how the Heavens and Earth
> Rose out of Chaos; or if Sion Hill
> Delight thee more, and Siloa's brook that flowed
> Fast by the oracle of God, I thence
> Invoke thy aid to my adventurous song,
> That with no middle flight intends to soar
> Above the Aonian mount.

See INSPIRATION.

IRISH LITERARY RENAISSANCE: In 1878, the publication of Standish O'Grady's *History of Ireland: Heroic Period* marked the beginning of the Irish Literary Renaissance. The work, an account of the heroic exploits of such mythological figures as Finn MacCool and Cuchulain, stirred a new spirit of nationalism among Irish intellectuals and writers who looked forward to an art within the Celtic tradition and to the restoration of Ireland's cultural position. Attempting to divorce themselves from the dominance of British literature, Irish writers turned to their own heritage and wrote of past heroes and of the glories of Ireland's Golden Age. Yeats, for example, deals with a mythic odyssey in the legendary "The Wanderings of Oisin" (1889); other poems are populated by Fergus, Cuchulain and other figures of Irish folklore. Though some Irishmen, such as Douglas Hyde, championed the use of Gaelic as appropriate for verse, others felt that English was a suitable instrument for expression provided Irish material was used.

In 1891, feeling that Ireland was ready for a "new literary consciousness," Yeats, with other prominent poets, founded the Irish Literary Society in London, and in the following year the Irish National Literary Society in Dublin. Now that the Irish Leader Parnell was dead and resistance to British rule was split into factions, Irish writers turned their energies to the cultural revival and supported the two societies. The two organizations established libraries, published books on Irish subjects, sponsored lectures, and attempted to stimulate the public's interest in the movement.

In 1899, encouraged by the revival, Yeats, George Moore, and Edward Martyn founded the Irish Literary Theatre, which lasted for three seasons. It was discontinued because of disagreement over the repertory. Martyn and Moore preferred modern realistic drama; Yeats wanted verse and legend.

Determined to have a national drama, Frank and William Fay established another Irish theater in 1901 which was later known as the Abbey or the National Theatre Society. Under the direction of Yeats and Lady Gregory, the theater presented plays depicting peasant life as well as the legendary deeds of past heroes. Such plays as A.E.'s *Deirdre* and Yeats' *Cathleen Ni Houlihan,* acted by native performers, established an indigenous Irish theater. Perhaps the greatest playwright of the group was John Millington Synge. His *Playboy of the Western World,* which provoked riots in the theater for an entire week because of its unorthodox view of Irish life, is often considered the most significant play to emerge from the Irish Renaissance.

The early plays of Sean O'Casey, though produced at the Abbey Theatre in the 1920's, are outside the Irish literary revival, since they are concerned with social and political problems in urban, realistic settings rather than with folklore and rustic characters.

IRISH LITERARY REVIVAL: See IRISH LITERARY RENAISSANCE.

IRONY: A device by which a writer expresses a meaning contradictory to the stated or ostensible one. There are many techniques for achieving irony. The writer may, for example, make it clear that the meaning he intends is the opposite of his literal one, or he may construct a discrepancy between an expectation and its fulfilment or between the appearance of a situation and the reality that underlies it. Whatever his technique, the writer demands that the reader perceive the concealed meaning that lies beneath his surface statement.

It is this element of concealment or dissimulation from which irony developed. *Eironeia,* or "dissembling," was what characterized the *eiron,* a stock character of Greek comedy. Though small and weak, the *eiron,* by means of his wit and resourcefulness, was always able to prevail over the *alazon,* the bullying braggart.

The success of the *eiron* in defeating his opponent by seeming to retreat parallels that of Socrates, who, in the Platonic dialogues, pretends to be ignorant and willing to adopt his opponents' views but does so only to display their flaws. This technique of apparent self-denigration is called *Socratic irony.*

Of the various types of irony, probably the simplest and the most commonly used is verbal irony, also called *rhetorical irony.* It occurs when the attitude of the writer or speaker is the opposite to that which is literally stated. When Horatio mentions that the marriage of Hamlet's mother followed closely the funeral of his father, Hamlet replies: "Thrift, thrift, Horatio! the funeral bak'd meats / Did coldly furnish forth the marriage tables." Hamlet offers a ridiculous explanation of his mother's hasty marriage so that the irony will intensify his expression of revulsion at the lust which he and Horatio both recognize as the real explanation. Again, when Hamlet, feigning madness, says that his father has been dead for less than two hours, Ophelia corrects him: "Nay, 'tis twice two months, my lord."

Hamlet: So long? . . . O heavens! die two months ago and not for-
gotten yet? Then there's hope a great man's memory may
outlive his life half a year.

Hamlet's ironical delight is more expressive of his grief than
any outburst of anger.

Dramatic or tragic irony depends on the structure of the play
more than on the actual words of the characters. An extraordinary example of sustained dramatic irony is Sophocles' *Oedipus
Rex,* in which Oedipus seeks throughout the play for the murderer of Laius, the former king of Thebes, only to find that he
himself is the guilty one. The term *dramatic irony* is also used
to describe the situation which arises when a character in a play
speaks lines which are understood in a double sense by the audience though not by the characters on stage. When Brabantio
warns Othello against being betrayed by Desdemona, the Moor
replies, "My life upon her faith." For an audience which knows
the story, Othello's remark presages the tragedy to come.

We speak of irony of situation when a set of circumstances
turns out to be the reverse of those anticipated or considered
appropriate. In Shelley's "Ozymandias," a traveler describes a
shattered statue lying in a desert:

And on the pedestal these words appear:
"My name is Ozymandias, king of kings;
Look on my works, ye Mighty, and despair!"
Nothing beside remains. Round the decay
Of that colossal wreck, boundless and bare
The lone and level sands stretch far away.

Romantic irony occurs when a writer builds up a serious emotional tone and then deliberately breaks it and laughs at his own
solemnity. Byron, the most noted practitioner of romantic irony
in English, does so in this stanza from Canto IV of *Don Juan:*

If in the course of such a life as was
    At once adventurous and contemplative,
Men, who partake all passions as they pass,
    Acquire the deep and bitter power to give
Their images again as in a glass,
    And in such colors that they seem to live;

> You may do right forbidding them to show 'em,
>> But spoil (I think) a very pretty poem.

Several of the New Critics (*q.v.*), especially Brooks and Warren, use the term *irony* in a more general sense to describe the way in which, in a complex poem, the total context qualifies the various elements which enter into it. A poem is "ironic" if it takes account of the complexities and incongruities of experience. Even among the New Critics, however, this usage is not universal.

IRREGULAR ODE: See COWLEYAN ODE.

ISSUE: See EDITION.

ITALIAN SONNET: See PETRARCHAN SONNET.

IVORY TOWER: A phrase suggesting the detachment and aloofness of the artist or the philosopher from the mundane preoccupations of mankind. The tower alone, as it appears, for example, in Milton's "Il Penseroso" and Yeats' "The Tower," suggests contemplation; the ivory tower, however, generally connotes isolation from life. As such, the term frequently has pejorative meaning, since it suggests a devitalization of the spirit.

J

JABBERWOCKY: Derived from a poem in Lewis Carroll's *Through the Looking Glass,* the term *jabberwocky* refers, by extension, to any unintelligible speech or writing. In the story, Alice, discovering a poem called "Jabberwocky" printed backwards in a looking-glass book, holds it up to a mirror so that she may read it and finds this:

> 'Twas brillig, and the slithy toves
>> Did gyre and gimble in the wabe:
> All mimsy were the borogoves,
>> And the mome raths outgrabe.

Explicating what appears to Alice as nonsense verse, Humpty Dumpty says that "brillig" means "four o'clock in the afternoon —the time when you begin *broiling* things for dinner." While some of his explanation of the poem is persuasive, part of it is very odd. "Wabe," a grass plot around a sun-dial, is referred to by that name because "it goes a long way before it, and a long way behind it . . . and a long way beyond it on each side."

In constructing the dream language of *Finnegans Wake,* in which Carroll is mentioned several times, James Joyce is partly indebted to the technique of jabberwocky.

JARGON: A term of contempt applied to speech or writing considered ugly sounding, unintelligible, or meaningless. Often the language of a trade or profession seems full of unnecessarily complex or inflated terminology, which is called *jargon.* Thus, we speak of medical jargon or the jargon of the New Criticism (*q.v.*).

JEREMIAD: A literary work or speech which contains prophecies of destruction in the manner of those in the *Book of Jeremiah:* ". . . for evil appeareth out of the north, and great destruction." However, the term may also refer to complaints similar to those in the *Lamentations* of Jeremiah. G. A. Greene's "A Mood" is an example of this kind of verse:

> They have taken away my Lord;
>> They have shattered the one great Hope;
>> They have left us alone to cope
> With our terrible selves: the sword
>
> They broke, which the world restored;
>> They have cast down the King from on high;
>> Their derision has scaled the sky;
> They have taken away my Lord
>
> The strength of immortal Love;
>> The comfort of millions that weep;
>> Prayer, and the Cross we adored—
> All is lost! there is no one above;
>> We are left like the beasts that creep;
>> They have taken away our Lord.

JEST-BOOKS: Collections of witty and satirical anecdotes, widely read in England and on the continent during and after the sixteenth century. Influenced by the medieval *fabliau* (*q.v.*) and other genres which were designed to instruct while they amused, the jests are short, frequently ending didactically. The stories, epigrams, and *exempla* (*q.v.*)—satiric, ribald, sometimes coarse —are populated by characters who are the dupes of practical jokes or the targets of witty remarks. *A Hundred Merry Tales* (ca. 1526) is the earliest example that exists in English.

JEU D'ESPRIT: French: "play of the mind." A witticism or flight of fancy characterized by graceful expression and urbane wit. In Oscar Wilde's *The Picture of Dorian Gray,* Lord Henry Wotton, recalls an acquaintance:

> "She is still *décolletée,*" he answered, taking an olive in his long fingers; "and when she is in a very smart gown she looks like an *édition de luxe* of a bad French novel. She is really wonderful, and full of surprises. Her capacity for family affection is extraordinary. When her third husband died, her hair turned quite gold from grief."

JONGLEUR: In medieval France, a minstrel or wandering entertainer. As a singer (Jongleurs also entertained by juggling or performing tricks), he might present his own material, but he often served merely as the interpreter for the verses of the *trouvère* or troubadour poet (*qq.v.*).

JOURNAL: 1. A magazine or periodical, especially of a serious or learned nature, such as the *Publications of the Modern Language Association.*

2. A daily record of occurrences. Among the most noted private journals are those of James Boswell, in the eighteenth century, and of André Gide, in the modern period.

JOURNALESE: A cliché-ridden or elaborately pretentious style once used widely by journalists. In the past, newspapers were not always able to maintain a high stylistic standard in their staffs; as a result, newspaper writing was often marked by affectations and the use of hackneyed phrases. A suicide, for example, was regularly converted into "the desperate act." As standards of style rose, newspapermen removed worn-out expressions and strove for simplicity and directness. Nowadays, the word *journalese* is often extended to the sort of semaphore style adopted by space-conscious headline writers who convert the fact that a police commissioner has declined to attend a conference into "TOP COP NIXES CHAT."

K

KABUKI: In Japan, *Kabuki* began, according to tradition, early in the seventeenth century when a former priestess named O-Kuni gave dance performances, accompanied by the ringing of a little bell, and sang religious songs. Previously, the popular theater had consisted of public recitations of legends accompanied by a guitar and rhythmic tappings of a fan. With another actor, who also functioned as her manager and lover, O-Kuni organized a troupe which included men who were female impersonators. The extraordinary popularity of *Kabuki* as popular entertainment resulted in numerous companies of male and female prostitutes, who created such scandals that *Onna* (woman) *Kabuki* was suppressed in 1629. By the middle of the nineteenth century, the law against women performers was relaxed, but female impersonators continued to perform in *Kabuki* plays.

Unlike the performers of aristocratic *Nō* drama (*q.v.*), *Kabuki* actors wear no masks. Moreover, in staging, instead of the bridge of the *Nō* play leading from the actors' dressing room, the *Kabuki* theater has a flowery runway leading from the rear of the audience to the stage so that actors make their appearances not from the side of the stage but directly from the rear of the theater.

Characteristically violent and melodramatic, the elaborately plotted *Kabuki* drama may be shorter or longer than the Western three-act play. Performances frequently continue throughout an entire day, and if spectators remain in the theater, meals are served to them. See NŌ DRAMA.

KATHARSIS: See CATHARSIS.

KENNING: A standard phrase or metaphor used in Anglo-Saxon and other Germanic verse, such as "the leavings of hammers" for swords or "the whale-road" for the sea. It is analogous to the Homeric epithet (*q.v.*).

KING'S ENGLISH: Correct usage, that of the royal family being presumably beyond question.

KÜNSTLERROMAN: A novel which traces the development of the

artist (German: *Künstler*, "artist"; *roman*, "novel"), usually from childhood to his maturity. Generally, the pattern of these novels is similar: a sensitive young man, artistically inclined, finds that he must struggle against the misunderstandings and bourgeois attitudes of his family, which is unsympathetic towards his creative desires. Attempting to preserve his "artistic integrity," he leaves home, determined, like Stephen Dedalus in James Joyce's *Portrait of the Artist as a Young Man*, to "forge in the smithy of [his] soul the uncreated conscience of [his] race."

L

LAI: See LAY.

LAKE POETS: Wordsworth, Coleridge, and Southey, so called because, at one time or another, each lived in the Lake Country of northwestern England. Wordsworth settled in the Lake Country in 1799, Southey in 1803; both spent the rest of their lives there. Coleridge lived at Greta Hall, Keswick, from 1800 to 1804, and in 1809-10 stayed with the Wordsworths at Grasmere but then left the Lake Country and never returned. With its lakes and pleasant valleys, the area gave to the poets an example of the serene and gentle nature which they admired.

LAMENT: A work, usually a poem, expressing intense grief. The *complaint* (*q.v.*) is a mournful poem, but its circumstances are less tragic and the emotions it evokes less painful. The *Lamentations of Jeremiah* are among the most famous laments. In English, there are several laments in Anglo-Saxon literature, such as "The Wanderer," "Deor's Lament," etc. A modern example is Shelley's "Lament":

> O world! O life! O time!
> On whose last steps I climb,
>   Trembling at that where I had stood before;
> When will return the glory of your prime?
> No more—Oh, never more!

LAMPOON: A satirical attack on a person, usually a malicious character sketch. Lampoons, which can be either prose or verse, were widespread in seventeenth- and eighteenth-century England, but their flowering was cut short by the development of libel laws. In these verses, Alexander Pope lampoons the scholars Richard Bentley and Lewis Theobald:

> Yet ne'er one sprig of laurel graced these ribalds,
> From slashing Bentley down to piddling Tibbalds:
> Each wight, who reads not, and but scans and spells,
> Each word catcher, that lives on syllables,
> Even such small critics some regard may claim,
> Preserved in Milton's or in Shakespeare's name.
> Pretty! in amber to observe the forms
> Of hairs, or straws, or dirt, or grubs, or worms!
> The things, we know, are neither rich nor rare,
> But wonder how the devil they got there.
>   "Epistle to Dr. Arbuthnot"

LAUREATE: See POET LAUREATE.

LAY: In medieval French literature, tales of romance and adventure composed in octosyllabic couplets. The *lais* of Marie de France, who wrote at the court of Henry II during the latter part of the twelfth century, were said to be based upon Celtic legends as sung by the minstrels of Brittany. Some of these "Breton lays" deal with the characters of Arthurian legend.

The Provençal *lai,* usually a love poem, was designed to be sung to a popular tune of the day and as a result had greater metrical variety. In fourteenth-century England, the term *lay* could be used to describe any short narrative poem resembling the Breton lays. The most famous of these is Chaucer's "Franklin's Tale" from *The Canterbury Tales;* its prologue begins:

> Thise olde gentle Britouns in hir dayes
> Of diverse aventures maden layes,
> Rymeyed in hir firste Briton tonge;
> Whiche layes with hir instrumentz they songe.

The term has since been used to describe any simple song or verse narrative of adventure, such as Macaulay's *Lays of Ancient Rome* and Scott's *Lay of the Last Minstrel.*

LEAF: A part of a book comprising two pages, printed or blank, one on each side. See FOLIO.

LEGEND: 1. A story, sometimes of a national or folk hero, which has a basis in fact but which also includes imaginative material. The story of Paul Bunyan is regarded as legend, for it is believed that there was an extraordinary lumberjack who served as the model. The story of Casey Jones is in process of becoming a legend, for stories of Casey's devotion have grown up around the historical facts of his death.

2. An account of a life. Chaucer's *Legend of Good Women* contains the stories of both historical and mythological figures, such as Cleopatra and Medea, who are united by a single theme —the praise of faithful women.

3. An account of a saint's deeds. The famous *Legenda Aurea,* or *Golden Legend,* a thirteenth-century collection of saints' lives by Jacobus de Voragine, is the most notable example. See MYTH.

LEGITIMATE THEATER: Any theatrical presentation by actors in a theater, performed solely for the audience present. In 1737, the Licensing Act, passed by Parliament through the efforts of Prime Minister Walpole, authorized Covent Garden, Drury Lane, and the Haymarket as the sole legal theaters, though other theaters evaded the law by calling their dramatic presentations "concerts" or pantomimes. The law continued with some modification until 1843, when restrictions on the number of "legitimate" theaters were abolished. Because the plays presented in the unlicensed houses were musicals, the term *legitimate theater* came to be associated with non-musical plays, but as it is used today, it includes both types of theatrical presentation.

LEONINE RHYME: That type of internal rhyme (*q.v.*) in which the word before the caesura (*q.v.*) rhymes with the concluding word. According to tradition, it is so called from Leoninus, Canon of the church of St. Victor in Paris, whose Latin verses are marked by this kind of rhyme. Although the term is sometimes limited to pentameters and hexameters (lines of five and six metrical units), as used by Leoninus, it can be extended to describe the rhymes in the first, third, fifth and seventh lines of this stanza from W. S. Gilbert's *The Yeoman of the Guard:*

Oh! a private *buffoon* is a light-hearted *loon,*
If you listen to popular rumor;

From the morn to the *night* he's so joyous and *bright,*
And he bubbles with wit and good humor!
He's so quaint and so *terse,* both in prose and in *verse,*
Yet though people forgive his transgression,
There are one or two *rules* that all family *fools*
Must observe, if they love their profession.

LETTER: 1. In the plural, a synonym for literature or scholarship: "a man of letters." See BELLES-LETTRES.

2. The personal letter, though not primarily a literary form, has many relations to literature; in fact, some writers, such as Sydney Smith and Lord Chesterfield, are remembered largely for their letters. A scholar or biographer reads the available letters of a writer and his associates for information about his life and the composition of his works. Letters, moreover, among the most revealing of documents, often display aspects of an author's psychological make-up not immediately apparent in his more public writings. But it is when the letter, by the force of its style and the importance of its statements, becomes an object of interest in its own right that it may be called a literary work. Some letters of this type, such as the one in which Petrarch describes the ascent of Mount Ventoux to Dionisio da Borgo San Sepolcro, are meant for publication, but many of the greatest letters were meant to be seen only by their recipients. When the letters of a great figure are at once vivid, revealing, and significant, as, for example, those of Keats, Mozart, and Flaubert, they become cultural documents of the first importance. See EPISTLE, EPISTOLARY NOVEL.

LEVEL STRESS (EVEN ACCENT): Occurs when the stress falls evenly on two syllables in the same word or on two monosyllabic words which are closely linked, as *daybreak, snow storm.* For the use of this phenomenon in verse, see HOVERING ACCENT.

LIBRETTO: Italian: "little book." A text of an opera, operetta, or other long vocal composition, containing dialogue or narrative. Traditionally opera librettos, with such exceptions as Da Ponte's libretto for *Le Nozze di Figaro* and Boito's for *Otello* and *Falstaff,* have been of limited literary interest, but in the modern operatic theater, there has been an effort to produce texts of such quality that the music and the libretto may form an organic whole. The collaboration between Richard Strauss and Hugo von Hofmannsthal, for example, has resulted in such unified works.

LIGHT ENDING: A term used as a synonym for both weak and feminine ending (*qq.v.*).

LIGHT RHYME: Occurs when one of a pair of rhyming syllables is unstressed. This type of rhyme is frequent in ballad literature; in the following stanza, the second syllable of the word *also*, which rhymes with *go*, is unstressed:

> "If I was to leave my husband, dear,
>   And my two babes also,
> O what have you to take me to,
>   If with you I should go?"
>
> "The Demon Lover"

LIGHT STRESS: In verse, a stress on a word not normally accented in speech. In the following stanza, the word *and* in the last line is so stressed:

> My notion was that you had been
>   (Before she had this fit)
> An obstacle that came between
>   Him, and ourselves, and it.
>
> *Lewis Carroll*

LIGHT VERSE: Poetry written to entertain. Light verse may be brief, as in the lyric, epigram, or limerick, or long, as in Lewis Carroll's "The Hunting of the Snark." The use of French fixed forms, such as the triolet, ballade, and the rondeau (*qq.v.*), for light verse was common in the nineteenth century in England, but they have since lost favor.

Although light verse is designed principally to entertain, there may also be a serious side to the poet's play of the mind, for the term *light verse* includes parodies, occasional verse, and satire which may, under the appearance of humor, have a serious intention. In such writers as Swift and T. S. Eliot, light verse has intellectual bite.

LIMERICK: A type of light verse. The limerick, one of the few fixed forms to become genuinely popular in English, consists of five anapestic lines rhyming *aabba*. The first, second, and fifth lines are trimeter and the third and fourth dimeter though these two may be printed as a single line with internal rhyme. Although there have been several explanations for this term, the most common is that the refrain "Will you come up to Limerick?" was sung at parties at which these verses were extemporized; its origin, however, is not definitely known. In an early limerick, the nursery rhyme "Hickory Dickory Dock," the last line and the first lines are the same; in the limericks of Edward Lear, whose *Book of Nonsense* (1846) popularized the form, the last line is usually a variation on the first:

> There was a young lady of Lucca,
> Whose lovers completely forsook her;
> She ran up a tree, and said "Fiddle-de-dee!"
> Which embarrassed the people of Lucca.

The modern limerick reserves the last line for some climactic or surprising twist:

> There was a young lady from Spain,
> Who was exceedingly sick on a train,
> Not once but again
> And again, and again
> And again, and again, and again.

Always vigorous and often bawdy, the limerick may be the last surviving folk poetry in the machine age.

LINGO: A term applied either humorously or in contempt to any strange speech or foreign language.

LINGUISTICS: The scientific study of language. Descriptive linguistics is concerned with classifying the characteristics of a language, and comparative or historical linguistics with its development. Among the major divisions of the field of linguistics are etymology, the history of word forms; semantics, the study of the meanings of words; phonetics, the study of speech sounds; morphology, the study of the forms or inflections of words; syntax, the study of the groupings of words into sentences or units of meaning.

LINKED RHYME: See RHYME.

LINK SONNET: See SPENSERIAN SONNET.

LITERARY BALLAD: See BALLAD.

LITERARY EPIC: See EPIC.

LITERATURE: Such genres as the novel, the short story, the epic poem, the lyric, and the play clearly fall within the boundaries of literature; as embodiments of some of man's feelings and thoughts, they are experiences shaped into aesthetic forms. The distinction between literature and other forms of communication is often tenuous. A historical work such as Douglas S. Freeman's monumental biography of George Washington presents the facts and conditions of the subject's life, whereas a work such as Lytton Strachey's *Elizabeth and Essex*, while purporting to be history, is in reality a highly imaginative account written in a style which creates the atmosphere of a historical romance. Sometimes, as a work ceases to have scholarly authority in a field, it acquires distinctly literary value. Thus, because of its impressive Neo-Classic style and subjective point of view, Gibbon's *Decline and Fall of the Roman Empire* has perhaps come to be read more as literature than as history.

Whatever its form, however, literature has at least four major functions. Many readers go to literary works for entertainment, which may be elevated and intellectual or which may be of a comparatively less exalted nature. For example, the plays of Shaw are witty, cerebral entertainment, whereas an ordinary farce offers a different quality of amusement. The desire to escape from an oppressive or dull environment may impel the reader to seek the fantasy of science fiction, the remoteness of a Western, or the excitement of a detective story. On the other hand, literature may be valued for its capacity to inculcate moral and spiritual values. The didacticism of a literary work may thus be direct, as in Bunyan's *Pilgrim's Progress,* or indirect, as in Shakespeare's *Macbeth.* One of the greatest values which we can attribute to literature is its capacity to acquaint us with the forces which motivate men, the place of man in society and in the universe. In the final analysis, it provides a reader with intense and unique experiences ordered to give him the aesthetic pleasure which accompanies his apprehension of the work.

LITOTES: A form of meiosis (*q.v.*) in which an idea is expressed by the denial of its opposite. A scholar who wishes to recommend his work while retaining his modesty may remark that during his researches he has learned "not a little" to signify that he has in fact learned a good deal. Milton makes use of this device when, at the beginning of *Paradise Lost,* he asks the muse to aid his adventurous song "that with no middle flight intends to soar," indicating that in reality his poem will soar to the highest levels of imagination.

LITTERATEUR: One who devotes himself to the study or writing of literature; a man of letters. The term sometimes suggests the amateur or dilettante rather than the professional.

LITURGICAL DRAMA: Plays performed as part of the liturgy of the medieval church. When these were merely tropes, or brief interpolations in the service, they were in Latin and chanted by members of the clergy. As these plays became popular, they were expanded, and the vernacular was introduced. After they were moved out of the church buildings, their production was placed in the hands of the laity, and although the plays still dealt with religious themes, they ceased to be liturgical in character. See MIRACLE and MYSTERY PLAYS.

LIVING NEWSPAPER: A type of didactic play produced by the Federal Theater project in the 1930's. These plays dramatized social and economic problems of the time in productions that were elaborate and often experimental in theatrical technique. Episodically constructed and peopled by symbolic characters, the plays made their points not only through acting but also through such devices as dance, mime, film, and the use of extracts from newspapers and political speeches. *One Third of a Nation* and *Triple-A Ploughed Under* were among the best-known living newspapers.

L.M.: The abbreviation for long measure (*q.v.*).

LOCAL COLOR: The use of regional detail to add interest to a narrative. Local color, as the term implies, is generally not of crucial importance to the plot or for an understanding of motivation; it is, rather, in descriptions of locale, dress, and customs, concerned with the quaint and the picturesque. In this sense, local color is mere decoration. When, however, description of a region becomes an intrinsic and necessary part of the work, the emphasis on the relationship of region to the action is characteristic of what is called regional literature (*q.v.*).

LOGAOEDIC: In Greek and Latin prosody, a meter composed of anapests and iambs or of dactyls and trochees. The term is sometimes extended to refer to any mixed meter. The following lines of Edward Lear's "The Jumblies" are logaoedic:

> Far and few, far and few,
>   Are the lands where the Jumblies live;
> Their heads are green, and their hands are blue,
>   And they went to sea in a Sieve.

LOGICAL STRESS: Also called rhetorical stress and rhetorical accent. See ACCENT.

LONG MEASURE (L.M.): A hymnal stanza (*q.v.*) in which all four lines are tetrameters.

LOOSE AND PERIODIC SENTENCE: A loose sentence is one in which a main clause comes first, followed by further dependent grammatical units: "Hotchkiss rose slowly from his seat with a shy smile, determined to show the class that he could, for once, answer the instructor's question." A periodic sentence is one in which the main clause is withheld until the end: "Delighted by Hotchkiss' resolve, the class and the instructor burst into applause." In formal writing, the periodic sentence is used for structural variety and rhetorical emphasis. The loose sentence, however, a more relaxed construction, is more frequently used in informal writing and in conversation.

LOW COMEDY: In a play, the coarse elements designed to arouse the audience's laughter. Frequently, low comedy consists of off-color jokes or physical action, such as slapstick. In medieval English drama, low comedy commonly made its appearance as added stage business. The character of Vice, for example, often the object of practical jokes, himself engaged in clownish behavior to relieve the solemnity of the play. The Elizabethan playwrights inherited the traditions of medieval drama. In Shakespeare's *The Merry Wives of Windsor,* for instance, Falstaff, getting into a basket to hide from a suspicious husband, has "foul linen" piled atop him. The basket is then carried off-stage to be dumped into the Thames.

LOWER CRITICISM: See HIGHER CRITICISM.

LYRIC: In Greek poetry, a lyric was a poem sung to the accompaniment of a lyre. We still refer to the words of a song as "the lyrics," but in general the term *lyric* denotes a poem of limited length expressing the thoughts and especially the feelings of a single speaker. This term, which is widely used, designates such disparate works as Wordsworth's "Tintern Abbey," an extended philosophic poem, as well as this anonymous sixteenth-century song:

> Western wind, when wilt thou blow
> The small rain down can rain?
> Christ, if my love were in my arms
> And I in my bed again!

M

MACARONIC VERSE: Light verse written in two or more languages. Macaronics are usually made by mixing a modern language with Latin or Greek. English is most commonly mixed with Latin, often to the extent of giving English words Latinate endings, as in the following:

> Qui nunc dancere vult modo,
> Wants to dance in the fashion, oh!
> Discere debet ought to know
> Kickere floor cum heel and toe.
>   One, two, three,
>   Come hop with me,
> Whirligig, twirligig, rapidee.
>   "Polka," *G.A. à Beckett*

MADRIGAL: A song designed for several voices, the madrigal may be pastoral, satiric, or concerned with love. Italian in origin and influenced by the Tudor court song cultivated during the reigns of Henry VII and Henry VIII, the English madrigal flourished for less than a quarter of a century, reaching its height around 1600. Some of the great English madrigal composers were Thomas Morley, John Wilbye, and Thomas Weelkes. The madrigal is used in a number of Gilbert and Sullivan operas, such as *The Mikado* and *Ruddigore*.

MAGNUM OPUS: Latin: "a great work." A major literary work, a writer's masterpiece. Today the term often carries ironic connotations.

MALAPROPISM: A blunder in speech or writing caused by the substitution of a word for another similar in sound but different in meaning. Shakespeare's Dogberry of *Much Ado about Nothing* is greatly addicted to malapropisms ("O villain! thou wilt be condemned into everlasting redemption for this"), but it is from Mrs. Malaprop of Sheridan's *The Rivals*, that the term derives. In this speech, she explains to Sir Anthony Absolute her ideas on the education of women:

> Observe me, Sir Anthony, I would by no means wish a daughter of mine to be a progeny of learning . . . But, Sir Anthony, I would send her at nine years old to a boarding school, in order to let her learn a little ingenuity and artifice. Then, sir, she should have a supercilious knowledge in accounts;—and as she grew up, I would have her instructed in geometry, that she might know something of the contagious countries;—but above all, Sir Anthony, she should be mistress of orthodoxy, that she might not mis-spell and mis-pronounce words so shamefully as girls usually do; and likewise that she might reprehend the true meaning of what she is saying.

MARCHEN: See FOLK TALE.

MARGINALIA: Notes written in the margin by a reader as a commentary on the text. Sometimes, marginalia may be of significance if the reader is a distinguished author or scholar.

MARINISM: A style named for the Italian poet G. B. Marino (1569-1625), whose writing was characterized by flamboyant figures of speech designed to astonish the reader. Marino's extraordinary poem *L'Adone,* which contains twenty cantos, abounds in strained metaphors, bombast, and ingenious conceits. The style influenced some of the Metaphysical poets (*q.v.*), notably Crashaw and Herbert.

MARIVAUDAGE: Writing characterized by psychological subtlety and stylistic elegance approaching affectation, in the manner of the eighteenth-century French playwright and novelist Pierre de Marivaux. In the refined and subtle world of Marivaux's plays, his characters, elegant and graceful, take part in an elaborate courtship during which Marivaux analyzes with great subtlety the conflicting impulses and hesitations of his lovers. Among the best of his plays, which have influenced such dramatists as Musset and Giraudoux, are *Arlequin poli par l'amour* (1720), *La Surprise de l'amour* (1722), and *Le Jeu de l'armour et du hasard* (1734).

MASCULINE ENDING: Occurs when the final syllable in a line of verse is stressed.

MASCULINE RHYME: A rhyme limited to a single terminal syllable, always stressed. In this stanza from Edward Lear's description of himself, the rhymes of the first and third lines are feminine (*q.v.*), those of the second and fourth masculine:

> He has many friends, laymen and clerical;
>   Old Foss is the name of his cat;
> His body is perfectly spherical,
>   He weareth a runcible hat.

MASKED COMEDY: See COMMEDIA DELL'ARTE.

MASQUE: During the first half of the seventeenth century in England, a courtly form of entertainment characterized by song, dance, lavish costumes, and extraordinary spectacle. Introduced into England from Italy, the masque flourished in the latter part of Elizabeth's reign, continued at the court of James I, and reached its highest development in the time of Charles I, who was its most devoted admirer. Astonishing sums were spent on the productions of masques for the entertainment of nobility and distinguished foreign visitors.

Elaborate stage machinery designed by Inigo Jones (1573-1652), the great theatrical architect, produced such effects as splitting mountains, growing trees, clouds in motion, through which a *deus ex machina* (*q.v.*) could descend. The masques themselves usually had only slight dramatic interest. Dealing largely with mythological and pastoral figures, the action served as a vehicle for spectacle and for the appearance of masked dancers who joined the actors. Except for the dancers of the anti-masque, a light or grotesque interlude often featuring bawdy humor (an innovation introduced by Ben Jonson, the greatest of the masque writers) all the performers were from the nobility and even, on occasion, from royalty.

In the popular theater of the time, many Elizabethan play-wrights incorporated elements from the courtly masque into their plays. In Act IV of Shakespeare's *The Tempest*, for example, Prospero provides a masque for Ferdinand and Miranda in which mythological and pastoral figures appear accompanied by song and dance celebrating marriage. A later masque, Milton's *Comus* (1634), depends more on poetry than on spectacle for its effects. With the Civil War and the closing of the theaters in 1642, this form of entertainment ended.

MAXIM: See APHORISM.

MEANING: Two types of meaning, emotive and cognitive (or referential), are usually distinguished. The emotive meaning of the word *thug*, for example, is its tendency to induce fear or anger; its cognitive meaning is a thought process, namely its suggestion of a man who perpetrates crimes of violence.

Cognitive meaning may be further considered under the headings *extension* and *intension*. In formal logic, the extension of a word is the aggregate of all the individual objects or concepts to which it may be applied. Thus, the extension of the word *chair* is the chair on which the reader is sitting and all other particular chairs. The intension of a word is the group of attributes comprised by it. Thus, the intension of *chair* is the sum of its attributes, such as "being inanimate, having four legs, a back, and a seat," etc. The extension and intension of a word are sometimes called the denotation and connotation respectively, but the latter set of terms so used are technical terms in logic and are not to be confused with the usual senses of denotation and connotation as given under those entries in this book.

MEANING, FOUR LEVELS OF: See FOUR LEVELS OF MEANING.

MEDIEVAL DRAMA: In the ninth century, when words were added to the elaborate Hallelujahs chanted during church services, medieval drama began. Soon these words took the form of playlets performed in Latin by members of the clergy. As these plays grew in popularity and in length, the vernacular was introduced to make them more readily comprehensible. When the performances were moved out of the church and placed in the hands of the laity, a secular drama came into existence. Under the sponsorship of the guilds, cycles of plays arose in which scriptural

history from the fall of Lucifer to the Last Judgment was dramatized. There were also plays dealing with the lives of the saints
and the miracles they performed. Morality plays, moral allegories, were given as community performances, as, on a different
level, were folk plays about such figures as Robin Hood and St.
George. From these plays and from the rediscovery of the classic
theater, the modern drama developed. See LITURGICAL DRAMA,
MIRACLE PLAY, MORALITY PLAY, MYSTERY PLAY.

MEDIEVAL ROMANCE: Stories of love and chivalric adventure, either
in prose or in verse, popular during the later Middle Ages. The
major sources for these romances were ancient history and literature, the stories that centered around Charlemagne, and the Arthurian legends. Among the most famous of the English romances are *Sir Gawain and the Green Knight, Le Morte
d'Arthur,* of Sir Thomas Malory, and Chaucer's *Troilus and
Criseyde.*

MEIOSIS: Understatement, the device of presenting something as
less significant than it really is, as in a description of *Hamlet* as
"a play of some interest."

MELIC POETRY: Greek: *melos,* "song." Verse written for musical
accompaniment on the lyre or flute. Greek melic poetry, which
flourished particularly between the seventh and fifth centuries
B.C., was composed by such poets as Sappho, Anacreon, and Pindar.

MELODRAMA: Greek: *melos,* "song" + *drama.* During the Italian Renaissance, there was no distinction between opera and
melodrama. The fusion of music and drama was, in intention, a
revival of the Classical theater. In the eighteenth century, Han-
del referred to some of his works with both terms, *opera* and
melodrama. During this time, French playwrights wrote plays
which emphasized music, sensationalism, spectacle, and the
happy ending. In time, melodrama depicted the conflict of de-
spicable evil and extraordinary good, as personified in the hero
(or heroine), who was always a model of magnanimous virtue,
and the villain, who existed in the play for the express purpose of
making other people's lives wretched. The broad, forceful style
of acting employed emphasized this conflict with perhaps excessive clarity. In nineteenth-century England, melodrama flour-

ished in a variety of plays which ranged in subject from the supernatural to domestic life. While disappearing skeletons, conjuring wizards, or infernal demons furnished the playgoer with suitable thrills, his moral indignation was pleasurably aroused by improbable spectacles of the evils of drunkenness, the cruelties of a foreclosed mortgage, or the machinations of a fiendish murderer. Such well-known plays as *Sweeney Todd, the Demon Barber of Fleet Street* (1842) and *Ten Nights in a Bar-room* (1858) are characteristic of the popular melodramas of the day.

At the end of the nineteenth century, Shaw incorporated melodramatic elements in *The Devil's Disciple,* which, in fact, he subtitled "A Melodrama." In the last act of the play, as Dick Dudgeon is about to be hanged by General Burgoyne, Pastor Anderson appears at the crucial moment and saves Dudgeon. Witty and urbane, Shaw uses the action for his own comic purposes.

In the modern theater, melodrama has given way to more sophisticated treatments of character and situation, though melodramatic elements are still found, on occasion, to be theatrically effective.

MEMOIR: An account of a person's life and experiences written by himself. Where the autobiography is concerned primarily with the writer, his personal experiences, and the delineation of his character, the memoir centers more on the world in which he has lived. Sometimes the writer of a memoir is a person of no great significance but one who has come into contact with noteworthy people and events; he himself may play a relatively minor part in his book. Since World War II, innumerable memoirs have appeared in which high-ranking officers describe their roles in that conflict.

MESOSTICH: See ACROSTIC.

METAPHOR: A figure of speech in which two unlike objects are compared by identification or by the substitution of one for the other. Metaphors, like many other figures of speech, are common in everyday conversation. We say, for instance, "Hotchkiss is a dead duck," fully aware that Hotchkiss is nothing of the kind, but for rhetorical force we compare Hotchkiss and the dead duck by identifying them. In the same way, Wordsworth, in one of his sonnets, says of England, ". . . she is a fen of stagnant waters." The comparison, however, is not always so direct. In the following stanza, Blake also speaks about the state of England:

> And did the Countenance Divine
> Shine forth upon our clouded hills?
> And was Jerusalem builded here
> Among these dark Satanic Mills?

Here only half a metaphor is directly expressed. Jerusalem is substituted for a state of Godly peace supposed to have once existed. Another metaphor is concealed in the word *clouded.* Not only are the hills covered by cloudlike gusts of smoke from the Satanic mills, the instruments of industrialism blighting the English countryside, but the squalor and evil which they cause shut off from the land the light of the Countenance Divine as clouds shut it off from the sun.

When a metaphor serves to illustrate an idea which can be expressed in other ways, it is merely decorative, as when we speak of the "ship of State." When, however, a metaphor expresses a complex of thought and feeling that is so subtle or precise that it cannot be expressed in any other way, it is called a functional, organic, or structural metaphor. In the octet of Sonnet CXLVI, Shakespeare portrays the relationship between the soul and the body in a series of such metaphors. First, the body is the earth, of which the soul is the center; then it is a rebel army surrounding a rightful king, and finally a house upon which the owner wastes his substance:

> Poor soul, the centre of my sinful earth,
> Thrall to these rebel pow'rs that thee array,
> Why dost thou pine within and suffer dearth,
> Painting thy outward walls so costly gay?
> Why so large cost, having so short a lease,
> Dost thou upon thy fading mansion spend?
> Shall worms, inheritors of this excess,
> Eat up thy charge? Is this thy body's end?

When a metaphor, such as "the arm of a chair," has become so common that it is no longer recognized as such, it is called a dead metaphor. If the two elements in a metaphor are startlingly disparate, we call it a mixed metaphor. This is usually a fault, as in the following instance: "The long arm of the law has two strikes against it." Under extraordinary circumstances, however, it may be highly effective, as in Milton's famous description of the corrupt clergy in "Lycidas": "Blind mouths! that scarce themselves know how to hold a sheep-hook."

In *The Philosophy of Rhetoric* (1936), I. A. Richards distinguished the two parts of a metaphor by the terms *tenor* and *vehicle*. The tenor is an idea with which another idea (the vehicle) is identified. It is in the vehicle that the force of such a comparison lies. When Macbeth says that life is but a walking shadow, *life* is the tenor of a metaphor in which *walking shadow* is the vehicle. See SIMILE.

METAPHYSICAL CONCEIT: See CONCEIT.

METAPHYSICAL POETRY: Although the term *metaphysical* may be applied to any poetry dealing with spiritual or philosophic matters, it is usually limited to the work of a group of seventeenth-century English poets, of whom John Donne was the most disguished. Other Metaphysical poets were Marvell, Cleveland, Cowley, and the religious poets Crashaw, Herbert, and Vaughn. Dryden said that Donne "too much affects the metaphysics," meaning that he was too much given to intellectual analysis. Dr. Johnson extended the term *metaphysical* to designate the group of poets. The work of these men is characterized by the use of ordinary speech ("For God's sake hold your tongue, and let me love") coupled with paradoxes, elaborate conceits (*q.v.*), and abstruse terminology often drawn from the science of the day. The poems sometimes take the form of arguments, for the Metaphysicals characteristically link intense emotion with intellectual ingenuity. In the eighteenth and nineteenth centuries, changes in taste made the Metaphysicals unfashionable, but in the twentieth century, with its admiration for intellectual clarity and psychological exploration, there has been a revival of interest in their poetry.

METER: In English verse, which is based on accent rather than quantity (*q.v.*) the term *meter* refers to the pattern of stressed and unstressed syllables. The number of syllables in a line may be fixed while the number of stresses varies, or the stresses may be fixed with variation in the number of unstressed syllables. In the most frequent form of meter in English, the number of both stresses and syllables is fixed. In actuality, a meter, while retaining its basic pattern, frequently varies in a poem so that the sequence of stressed and unstressed syllables does not resemble the ticking of a metronome. In much modern verse, the regularity of meter is abandoned; instead, cadences (*q.v.*) approximating the flow of speech, are employed.

In English verse, the following meters are the most commonly used:

Iambic:	control	Anapestic:	contradict
Trochaic:	stupid	Dactyllic:	clumsiness
	Spondaic:	snow storm	

These meters are illustrated in a poem by Coleridge:

Trochee trips from long to short.
From long to long in solemn sort
Slow Spondee stalks; strong foot! yet ill able
Ever to come up with Dactyl trisyllable.
Iambics march from short to long.
With a leap and a bound the swift Anapests throng.

When a line is divided into metrical units, or feet, the following terms are used to indicate the number of feet to a line:

Monometer (one)	Pentameter (five)
Dimeter (two)	Hexameter (six)
Trimeter (three)	Heptameter (seven)
Tetrameter (four)	Octometer (eight)

For further discussion and illustrations, see individual entries. See also FOOT, FREE VERSE, QUANTITATIVE VERSE, SPRUNG RHYTHM.

METONYMY: A figure of speech in which the name of some object or idea is substituted for another to which it has some relation, as a cause for its effect, a writer for his work ("Hotchkiss has never read Browning"), etc. Milton makes use of the device in the line "When I consider how my light is spent," where he substitutes *light* for the related word *vision*. See SYNECDOCHE.

METRE: See METER.

METRICAL ACCENT: See ACCENT.

METRICAL FOOT: See METER, FOOT.

METRICAL ROMANCE: A story of adventure in verse. Chaucer's "Knight's Tale" in the *Canterbury Tales* is a metrical romance, as is Scott's *The Lady of the Lake* and Byron's *The Giaour* and *The Corsair*.

MIDDLE COMEDY: The Athenian comedy which flourished during the last three quarters of the fourth century B.C. It avoided the political satire of the Aristophanic Old Comedy and concentrated on love intrigue and burlesques of mythological stories. No examples of this form are extant.

MILES GLORIOSUS: A play by the Roman dramatist Plautus (approximately 254-184 B.C.) which has given its name to one of the stock characters of comedy, the braggart soldier, a swaggerer and a coward at heart who is regularly duped and made the butt of the other characters' laughter. In English drama, he first appears as the title character of Nicholas Udall's *Roister Doister*. A typical incarnation is Bobadil in Ben Jonson's *Everyman in his Humour*. Shakespeare's Falstaff is at once a standard *miles gloriosus* and an example of how the limitations of a type may be transcended and an individualized character created.

MILTONIC SONNET: A form, introduced by Milton, which retains the octave rhyme scheme of the Petrarchan sonnet, *abbaabba*, but which does not have any pause or turn in the meaning at the beginning of the sestet or an invariable rhyme scheme within it:

Avenge, O Lord, thy slaughtered saints, whose bones
Lie scattered on the Alpine mountains cold;
Ev'n them who kept thy truth so pure of old,
When all our fathers worshipped stocks and stones,
Forget not: in thy book record their groans,
Who were thy sheep, and in their ancient fold
Slain by the bloody Piedmontese, that rolled
Mother with infant down the rocks. Their moans

The vales redoubled to the hills, and they
To Heav'n. Their martyred blood and ashes sow
O'er all th'Italian fields, where still doth sway
The triple Tyrant that these may grow
A hundredfold, who, having learnt thy way,
Early may fly the Babylonian woe.

> "On the Late Massacre in Piedmont"

MIME: A type of short comedy which originated in Sicily and southern Italy about the fifth century B.C. It dealt with events from ordinary life or burlesqued the gods and heroes. The actors, who wore grotesque masks and the padded *phalli* of ancient comedy, indulged in slapstick and coarse dialogue. Although performances of the mimes were frowned on by the church, they survived into the Dark Ages. Many of the traditions of the mime appear in the *commedia dell'arte* (*q.v.*) and have been characteristic of low comedy ever since.

MIMESIS: Greek: "imitation." In the *Poetics,* Aristotle states that tragedy is an imitation of an action. Such a statement, however, does not imply that art and life are synonymous. In his discussion, Aristotle makes it clear that the imitation is achieved not through simple mimicry but by the careful construction of the play; selection and arrangement, consequently, are the primary tasks of the playwright.

In acting, the concept of mimesis has also been used to characterize the relationship of art to life. Hamlet's speech to the players advises them concerning the "purpose of playing, whose end, both at first and now, was and is, to hold, as 'twere the mirror up to nature; to show virtue her own feature, scorn her own image, and the very age and body of the time his form and pressure."

MINNESINGER: German: "singer of love." In the Middle Ages, especially the twelfth and thirteenth centuries, the lyric poet in Germany who sang of courtly love. In their choice of subject matter, the German poets were perhaps influenced by troubadour verse (*q.v.*). The most notable *minnesinger* of his time was Walter von de Vogelweider.

MINSTREL: A wandering poet or musician of the later Middle Ages. See JONGLEUR.

MIRACLE PLAYS: In English, the term *miracle play* has generally referred to the medieval religious drama which dramatized saints' lives and divine miracles as well as stories from the Scriptures. Sometimes, however, the term *mystery play,* as it was used in France, is employed to designate those plays containing Biblical stories, as distinct from those about lives of the saints. English medieval writers referred to all of these plays as "Corpus Christi plays," "Whitsuntide plays," "pageants," and occasionally "miracle plays."

The miracle plays, to use the inclusive term, were first presented in connection with saints' days and religious processions, the most notable being the festival of Corpus Christi held in the spring. At first, these plays were given in Latin as part of the church services. Later, as secular and ribald material entered into the performances, they were moved out into the streets. In France, the plays became the property of the town, which continued to present them in more elaborate form on various religious occasions. In England, the trade guilds of each town assumed the responsibility for presenting one play each so that a series of performances could present the story of the creation of the world through the fall of man, or some other "cycle." These so-called craft cycles became enormously popular. Combining serious themes with farce, buffoonery, and coarse humor, medieval religious drama flourished for over four hundred years. A major theatrical entertainment of the time, it reached its highest development in the fifteenth and sixteenth centuries. In England, the cycles grew to considerable size, the Wakefield cycle, for example, having thirty-two plays; the other important groups were the York, Chester, and Coventry cycles.

The cycle was presented with each play mounted on a wagon with a high curtained scaffold, the lower part of the wagon serving as a dressing room. After the play was performed at a stated time in a pre-arranged place, the wagon moved on to follow another play in another street; thus, a series of wagons moved through the city so that the entire population might see the complete cycle.

The settings of the plays were elaborate. Heaven, where God the Father made his appearance, was designed to be awe-inspiring, whereas "Hell-mouth," shaped to resemble a dragon's mouth, contained costumed devils whose principal function was to entertain. Trap doors, pulleys, and other mechanical devices served to create ingenious theatrical effects. Costuming was frequently ornate, and lighting effects highly imaginative. A nativity scene might thus be brilliantly illuminated in an evening performance to create the proper effect. As many as three hundred actors, members of the guilds, might be used for one cycle of plays.

MISCELLANIES, POETICAL: Collections of poems by various authors. In 1557, Richard Tottel published a collection called *Songs and Sonnets,* usually known as *Tottel's Miscellany,* which contained the work of Wyatt and Surrey, among others. The publishing of poetical miscellanies, begun by Tottel, was extremely popular in the Elizabethan period and has continued ever since. The Elizabethan miscellanies often have elaborate titles, such as *The Paradise of Dainty Devices* or *A Gorgeous Gallery of Gallant Inventions.* The authors of the various poems are sometimes unnamed, sometimes identified by initials. When a poem is ascribed to a particular author, the ascription is not always accurate. Nevertheless, it was through the miscellanies that some of the best Elizabethan verse was published.

MISE EN SCENE: The scenery, costumes, properties, etc., of a theatrical production.

MIXED METAPHOR: See METAPHOR.

MOCK EPIC: A work in which a trivial subject is made ridiculous by being treated with the elaborate and dignified devices of the epic (*q.v.*). The masterpiece of the mock epic in English is Pope's *The Rape of the Lock,* in which the theft of an elegant lady's lock of hair by one of her beaus is treated as if it were an event of momentous importance. Pope begins with a solemn statement of his theme ("What dire offense from amorous causes springs") and proceeds to introduce all the usual epic features, such as supernatural machinery, epic similes, a voyage to the underworld, grandiose orations, and mighty battles, all used to describe the trivia of an elegant afternoon, as here, where the heroine's victory in a card game is seen in terms of a Homeric battle:

An Ace of Hearts steps forth: the King unseen
Lurked in her hand, and mourned his captive Queen:
He springs to vengeance with an eager pace,
And falls like thunder on the prostrate Ace.
The nymph exulting fills with shouts the sky;
The walls, the woods, and long canals reply.
   Oh thoughtless mortals! ever blind to fate;
Too soon dejected, and too soon elate.
Sudden, these honors shall be snatched away,
And cursed for ever this victorious day.

See BURLESQUE, PARODY, TRAVESTY, SATIRE.

MOCK HEROIC: The style of the mock epic (*q.v.*) and other works which satirize their subjects by inflating them with false dignity. Many works besides strict mock epics make use of the mock heroic style. Fielding's *Tom Thumb,* for example, is a mock heroic play. Byron has mock heroic passages in *Don Juan,* and Wilde uses the style in *The Importance of Being Earnest,* where the characters discuss ridiculous events, such as being born "or at any rate, bred" in a handbag, with portentous solemnity.

MONODRAMA: A theatrical presentation featuring only one character. Ruth Draper and Cornelia Otis Skinner have achieved considerable success in this form of entertainment. The term *monodrama* has also been used by Tennyson in characterizing his poem "Maud," a soliloquy which begins:

Come into the garden, Maud,
  For the black bat has flown,
Come into the garden, Maud,
  I am here at the gate alone . . .

MONODY: In Greek poetry, a poem, especially of mourning, presented by one singer. Matthew Arnold called his elegy on Arthur Hugh Clough "Thyrsis, a Monody," and "Lycidas" is so referred to in Milton's introduction, added to the poem in 1645.

MONOGRAPH: An essay usually on a scientific subject or of a scholarly nature.

MONOLOGUE: An extended speech by one person. A remarkable use of the monologue occurs in Strindberg's one-act play *The*

Stronger, which consists entirely of the speech of one character. For subtypes of the monologue, see DRAMATIC MONOLOGUE, SOLILOQUY, STREAM OF CONSCIOUSNESS.

MONOMETER: A line of verse consisting of one foot; also called *monopody.* See AMPHIMAC for an example.

MONOPODY: See above.

MONOSTICH: 1. A line of verse. 2. A poem of one line.

MOOD: In a literary work, the predominating atmosphere or tone. The mood of Suckling's "The Constant Lover," for example, is graceful and ironically witty.

MORA: A unit of measure in quantitative verse. A mora is the time taken up by a short syllable. A long syllable is equal to two morae. In quantitative verse, a metrical foot can be substituted for another without changing the speed of the verse only if the two feet have equal numbers of morae. Iambs and trochees, for example, each having three morae, can be readily substituted for each other. A spondee may replace a dactyl or an anapest, since each of these feet has four morae.

MORAL, THE: The "teaching" or "lesson" in a literary work which is either implied or specifically stated. Many critics avoid discussing "the moral" since the value of a literary work, a complex aesthetic experience, does not depend on the "lesson" which may be extracted from it. See DIDACTIC.

MORALITY PLAY: A form of late medieval and early Renaissance drama containing allegorical figures who are frequently involved in the struggle over a man's soul. The term *morality play* was not used at the time; usually the terms *moral, pithy,* or *goodly Interlude* referred to this type of theatrical presentation. The moralities developed from a combination of the medieval religious drama and such allegories as the *Roman de la Rose.*

The first known moralities, called the *Paternoster* plays, performed in York and elsewhere in the latter part of the fourteenth century, dealt with the conflict between the Seven Moral Virtues and the Seven Deadly Sins, which try to lead Man astray. The most notable morality is *Everyman* (early sixteenth century), which, instead of the vices and virtues, contains the characters of God, Death, Good Fellowship, Good Deeds, etc., who are concerned with the future of Everyman's soul.

Unlike the mystery and miracle plays (*q.v.*), the morality play, instead of being mounted on wagons, was staged on simple platforms. Moreover, it lacked the elaborateness of production and ingenuity of staging that characterized the miracle plays.

In the sixteenth century, the morality play served as a vehicle for religious and political propaganda. By the middle of the century, the popularity of the morality play had waned. However, the survival of elements of the form may be seen in *Cambises* (1569), which contains such allegorical figures as Shame, Diligence, Preparation, and Murder, in addition to other characters which are historical or pseudo-historical.

MOTIF: A theme, character, or verbal pattern which recurs in literature or folklore. The reveler who blasphemes upon a grave and is later dragged to damnation by the ghost of the man who was buried there is a widespread folklore motif which later becomes part of the Don Juan legend. A motif may be a theme which runs through a number of different works. The motif of the imperishability of art, for example, appears in Shakespeare, Keats, Yeats, and many other writers. A recurring element within a single work is also called a motif. Among the many motifs that appear and reappear in Joyce's *Ulysses*, for example, are Plumtree's Potted Meat, the man in the brown mackintosh, and the one-legged sailor.

MOTIVATION: The combination of circumstance and temperament which determines the actions of a character. If this combination is inadequate to account for these actions—if, for example, a timid and diffident soul suddenly and without apparent reason attacks the town bully—the character is insufficiently or implausibly motivated. In a work which purports to be psychologically realistic, the behavior of characters must be in keeping with their natures as acted upon by the circumstances of the plot.

MOVEMENT: A literary trend or development. The term may be used very broadly to describe a general literary tendency, as the Romantic Movement, or precisely to denote the work of a few writers, as the Imagist Movement.

MUMMERY: In the Middle Ages, celebration of such festive occasions as Christmas and New Year's frequently took the form of mumming, the wearing of masks or grotesque disguises and participation in dances and buffoonery. By extension, the term *mummery* refers to a theatrical presentation in which the actors or dancers are masked or in disguise. In addition, the term may also refer to acting in general.

MUSES: In Greek mythology, there were nine muses, the daughters of Zeus and Mnemosyne, or Memory. Though at first, one was not distinguished from another, they later had their individual provinces to preside over. Clio was the muse of history, Calliope of epic poetry, Erato of love poetry, Euterpe of lyric poetry, Melpomene of tragedy, Polyhymnia of songs to the gods, Terpsichore of the dance, Thalia of comedy, Urania of astronomy.

Traditionally, poets appealed to a particular muse for aid in assisting them to compose their works. In later literature, writers have used the notion of the muse but without invoking a specific Classical figure. In Shakespeare's *Henry V,* for example, the Chorus, in the opening lines of the play, exclaims:

> O! for a Muse of fire, that would ascend
> The brightest heaven of invention . . .

MUSICAL COMEDY: A theatrical form, developed in the United States during the twentieth century, mingling song and spoken dialogue. Deriving from vaudeville and operetta, the earliest musical comedies had conventional romantic plots interspersed with pleasant, if irrelevant, songs. Much of their effect derived from spectacular staging and low comedy. Although there were a few previous experiments, the modern musical comedy dates from the early 1940's. It is marked by a libretto of higher literary and dramatic quality, by the close integration of text and music, and often by the use of ballet in place of more popular dance forms. At its best, the musical comedy, or more precisely the musical play, has approached the status of true opera.

MYSTERY PLAY: As used in France, the term *mystère* referred to the medieval religious plays which dramatized stories taken from the Scriptures. Christ's passion, the fall of man, the story of Noah were some of the subjects used by playwrights. In England, the terms *miracle play* and *mystery play* were used interchangeably. See MIRACLE PLAY for a discussion of the form and its theatrical history.

MYTH: An anonymous tale, ostensibly historical, the origins of which are unknown. A mythology, which is a collection of such tales, may contain the story of the origin of the world, the creation of mankind, the feats of gods or heroes, or the tragedies which befell ancient families. For the primitive mentality, many myths provided explanations of natural phenomena; with an increase in scientific knowledge, however, this function is often supplanted and myths survive simply as stories.

Writers have always been fascinated by the remoteness, mystery, and heroism of myth. Blake, for example, created his own mythology. For him, spiritual realities existed in the visions, chiefly Christian, which he embodied in his verse. Like Blake, other writers, seeking aesthetically satisfying systems, have invented their own myths or have turned to those already established. Yeats, for example, employed Irish myths early in his poetic career, but later developed his own metaphysical system or mythology in *A Vision* (1926), which became the source for many images in his verse.

For other writers, established myth satisfied a metaphysical hunger and provided material for their art. D. H. Lawrence in *The Plumed Serpent* used both elements of Christianity and the myth of the Mexican god Quetzalcoatl to formulate his own vision. In Joyce's novels, elements of Classical, Christian, and Hebraic myth are fused to create a universal myth which, he felt, embodied the experiences of all men. On this point, C. G. Jung has declared that the materials of myths lie in the collective unconscious of the race; the widespread similarity between myths, he has stated, results from a common inheritance.

In *Moby Dick*, Melville created a significant story which, by extension, we may call a myth. The novel, to be fully understood, must be apprehended as a symbol of a primal conflict; the story emerges as myth, for it evokes, as Jung might say, responses from the unconscious which we regard as universal.

N

NAIVE AND SENTIMENTAL WRITING: A distinction developed by Schiller in his essay *Über naive und sentimentalische Dichtung* (1795). He felt that such writers as the ancient Greeks, Shakespeare, and Goethe were in harmony with nature and had produced a certain kind of literature which he called "naive" as opposed to his own "sentimental" writing and that of his contemporaries, who, out of touch with nature though longing to return to it, created works which lacked the harmony and serenity of "naive" poetry. In Schiller's usage, neither of these terms has the pejorative connotations which they carry in English.

NARRATIVE VERSE: Non-dramatic verse which tells a story. *The Canterbury Tales* is a notable example in English. Verse narratives, of such disparate types and quality as Marlowe's *Hero and Leander* and Kipling's *Ballad of the East and West,* were common in English literature up to the twentieth century. Today, such factors as the popularity of the novel and the disinclination of poets to use verse for subjects that can be adequately treated in prose have made narrative verse a rarity.

NATURALISM: 1. A literary movement related to and sometimes described as an extreme form of realism (*q.v.*) but which may be more appropriately considered as a parallel to philosophic naturalism. This doctrine holds that all existent phenomena are in nature and thus within the sphere of scientific knowledge; it maintains that no supernatural realities exist. In the first half of the nineteenth century, Comte applied the ideas of science to the study of society, and soon after, Taine applied them to literature, maintaining that psychological states as well as human actions were the results of material causes.

Carefully documenting their work, the Goncourt brothers produced *Germinie Lacerteux* (1865), a novel which examines in clinical detail the sordid life of a servant girl. This novel was admired by Emile Zola, the great theorist of naturalism. In his essay *Le Roman expérimental* ("The Experimental Novel"), dated 1880, Zola said that the novelist should be, like the scientist performing an experiment, independent of moral conventions or preconceived theories. In his novel, which is based on careful documentation, he should examine dispassionately certain phenomena and draw indisputable conclusions. Among the things that his experiments will confirm is the law that the actions of men are determined by heredity and environment. Zola carried out his theories in such novels as *Thérèse Raquin* (1868) and *L'Assommoir* (1877). To distinguish his work from the realism of Balzac and Flaubert, Zola called his novels "naturalistic." Although he wished by this term to characterize his theories and methods, it has often served only to denote his usual subject matter and that of his followers. Theoretically, there is no reason why the experimental or naturalistic method could not be applied to an investigation of the highest levels of society, but in fact naturalistic novels have usually concerned themselves with slums, poverty, disease, and dirt.

It was this preoccupation with ugliness that brought forth such comments as this by Tennyson in "Locksley Hall Sixty Years After":

Feed the budding rose of boyhood with the drainage of your sewer;
Send the drain into the fountain, lest the stream should issue pure.
Set the maiden fancies wallowing in the troughs of Zolaism,—
Forward, forward, ay, and backward, downward too into the abysm!

In these lines, Tennyson may have been referring to Zola's English disciple George Moore, who along with such writers as Gissing, Maupassant, and the early Huysmans, carried on the naturalistic tradition. In the drama, naturalistic plays were written by such playwrights as Gorky and Hauptmann.

2. The term *naturalism* is sometimes used to describe the work of a "nature" poet, such as Wordsworth, who deals sympathetically with the beauties of the countryside.

NEAR RHYME: See RHYME.

NEGATIVE CAPABILITY: An expression used by Keats in his letter of December 21, 1817, to his brothers George and Thomas. With the term *Negative Capability*, Keats described a quality which a man possesses when he is "capable of being in uncertainties, mysteries, doubts, without any irritable reaching after fact and reason." Coleridge, Keats said, often lacked Negative Capability, for he was incapable of negating the logical, rationalizing part of his mind and would often lose an intuition by attempting to make it part of a system, that is, by "being incapable of remaining content with half knowledge." When a poet possesses Negative Capability, he has no need to rationalize; "the sense of Beauty," Keats said, "overcomes every other consideration."

NEO-CLASSICISM: In its most general sense, a revival of the style and attitudes of a former literature. In English literature, the term generally refers to the theories and practices of certain writers from the latter part of the seventeenth century through the eighteenth. Though such Neo-Classicists as Dryden, Pope, Addison, Johnson, Goldsmith, and Swift differ in practice, some general principles on which Neo-Classicism rests can usually be agreed upon.

The Neo-Classicists regarded man as a creature limited by his innate nature and by the society of which he is a part. With Pope, they believed that the "proper study of mankind is man," the principal source of subject matter in art. From the Roman poet Horace, they derived the idea that art, especially poetry, should both instruct and delight. Opposed to unlimited novelty, the Neo-Classicists preferred tradition, for they were convinced that the Classical authors, particularly the Roman, had perfected the various literary forms. Study of the Roman writers and imitation (*q.v.*) of their achievements would, they felt, yield an equal measure of perfection. Craftsmanship was essential, the Neo-Classicists agreed; reason should control fancy, and the typical should be harmonized with the individual. In all matters, decorum would insure excellence. Whether in art or in life, Neo-Classicism emphasized restraint, balance, and proportion.

NEOLOGISM: A new word or a new meaning assigned to an old word. Frequently, the neologism is a word taken from a foreign language, as the word *sputnik,* which has become part of the English vocabulary. In fact, it is a neologism even in Russian, for the term, which means "fellow traveler," now refers to a satellite.

NEW COMEDY: Greek comedy of the third and fourth centuries

B.C. With the decline of Greek power and the rise of Macedonia, the biting personal and political satire of Aristophanic Old Comedy (*q.v.*) disappeared. Its place was taken by the New Comedy, which utilized stereotyped plots and characters. Courtesans, young lovers, parsimonious elders, and scheming servants were played off against each other in various combinations. After many complications, the love intrigues, which formed the bases of these plays, regularly ended in a happy marriage. Menander, along with Philemon and Diphilus, was the most famous writer of this genre. The Romans Plautus and Terence were much influenced by the New Comedy, which has, in fact, supplied the materials of most comedy since its day.

NEW CRITICISM: A movement, largely American, in literary criticism which dates from the 1920's, though it did not receive a name until John Crowe Ransom, one of its practitioners and theoreticians, published a book called *The New Criticism* in 1941. Although this term is sometimes limited to the work of a dozen or so leading modern critics, it is often extended to describe the tendency in recent criticism to emphasize the close reading and the explication of a text rather than biographical or historical study. Despite their common orientation toward textual analysis, the major New Critics have at no time agreed upon a single methodology or set of principles. They do, however, accept the idea that a poem should be considered as such and not as something else, an ornamented form of sociology, philosophy, or ethics, for example. In general, the New Critics, who have excelled in the interpretation of complex, highly intellectual poems, have centered their attention on the linguistic organization of poetry, though some have made use of such disciplines as psychology and anthropology.

The early semantic studies of I. A. Richards, which emphasized the nature of symbolic language, have been influential in the New Criticism, as has the work of Richards' disciple, William Empson. (See AMBIGUITY) Other major figures are Allen Tate, R. P. Blackmur, Yvor Winters, and Kenneth Burke. Through their book *Understanding Poetry* (1938), Cleanth Brooks and Robert Penn Warren have spread the doctrines of the New Criticism into American colleges. T. S. Eliot, though not strictly a New Critic, has been important in showing the value of subtle textual study.

NEW HUMANISM: A movement in letters and philosophy, primarily American, in the 1920's. Reacting against the excesses of Romantic individualism and realistic naturalism, such men as Irving Babbitt, Paul Elmer More, and Norman Foerster advocated a concern with "human" values. They insisted that man stood apart from nature and possessed free will. They advocated restraint, self-control, and the imitation of a model of typical human excellence. In both life and art, the nearest approach to their ideas of excellence had come, they felt, in the great epochs of the past and especially in the classical age of Greece. In general, the New Humanists were scholarly and, in both art and politics, conservative.

NINE WORTHIES, THE: In his preface to Malory's *Morte d'Arthur,* Caxton lists the Nine Worthies, or heroes, of Renaissance and late medieval literature: Hector, Alexander, and Julius Caesar are the pagan heroes; the Jewish are Joshua, David, and Judas Maccabaeus; and Arthur, Charlemagne, and Godfrey of Boulogne are cited as the Christian worthies. The clowns in Shakespeare's *Love's Labour's Lost* who set out to play the Nine Worthies include among them Hercules and Pompey the Great.

NOBLE SAVAGE, THE: The concept that primitive man is inherently good, or noble, and that evil results from the corrupting influence of civilization is one of the clichés of Romanticism. This widespread notion is especially prominent in such works as Chateaubriand's *Atala* and *René.* The idea of the Noble Savage, though it enters Romantic thought largely through the writings of Rousseau, goes back at least to the Renaissance, where it is utilized by Montaigne.

NŌ (NOH) DRAMA: A type of drama which developed in fourteenth-century Japan from a ritual dance associated with ancient Shinto worship. The plays, unlike those of the *Kabuki* drama (*q.v.*), were designed for aristocratic audiences, who welcomed the restraint and subtlety of the form.

Characteristically, the *Nō* play is mysterious and gloomy. The first character, or *shite,* generally meets a ghost (the *waki,* or second character) while on a journey to a shrine; recalling his past life in a stylized dance, the shade dramatizes his earthly struggles. The ghost frequently turns out to be the one to whose shrine the traveler is bound. The general theme, which is stated at the beginning of the play, is the illusion of life.

The actors of the Nō drama make their entrances by way of a bridge, actually a corridor with railings, leading from the actors' dressing rooms. Three symbolic trees, signifying heaven, earth, and humanity, are situated in front of the bridge; when playing on it, the performer stands at the appropriate tree. A pebble path separates the audience from the actors.

Performers employ a highly unrealistic style of acting, moving to the rhythmical thumping of feet on a wooden floor. Wearing masks, they speak or chant with high- or low-pitched voices to a musical accompaniment. Since women never act in Nō drama, male performers take their roles. During the performance, elaborate costume changes occur on stage; assisting the actors is the property man who, dressed in black, moves about the stage unobtrusively.

In such plays of W. B. Yeats as *At the Hawk's Well* (1917) and *The Only Jealousy of Emer* (1919), the influence of Nō drama is apparent.

NOM DE GUERRE: See NOM DE PLUME.

NOM DE PLUME: French: "pen name." A term used in English, but not in French, to indicate a fictitious name employed by a writer. "George Orwell," for example, is the *non de plume* of Eric Blair. In French, *nom de guerre* is the term used for an author's pen name.

NONCE WORD: A word invented for a particular occasion. Lewis Carroll's "Jabberwocky," for example, employs a number of nonce words. In *Finnegans Wake,* James Joyce made the nonce word a central element in his style.

NONSENSE VERSE: A type of light verse (*q.v.*) in which sense is subordinate to sound and absurdity is sought for its own sake. Among the most famous practitioners of nonsense verse are Lewis Carroll and Edward Lear, the author of the following lines:

On the Coast of Coromandel
Where the early pumpkins blow,
In the middle of the woods,
Lived the Yonghy-Bonghy-Bò.
                    "The Courtship of the Yonghy-Bonghy-Bò"

NOVEL, THE: Though the novel as a genre is of comparatively recent development, it has its roots in a number of forms which
may be traced back to the Classical epics, for the essence of the
novel is narrative. The epic, the medieval romance (*q.v.*), and
later, the short prose tale popular in Italy provided readers with
entertaining stories. Extended prose narratives, which had been
known in antiquity, became increasingly popular. They were
chiefly sequences of episodes held together by one central character. As the prose tale developed, verse narrative declined in
popularity until today it is virtually nonexistent.

In England, the novel established itself as a distinct genre
with the works of Defoe and Richardson in the eighteenth
century. Though character study became a major preoccupation
of the novelist, the element of romance was not lost, for side by
side with the development of realism in the novel, the exotic
and the adventurous continued to be popular.

In the late nineteenth and the twentieth centuries the novel,
as an art form, has reached its fullest development. Concerned
with their craft, novelists such as Flaubert, Henry James, Virginia Woolf, James Joyce, E. M. Forster, and Thomas Mann
have utilized various devices to achieve new aesthetic forms
within the genre.

NOVELETTE: See SHORT NOVEL.

NOVELLA: Italian: "a story." As used in connection with such
works as Boccaccio's *Decameron,* the term *novella* refers to a
short prose narrative. In the Elizabethan period, many writers,
including Shakespeare, drew upon Italian *novelle* for their plots.

NOVEL OF SENSIBILITY: See SENTIMENTAL NOVEL.

NOVEL OF THE SOIL: A narrative depicting man's struggle against
nature. Set in a rural environment, the novel of the soil has
emerged as a distinct genre during the twentieth century. In
American literature, such novelists as O. E. Rolvaag (*Giants in
the Earth*) and Ellen Glasgow (*Barren Ground*) have written

of hardship endured by those who must live from the earth. NUMBERS: Refers to either meter, feet, or verse. In Wordsworth's "The Solitary Reaper," for example, the term designates verses:

> Will no one tell me what she sings?—
> Perhaps the plaintive numbers flow
> For old, unhappy, far-off things
> And battles long ago . . .

NURSERY RHYME: A brief poem, usually anonymous, for a child's enlightenment. "There was an old woman who lived in a shoe," while depicting the horrors of a housing shortage, offers instruction on the care and feeding of children.

O

OBJECTIVE CORRELATIVE: In his essay "Hamlet" (1919), T. S. Eliot wrote that "the only way of expressing emotion in art is by finding an 'objective correlative'; in other words, a set of objects; a situation, a chain of events which shall be the formula of that *particular;* such that when the general facts, which must terminate in sensory experience, are given, the emotion is immediately evoked." Regarding *Hamlet* as an artistic failure, Eliot feels that the emotions which dominate Hamlet are in excess of the chain of events which he experiences. Eliot's dictum, disputed by many, has nevertheless had wide popularity, especially among the New Critics (*q.v.*).

OBJECTIVITY: A quality assigned to a work in which the author seems to be presenting his characters in an impersonal, noncommittal fashion without offering any judgment of them or their actions. Much modern poetry, reacting against the intensely personal writing of the Romantics, seeks to be impersonal and objective. In "Sweeney Among the Nightingales," for example, T. S. Eliot makes little comment on the sinister scene which he presents. The term *objectivity,* if handled with discretion, can be useful, although it is doubtful if strict objectivity exists in literature. Flaubert makes no comment on Madame Bovary, but the intensity of his feeling for her is as apparent as

the intensity of Eliot's revulsion from the world of Apeneck
Sweeney. See SUBJECTIVITY.

OBLIGATORY SCENE: (French: *scène à faire*.) An episode, usually
highly emotional, the circumstances of which are so strongly
anticipated by the audience that the dramatist is obliged to write
it. In Ibsen's *Ghosts,* the audience, aware that Oswald and
Regina are half brother and sister, sees the sexual interest developing between them and anticipates the scene in which they
are confronted with their relationship.

OBLIQUE RHYME: See RHYME.

OCCASIONAL VERSE: Poetry written in commemoration of an
event. Though much occasional verse succumbs to time, a number of well-known examples have, by their intrinsic literary
value, survived the occasions for which they were written.
Among the most notable instances are Marvell's "Horatian Ode
upon Cromwell's Return from Ireland," Milton's "On the Late
Massacre in Piedmont." Modern examples are Yeats' "Easter
1916," and Hopkins' "The Wreck of the Deutschland." Occasional verse sometimes takes the form of *vers de société (q.v.)*
when the sentiments are witty or satiric.

OCTAMETER: See OCTOMETER.

OCTASTICH: A stanza of eight lines.

OCTAVE (OCTET): 1. The first section of a Petrarchan sonnet (*q.v.*).
In this verse form, the octave (eight lines) is contrasted with the
sestet (six lines) by a change in the rhyme scheme and some
important turn of thought.

　　2. An eight-line poem or stanza, especially *ottava rima (q.v.)*.

OCTAVO: (Abbr. 8vo or 8°) A book in the manufacture of which
the printer's sheets have been folded three times, making eight
leaves or sixteen pages. As a rough indicator of the dimensions
of a volume, this term designates a book of average size.

OCTET: See OCTAVE.

OCTOMETER: A verse made up of eight metrical feet. The length
of this line, which is often broken into two tetrameters, makes it
rare. Tennyson, however, uses it in *Frater Ave Atque Vale:*

Row us out from Desenzano, to your Sirmione row!
So they rowed, and there we landed—"O venusta Sirmio!"

OCTOSYLLABLE: A verse containing eight syllables.

ODE: In English, a lyric poem of some length, serious in subject and dignified in style. The term, now loosely used, has lost any necessary reference to the odes of the Greek poet Pindar, to whom the form is usually traced. Originally an ode was a choral song to be sung and danced at a public occasion, such as the celebration of a victory in the Olympic games. The stanzas were arranged in groups of three. The strophe was sung while the chorus moved in one direction, the antistrophe, which had the same metrical form, while it moved in another, and the epode, which had a different form, as it stood still. Pindaric odes in English are rare; an example is Thomas Gray's "The Progress of Poesy." See COWLEYAN ODE, HORATIAN ODE.

OLD COMEDY: Greek comedy of the fifth century B.C. The Old Comedy, which derives from the fertility festivals in honor of the god Dionysus, combines Rabelaisian humor, lyric beauty, and biting personal and political satire. The chorus, which disappears by the period of the New Comedy (*q.v.*), takes an important part in the action and delivers the long speech called the *parabasis,* which expresses the views of the playwright. The works of such writers of Old Comedy as Crates and Eupolis have been lost; only the plays of Aristophanes survive.

OMNIBUS: A volume of works, usually reprints, by one author or on related subjects.

ONE-ACT PLAY: In the history of drama, there have been many short, unified dramatic works which may be properly called one-act plays, but the term is usually employed for those written since the late nineteenth century. Interest in this genre grew at that time as dramatists saw the possibilities for its development. The writing of such dramas was given impetus in Europe and in the United States by the "little theater movement," which emphasized experimental, noncommercial plays. Dramatists such as Hauptmann, Strindberg, Shaw, and O'Neill contributed a number of such plays in the early part of the twentieth century.

As a distinct dramatic type, the one-act play is generally limited in the numbers of characters as well as in scene changes. Two or three characters in one setting is typical. A single incident, with only a sufficient amount of exposition to establish the chain of events leading up to it, is presented without complicating subplots. The climax frequently occurs in the closing moments of the play.

In the current professional theater, curtain raisers, one-act plays presented prior to longer productions, are not common. However, in small amateur theaters, programs of one-act plays continue to be performed.

ONOMATOPOEIA: The use of words whose sounds seem to express or reinforce their meanings. Certain words, such as *hiss, bang, bowwow,* imitate the sounds they represent. In the strictest sense, onomatopoeia can only occur when the writer is imitating sounds, as in "Hotchkiss dropped to the carpet with a dull thud," or more subtly, as in this line from Alfred Noyes' "The Highwayman," where the explosive *k's* and *t's* suggest the sound of a horse's hoofs on cobblestones: "Over the cobbles he clattered and clashed in the dark innyard." It has been suggested that certain sounds bring to mind, perhaps by the process of pronunciation, certain qualities and thus tend to be associated with them, as, for example, the short "i" sound with smallness (*little, slit, midget,* etc.). However, this theory is still unproven.

ONTOLOGY: See STRUCTURE.

OPEN COUPLET: A couplet of which the second line is not complete in meaning but depends upon the first line of the following one, as in the second of these couplets from Milton's "L'Allegro":

> And ever against eating cares,
> Lap me in soft Lydian airs,
> Married to immortal verse,
> Such as the meeting soul may pierce
> In notes with many a winding bout
> Of linkèd sweetness long drawn out.

ORATION: A formal address delivered on a special occasion. Perhaps the most famous oration in literature is Mark Antony's speech to the crowd in Shakespeare's *Julius Caesar*.

ORGANIC FORM: That which is derived from the nature of a literary work's subject and materials rather than from rules externally imposed. In the theory of organic form, the work is said to grow from its inspiration like a plant from its seed, as opposed to a work which, governed by mechanical form, is fitted arbitrarily into a preconceived mold. The concept of organic form originated with Coleridge, who used it to reply to the Neo-Classical critics of Shakespeare, whose plays, these critics contended, lacked "form."

OTTAVA RIMA: In English, a stanza consisting of eight lines in iambic pentameter rhymed *ababababcc*. Used by such noted writers as Boccaccio, Pulci, and Tasso, it was a favored stanza for narrative and epic verse. Adopting the form for his mock epic, Byron uses *ottava rima* in *Don Juan,* which opens:

> I want a hero: an uncommon want,
>> When every year and month sends forth a new one,
> Till, after cloying the gazettes with cant,
>> The age discovers he is not the true one:
> Of such as these I should not care to vaunt,
>> I'll therefore take our ancient friend Don Juan—
> We all have seen him, in the pantomime,
> Sent to the devil somewhat ere his time.

In modern verse, W. B. Yeats uses *ottava rima* in "Sailing to Byzantium" and "Among School Children."

OXFORD MOVEMENT: The Anglican High-Church reaction to religious laxity began at Oxford University in 1833 with a sermon by John Keble. The movement, important in nineteenth-century English literary and intellectual history, was led by Newman and included such men as R. H. Froude and E. B. Pusey. It was also called the Tractarian Movement because the ideas it advocated were presented in a series of papers called *Tracts for the Times.* Newman and his colleagues wished to restore to the services of the Church of England the ardor and beauty which they believed had been lost. In seeking a historical basis for their reforms, they adopted certain doctrines considered too near those of Roman Catholicism. Finally, Newman left the Church of England and became a Catholic priest and eventually a cardinal. The Oxford Movement was attacked by such men as Kingsley, Arnold, and Carlyle. In reply to Kingsley's attack on him, Newman wrote his *Apologia pro Vita Sua.*

OXYMORON: Greek: *oxymoros,* "pointedly foolish." A figure of speech consisting generally of two apparently contradictory terms which express a startling paradox. The oxymoron is sometimes used in everyday speech, as in the phrase "conspicuous by his absence." In literature, a remarkable use of the oxymoron occurs in Shakespeare's *Romeo and Juliet,* Act I, in which Romeo, declaring that he is out of favor with Rosalind, jests about the nature of love:

> Alas! that love, whose view is muffled still,
> Should, without eyes, see pathways to his will.
> . . . .
> Here's much to do with hate, but more with love:
> Why then, O brawling love! O loving hate!
> O any thing! of nothing first create.
> O heavy lightness! serious vanity!
> Mis-shapen chaos of well-seeming forms!
> Feather of lead, bright smoke, cold fire, sick health!
> Still-waking sleep, that is not what it is!
> This love feel I, that feel no love in this!
> Dost thou not laugh?

P

PÆAN: Any song or hymn of joy, praise, or triumph. It is probably so called from Paian, the physician of the Greek gods, who was later identified with Apollo. The pæan, sung in gratitude for Apollo's aid, was later used to honor other gods and then sung on various appropriate occasions. An example of the pæan can be found in Sophocles' *Antigone.*

PÆON: In Classical prosody, a foot of one long and three short syllables, called the first, second, third, or fourth pæon depending on the position of the long syllable.

PAGEANT: The movable stage or platform upon which the medieval mystery plays (*q.v.*) were presented. The pageant was built on wheels and consisted of two rooms, the lower used as a dressing room, and the upper, which was open, used as a stage. The mystery play itself was also called a pageant. In modern times the term is applied to any elaborate outdoor performance or procession.

PALIMPSEST: A parchment or papyrus from which the original text has been removed and upon which a second (and sometimes a third) text has been imposed. Before the introduction of paper made good writing surfaces inexpensive, a parchment or papyrus was often used more than once. Sometimes, the original text can still be read because it was incompletely erased or has become visible with age. Upon occasion, modern chemical methods can restore the original text.

PALINDROME: A word, sentence, or verse which reads the same either backwards or forwards. Common palindromes are "Madam, I'm Adam" or "Able was I ere I saw Elba."

PALINODE: A poem in which the writer recants a statement made in a previous poem. The practice of writing palinodes was common in Classical and Renaissance literature. The most famous palinode in English is Chaucer's *Legend of Good Women*, written, as Chaucer tells us, to atone for the story of false Cressida.

PAMPHLET: A small book, unbound, usually having paper covers. Many pamphlets are tracts advocating a point of view in an argument. Most are ephemeral, but some, such as those written by Milton and Swift, are of permanent interest.

PANEGYRIC: A piece of writing or a formal speech praising someone. See ENCOMIASTIC VERSE.

PANTOMIME: 1. A performance consisting of action without speech.

2. A type of spectacular theatrical entertainment which developed in England in the early part of the eighteenth century. The story of the pantomime, which was acted out in song and dance, involved characters from both Classical mythology and the *commedia dell'arte* (*q.v.*). In production, the pantomime was lavish and elaborate, with much use of theatrical machinery and many changes of scene. The form still survives in England in the spectacular Christmas entertainments designed for children.

PANTOUM: A Malayan verse form which has been used in French and occasionally in English. There are an indefinite number of stanzas, each consisting of a quatrain rhyming *abab*. The second and fourth lines of each stanza become the first and third lines of the next. In the last stanza, the second and fourth lines are the first and third lines of the opening stanza reversed; thus, the poem ends with the same line with which it began.

PARABASIS: In the Greek Old Comedy (*q.v.*), the long speech delivered by the chorus or its leader near the close of the play. In this speech, which was full of witticisms and topical references, often personal, the playwright gave his advice and opinions directly to the audience.

PARABLE: A short, simple story illustrating a moral lesson. In a parable, the story is developed not for its own sake but only in so far as it reinforces the moral which is always explicit. The parables of Christ, such as those of the Good Samaritan and the Prodigal Son, are the most famous examples of this genre.

PARADOX: A statement which, though it appears self-contradictory, contains a basis of truth which reconciles the seeming opposites. The apparent contradiction of the paradox often concentrates the reader's attention on a particular point, as here where Pope uses paradoxes to say that a great writer may make a virtue of something that would be a flaw if handled less skillfully:

> Great wits sometimes may gloriously offend,
> And rise to faults true critics dare not mend.
> > "An Essay on Criticism"

Sometimes a paradox forms the basis of an entire poem, as in Lovelace's "To Althea, from Prison," where each stanza describes a different way in which the speaker is free though confined:

> When love with unconfined wings
> > Hovers within my gates,
> And my divine Althea brings
> > To whisper at the grates;
> When I lie tangled in her hair
> > And fettered to her eye,
> The birds that wanton in the air
> > Know no such liberty.

Some of the New Critics (*q.v.*), especially Cleanth Brooks, have emphasized the importance of paradox, holding it to be not an illustrative device but one of the essential characteristics of poetic speech.

PARALLELISM: The arrangement of the parts of a piece of writing so that elements of equal importance are balanced off in similar grammatical constructions. Parallelism, which acts as an organizing force directing the reader's attention to the elements which the writer wishes to emphasize, also can help give a polished effect to a piece of writing. It is one of the most persistent rhetorical devices and appears in many disparate types of literature, as these two quotations, one from the Bible and the other from Pope's "An Essay on Man," illustrate:

> The law of the Lord is perfect, converting the soul: the testimony of the Lord is sure, making wise the simple.
> The statutes of the Lord are right, rejoicing the heart: the commandment of the Lord is pure, enlightening the eyes.

> All Nature is but art, unknown to thee;
> All chance, direction, which thou canst not see
> All discord, harmony not understood;
> All partial evil, universal good;
> And, spite of pride, in erring reason's spite,
> One truth is clear, Whatever is, is right.

See ANAPHORA.

PARAPHRASE: The restatement in different words of the sense of a piece of writing. A paraphrase may be a general statement of the ideas of a work or a clarification of a difficult passage. Usually, it approximates the original in length. Below is a stanza from Donne's "A Valediction: Forbidding Mourning" and a paraphrase of it:

> Moving of th'earth brings harms and fears;
>   Men reckon what it did and meant;
> But trepidation of the spheres,
>   Though greater far, is innocent.

> An earthquake causes a great deal of destruction and arouses fear. Men assess the damage it did and speculate about its significance. However, a movement of the heavenly bodies, though a phenomenon far more vast, does not show itself so directly or appear to have such terrible consequences.

It should be remembered that a paraphrase is never adequate for the understanding of a good poem. The function of the word *innocent* in the stanza above, for example, is far more complex than any paraphrase can suggest.

PARNASSIANISM: As a reaction to the earlier romanticism of Hugo, Vigny, and Lamartine, French Parnassianism emerged under the leadership of Théophile Gautier in the 1830's. Turning their backs on the subjectivism and the social concerns of the Romantics, the Parnassians devoted themselves to objective poetry, from which the personality of the writer was removed, and to poetry which had "hardness" and clarity of outline. "Le poète est le sculpteur"—this statement by Gautier became, for the Parnassians, an emblem for craftsmanship in verse. By emphasizing craft and by using analogies with the other arts, Gautier attempted to place poetry on an equal basis with the plastic arts: the poem, too, should be carved, wrought into a tangible form, for the form was the idea given shape.

Preoccupation with form, among the Parnassians, gave rise to a style which has been called *lapidary*. Gems, porcelains, marble statues and tombs, and exquisitely painted miniatures came to be conventional images in their verse.

In limiting their subject matter and by excluding moral and social concerns, the Parnassians declared that they were concerned with art for its own sake—*l'art pour l'art*. In the preface to his novel *Mademoiselle de Maupin* (1835), Gautier advanced the idea that art could not be "used," opposing the dictum held throughout the nineteenth century by political radicals and bourgeois writers that art was a means to an end.

In the 1870's, the doctrines of Parnassianism began to be felt in England through the influence of Théodore de Banville, whose *Petit traité de poésie française* (1872) was read widely. He was in correspondence with Swinburne, Austin Dobson, Edmund Gosse, and Andrew Lang, who all admired his essay on French verse which urged a return to older French fixed forms such as the ballade, the villanelle, the rondeau, etc. The English Parnassians, notably Dobson, Gosse, and Lang, followed their French colleagues closely in matters of style and form, but the doctrine of *l'art pour l'art* was alien to their temperaments. Essentially moral in their attitudes, they adopted the poetic fashions of Parnassianism and ignored French slogans.

PARADOS: See GREEK TRAGEDY, STRUCTURE OF.

PARODY: See BURLESQUE.

PARONOMASIA: See PUN.

PASQUINADE: A lampoon posted in a public place. The term derives from the name Pasquino, given to an ancient statue which was exhumed in Rome during the Renaissance and to which satirical attacks were customarily affixed.

PASSION PLAY: A play which depicts the life, in whole or in part, of a god. Passion plays were performed in ancient Egypt and in the Near East. In western Europe, many of the medieval mystery plays (*q.v.*) presented episodes from the life of Christ and so are called passion plays. A few of these plays, especially the passion play given by the Bavarian town of Oberammergau, are still performed.

PASTICHE: Literally, a work made by pasting together scraps from different parts of an artist's work or from the works of various artists. Sometimes such a combination aims at creating a new work, as when a number of airs are strung together in a medley. Usually, however, the intention is satirical, and in its most common English usage, the word *pastiche* is a synonym for *parody*

PASTORAL: A term that covers a variety of literary forms. The only consistent characteristic of pastoral literature is that it concerns country life. In the third century B.C., the Greek poet Theocritus, writing of Sicilian shepherds, or "pastors," established the conventions of the pastoral world. In this world of trees, flowers, and meadows, it is always summer; no one performs the actual work of farming or sheep raising. Instead, the elegant shepherds and shepherdesses of this golden world occupy themselves with their love affairs or with composing and singing songs, which are usually of three types: the friendly singing contest between two shepherds, the song in which a single shepherd praises his mistress' beauty and laments her cruelty, and the elegy in which a shepherd laments the death of one of his comrades.

Theocritus' pastoral world, though unreal, was at least founded on that of the Sicilian shepherd, but since his time, the pastoral has been based on literary imitation. The most famous Classical writer of pastorals, Virgil, took Theocritus as a model and subsequent writers of pastoral verse have gone to at least one of these masters (or their imitators) for inspiration. In the Renaissance, two new forms, the pastoral romance and the pastoral drama, developed.

The pastoral romance, of which the *Arcadia*'s of Sannazaro and Sydney and the *Astrée* of d'Urfé are examples, is a long, complex prose tale of love and adventure set in the pastoral world. Influenced by the pastoral romance, the pastoral drama developed in Italy in the sixteenth century with such plays as Tasso's *Aminta* and Guarini's *Il Pastor Fido*. Elements of the pastoral drama appear in many English plays including Shakespeare's *As You Like It*. John Fletcher's *The Faithful Shepherdess* (1608), an attempt at pastoral drama, follows the traditions of Italian pastorals. The pastoral lyric and especially the pastoral elegy (*q.v.*) were popular in the Renaissance and remained so afterwards. Milton's "Lycidas" and Shelley's "Adonais" are the two most famous examples of the latter form.

In the Romantic period, when poets again turned directly to contemporary rural life, the popularity of the pastoral conventions declined. Recently, an attempt at a philosophical definition of pastoral was made by William Empson in *Some Versions of Pastoral* (1935). Empson discards the flowers and shepherdesses of tradition as superficial addenda and sees the essence of pastoral as a putting of the complex, such as courtly ladies and gentlemen, into the simple, such as a rustic setting. He then proceeds to analyze several different examples and types of literature, such as the proletarian novel, as examples of pastoral.

PASTORAL ELEGY: See ELEGY.

PASTORAL IDYLL: See IDYLL.

PASTOURELLE (PASTORELLA): A type of medieval lyric in dialogue form in which a knight or a man of equivalent social rank attempts to court a shepherdess. His suit is usually unsuccessful, though the wooing is sometimes terminated only by the arrival of a father or brother.

PATHETIC FALLACY: A phrase originated by Ruskin in *Modern Painters* (Vol. III, Part IV) to describe the attribution of human characteristics to inanimate objects. Such an attribution usually falls short of a full personification (*q.v.*). Quoting a phrase from Kingsley's "Alton Lock," "the cruel, crawling foam," Ruskin said, "The foam is not cruel, neither does it crawl. The state of mind which attributes to it these characters of a living creature is one in which the reason is unhinged by grief. All violent feelings . . . produce in us a falseness in all our impressions of external things, which I would characterize as the 'Pathetic Fallacy.' "

Ruskin qualified his condemnation by admitting that examples of the pathetic fallacy, though they gave a false picture of nature and were not characteristic of the greatest poets, were often very beautiful. Such examples, for instance, as Coleridge's "The one red leaf, the last of its clan / That dances as often as dance it can," were usually found, Ruskin said, in the work of poets of the second rank, men who felt strongly but who thought weakly. Great poets, such as Homer, Dante, or Shakespeare, men who both felt and thought strongly, would not so distort nature. An exception could occur when great poets, such as some of the writers of the Bible, under the stress of prophetic inspiration, attempted to express something so incomparably above them that neither theirs nor any other human minds could perceive it truly.

What Ruskin objected to most violently was the contrived use, by some eighteenth-century writers, of figures of speech involving the pathetic fallacy. "There is no greater baseness in literature," he wrote, "than the habit of using these metaphorical expressions in cold blood." Today, Ruskin's term is usually used descriptively and without any pejorative connotations.

ᵖATHOS: That quality in a work of literature which evokes from the reader feelings of pity, tenderness, and sympathy. The death of Desdemona is pathetic; that of Othello, however, is tragic. He is a character too heroic in scale, and his death is too great a fall to be described as pathetic. A pathetic object usually suffers helplessly, but a tragic hero, such as Othello, always achieves dignity and the resolution of his pain.

Sometimes, a writer, trying too hard for pathos or sublimity, stumbles into bathos (*q.v.*).

PAUSE: 1. A moment of rest in the rhythm of verse. The most commonly recognized pause, that which occurs within the line, is called a caesura (*q.v.*). There is often a pause at the end of a line and usually at the end of a stanza. These are sometimes called metrical pauses. A pause is often used in verse to offset a missing syllable. (See COMPENSATION.) Sometimes a pause is used for poetic rather than strictly metrical effects. In the final line of Hopkins' "God's Grandeur," the pause and the exclamation contribute to the power of expression:

> . . . the Holy Ghost over the bent
> World broods with warm breast and with ah! bright wings.

2. A moment of comparative calm in an action. Often such a moment precedes a climax and gives the reader or member of the audience a chance to catch his breath before being subjected to further strong emotional involvement. In *Macbeth,* the scene (Act IV, Scene iii) involving Malcolm and Macduff in England is a pause of this type.

PENNY DREADFUL: In England, a novel or novelette of mystery or adventure, cheaply printed and bound in paper, equivalent to the American dime novel.

PENTAMETER: A line of five metrical feet. The pentameter line, the most widely used in English poetry, is the basis of such special metrical forms as blank verse, the heroic couplet, and the sonnet (*qq.v.*). All the lines, except the first, in the following quatrain by Thomas Nashe are pentameter:

> Spring, / the sweet spring, / is the year's / pleasant king;
> Then blooms / each thing, / then maids / dance in / a ring,
> Cold doth / not sting, / the pret / ty birds / do sing:
> Cuckoo, / jug-jug, / pu-we, / to-wit / ta-woo!
> "Spring"

PENULT: The syllable next to the last in a word, as in "cru*ci*fy."

PERFECT RHYME: See RHYME.

PERIODIC SENTENCE: See LOOSE AND PERIODIC SENTENCE.

PERIPETEIA (PERIPETY): A sudden reversal of situation; a term usually limited to the drama. In the *Poetics,* Aristotle gives as an example of this phenomenon the scene in *Oedipus Rex* in which the messenger, believing he will relieve Oedipus of his fears, does the reverse. An instance from comedy will be found at the end of Congreve's *The Way of the World* when Fainall, apparently about to succeed in his aims, is suddenly discomfited by a crucial document produced by Mirabell. See ANAGNORISIS.

PERIPETY: See PERIPETEIA.

PERIPHRASIS: Circumlocution—using many words to express something which could be put more briefly. This is one of the devices by which a writer may avoid the commonplace and achieve an elevated style, though its indiscriminate use may lead not to elevation but to pomposity. In this passage from "The Rape of the Lock," Pope, for comic purposes, elaborates a simple statement, "Hampton Court is on the Thames near Hampton":

> Close by those meads, forever crowned with flowers,
> Where Thames with pride surveys his rising towers,
> There stands a structure of majestic frame,
> Which from the neighb'ring Hampton takes its name.

PERORATION: See SPEECH.

PERSONA: In poems such as Wordsworth's "I wandered lonely as a cloud," the "I" is not William Wordsworth but an imagined unidentified speaker. This speaker, called the *persona,* is not to be confused with the poet's private personality.

PERSONIFICATION: In Greek, *prospopoeia.* A figure of speech in which inanimate objects or abstract ideas are endowed with human qualities or actions. In morality plays, for example, characters are frequently given such names as Lust, Good Sense, etc., which indicate that ideas, not individualized persons, are being dramatized. Personification is often used in verse when the poet wishes to achieve certain effects, as in Gray's "Ode on a Distant Prospect of Eton College":

> These shall the fury Passions tear,
> The vultures of the mind,
> Disdainful Anger, pallid Fear,
> And Shame that skulks behind,
> Or pining Love shall waste their youth,
> Or Jealousy with rankling tooth,
> That inly gnaws the secret heart,

And Envy wan, and faded Care
Grim-visaged, comfortless Despair,
And Sorrow's piercing dart.

See PATHETIC FALLACY.

PETRARCHAN SONNET: A poem of fourteen lines divided into two parts: the first eight lines called the octave, or octet, rhyme *abbaabba;* the remaining six lines, or sestet, usually rhyme *cdecde.* The rhyme scheme of the sestet admits some variation but there are never more than a total of five rhymes in the poem. The octave generally contains the "problem" or theme which the sonnet will develop. Sometimes, an expression of indignation, desire, or doubt may occur in the opening lines which will be resolved in the sestet.

Originating in Italy in the thirteenth century, the Italian sonnet, as it is sometimes called, was brought to its fullest development by Petrarch (1304-1374). In England, Petrarch's sonnets were translated and imitated for the first time by Sir Thomas Wyatt in the sixteenth century. English imitators, using iambic pentameter, took liberties with the rhyme scheme, though they retained the division of the sonnet form into two parts, as in Keats' "On First Looking into Chapman's Homer":

> Much have I travelled in the realms of gold,
> And many goodly states and kingdoms seen;
> Round many western islands have I been
> Which bards in fealty to Apollo hold.
> Oft of one wide expanse had I been told
> That deep-browed Homer ruled as his demesne;
> Yet did I never breathe its pure serene
> Till I heard Chapman speak out loud and bold:
> Then felt I like some watcher of the skies
> When a new planet swims into his ken;
> Or like stout Cortez when with eagle eyes
> He stared at the Pacific—and all his men
> Looked at each other with a wild surmise—
> Silent, upon a peak in Darien.

PETRARCHISM: The style introduced by Petrarch (1304-1374) in his sonnets to Laura. It was a style marked by grammatical complexity, elaborate conceits (*q.v.*), and conventional diction. Its influence was widespread, extending to the Pléiade (*q.v.*) in France and the Elizabethan sonneteers in England.

PHILIPPIC: A speech or piece of writing which denounces someone in harsh and vituperative language. The term derives from the orations in which Demosthenes denounced Philip of Macedon.

PHILISTINE: One devoted to materialism, progress, and wealth with no concern for art, beauty, culture, or spiritual things. In a lecture entitled "Sweetness and Light," his last as Professor of Poetry at Oxford (1867), Matthew Arnold singled out as Philistines those Englishmen who believed that wealth indicated greatness. The lecture, subsequently printed as the first chapter of *Culture and Anarchy* (1869), cites culture as an antidote to the stultifying effects of Philistinism:

> Now, the use of culture is that it helps us, by means of its spiritual standard of perfection, to regard wealth as but machinery, and not only to say as a matter of words that we regard wealth as but machinery, but really to perceive and feel that it is so. If it were not for this purging effect wrought upon our minds by culture, the whole world, the future as well as the present, would inevitably belong to the Philistines . . . Culture says "Consider these people, then, their way of life, their habits, their manners, the very tones of their voice; look at them attentively; observe the literature they read, the things which give them pleasure, the words which come forth out of their mouths, the thoughts which make the furniture of their minds; would any amount of wealth be worth having with the condition that one was to become just like these people by having it?"

During the nineteenth century, aesthetes, identifying the term *Philistine* with the middle classes, attempted by their dress, behavior, and art to shock the unimaginative middle classes— *épater le bourgeois*. By the end of the century, the "struggle" between the disapproval expressed by the Philistines and the daring of the decadents culminated in the suspension of the *avantgarde* journal the *Yellow Book* and the trial of Oscar Wilde (1895). See DECADENCE.

PICARESQUE NOVEL: A narrative depicting the life of a *picaro* (Spanish: "rogue") or in English a "picaroon," whose knavery implicates him in adventures which take him from one social class to another. Frequently, he is a social parasite or a person of low estate who manages to exploit those in more elevated positions. A vehicle for satire, the picaresque novel, generally narrated in the first person, consists of unconnected episodes held together by the presence of the central character. Realistic detail, usually drawn from the life of the lower classes, tends to be coarse and bawdy.

Emerging as a distinct genre in sixteenth-century Spain, the picaresque novel became a popular form of entertainment following the success of an anonymous work *La vida de Lazarillo de Tormes* (ca. 1554). Later writers borrowed extensively from Spanish models, setting their stories in Spain and using similar incidents. A notable French example of the form is Lesage's *Gil Blas*. The first novel of this type in English was Thomas Nashe's *The Unfortunate Traveller* (1594), later followed by such well-known works as Defoe's *Moll Flanders* (which deals with a female picaroon), Fielding's *Jonathan Wild,* and Smollet's *Ferdinand, Count Fathom*.

PICAROON: See PICARESQUE NOVEL.

PIECE A THESE: See THESIS PLAY.

PIECE BIEN FAITE: See WELL-MADE PLAY.

PINDARIC ODE: See ODE.

PLAINT: A lament in verse. See COMPLAINT.

PLANH: In Provençal verse, a song of mourning for a deceased patron; it contrasts his virtues with the vices of those who survive. In aim and subject matter, the *planh* is related to the *sirventes* (*q.v.*). See TROUBADOUR.

PLATITUDE: A flat, stale, or trite statement uttered as though it were fresh and original. In *Hamlet,* Polonius, bidding goodbye to Laertes, instructs him in proper behavior with a series of pious platitudes:

> Give every man thine ear, but few thy voice;
> Take each man's censure, but reserve thy judgment.
> Costly thy habit as thy purse can buy,
> But not express'd in fancy; rich, not gaudy.
>
> . . . .
>
> Neither a borrower nor a lender be;
> For loan oft loses both itself and friend,
> And borrowing dulls the edge of husbandry.

> This above all,—to thine ownself be true;
> And it must follow, as the night the day,
> Thou canst not then be false to any man.

PLAY: A dramatized story designed to be performed on a stage by actors. For some of the major types of plays, see the following entries: CHRONICLE PLAY, COMEDY, COMEDY OF MANNERS, HIGH COMEDY, MIRACLE PLAY, MORALITY PLAY, THESIS PLAY, TRAGEDY, WELL-MADE PLAY.

PLEIADE: Originally a constellation named for the seven daughters of Atlas, the Pleiades has given its name to several groups of "stellar" poets, of which the most significant was the group that flourished in France in the middle of the sixteenth century. The members were Ronsard, du Bellay, Baïf, Belleau, Thyard, Jodelle, and Daurat. In the famous *Défense et illustration de la langue française,* du Bellay set forth the theories of the group. The *illustration,* or "making illustrious," of the language was to be achieved by expanding the vocabulary to include words from Greek and Latin, newly coined words based on these languages, and both antique and provincial words from French. The poet, accepting his task with high seriousness, was to create a French literature comparable to the literatures of Greece and Rome; and, to this end, he was to ignore the forms of medieval French literature such as the ballade, the villanelle, etc., and write sonnets in the manner of Petrarch, odes in the manner of Pindar, and in general take the writers of the Italian Renaissance and especially those of Classical antiquity as models. The *Pléiade* not only stimulated French literature but also influenced the poets of the English Renaissance as well.

PLEONASM: The unnecessary repetition or addition of words in the expression of an idea. Needless addition may make a statement ludicrous, as in "Hotchkiss, weary after walking *on foot* through the jungles, sat down for a breather." The scene from Shakespeare's *Julius Caesar* in which Antony addresses the crowd contains what is, by modern standards, a pleonastic line involving a double superlative, though it was perhaps not considered as such by the Elizabethans: "This was the *most unkindest* cut of all." Occasionally, a pleonasm may be used for rhetorical emphasis, as in "I saw it with my own eyes."

PLOT: The organization of incidents in a narrative or play. In the *Poetics,* Aristotle says that a good plot has a beginning, middle, and an end; he says further that it should be so constructed that no incident can be displaced or omitted without destroying the unity of the whole. The presence of a single hero is not sufficient, he continues, to give unity. A plot which consists of a series of disconnected incidents, even though it may center around one figure, he calls "episodic" and ranks as inferior. Many writers, however, have deliberately chosen the episodic plot for the freedom and scope which it gives. Whatever its structural arrangement, a plot usually contains conflict which provides a basis for the action. Characters are thus impelled to move from incident to incident—in the unified plot, the action reaches a climax, whereas in the episodic plot, it merely comes to a stop. In the latter, for example, the hero of a picaresque novel (*q.v.*), may become heir to a fortune and end his wanderings; in the former, however. the development of a major conflict provides the audience with suspense until all difficulties are resolved.

In the plot of Shakespeare's *Othello,* for example, the order of the incidents involving Iago's deception of Othello leads to a crisis (*q.v.*), the point at which the Moor decides to kill Desdemona. The conflicts of the play now intensified and heightened, the action moves toward the climax (*q.v.*), the discovery that Iago has misled Othello. Following this incident, the dénouement (*q.v.*) contains Othello's remorse and self-punishment, and Iago's capture and condemnation to torture. In the play, the rising action leading to the climax provides the greatest emotional intensity for the audience, while the falling action provides the spectators with relief. For a diagram of this type of plot structure, see FREYTAG'S PYRAMID. See also UNITIES.

POEM: A composition in which rhythmical, and usually metaphorical, language is used to create an aesthetic experience and to make a statement which cannot be fully paraphrased in prose. Such elements as meter, rhyme, etc., are usually but not necessarily present. See POETRY.

POETASTER: An incompetent versifier; a writer of inferior or mediocre verse.

POETIC DICTION: In the *Poetics,* Aristotle says that a writer's diction should be clear but that it should also be raised above the commonplace. To achieve this elevation, he maintains, the writer must introduce unusual words, metaphors, and various stylistic ornaments, "for by deviating in exceptional cases from the normal idiom, the language will gain distinction." In this part of the *Poetics,* Aristotle was defending poets who had been condemned for using expressions that would never be found in ordinary speech. A language made up entirely of deviations from the ordinary would, he said, be grotesque where one with no such deviations would be flat.

The debate on poetic diction—the type of language suitable to verse and the liberties allowable in it—has continued since Aristotle's time. In the English Renaissance, Spenser built an elaborate poetic style, using many words which were quaint or archaic even then. The eighteenth century saw the development of an ornate diction which, in addition to archaisms, utilized Latinisms, conventionally personified abstractions, and many periphrases (*q.v.*), such as "finny prey" for "fish."

At the beginning of the Romantic period, Wordsworth protested against this style. In the Preface to the *Lyrical Ballads,* he said that there was no essential difference between the language of prose and that of verse. The poet, since he was addressing other men, should employ a "selection of the language really used by men." Wordsworth said he had taken as much pains to avoid poetic diction as others had to achieve it. Nevertheless, to the modern ear, Wordsworth's speech is full of the conventions of nineteenth-century poetic style:

> Thrice welcome, darling of the spring!
> Even yet thou are to me
> No bird, but an invisible thing,
> A voice, a mystery.
> > "To the Cuckoo"

Such expressions as *thrice* for *three times, thou art* for *you are,* in this stanza, and *oft* for *often, whereso'er* for *wherever,* etc., seem to the contemporary reader marks of that "poetic diction" which Wordsworth sought to escape. The poets of the twentieth century have largely avoided the diction of Romantic poetry just as Wordsworth and his contemporaries attempted to avoid that of their predecessors, the Neo-Classicists. The language of poetry, never precisely the same as the language of prose, moves closer to it or further from it as the needs of the age demand.

POETIC JUSTICE: A term used by Thomas Rhymer in *Tragedies of the Last Age* (1678) to designate the idea that the good are rewarded and the evil punished. The use of poetic justice has been urged by many who regard the moral function of literature as primary. A writer, these critics say, should carefully distribute rewards and punishments so that the good may be inspired to further goodness and the wicked discouraged from evil. Despite the obvious observation that life does not have such a convenient arrangement, the doctrine is defended on the grounds that the universe is presided over by a beneficent deity who will, at the appropriate time, redress wrongs and punish the wicked who have prospered on earth. Literature, consequently, should present the true state of things.

In the eighteenth century, the critic John Dennis defended this idea of poetic justice by stating that literature which did not function as "a very solemn lecture" was either "an empty amusement, or a scandalous and pernicious libel upon the government of the world." Addison, however, called the idea a "ridiculous Doctrine." In modern times, the use of poetic justice is limited largely to melodrama (*q.v.*) and many motion pictures. In *The Importance of Being Earnest*, Oscar Wilde, ridiculing the notion of poetic justice, has Miss Prism declare that she has written a three-volume novel:

> Cecily: Did you really, Miss Prism? How wonderfully clever you are! I hope it did not end happily? I don't like novels that end happily. They depress me so much.
>
> Miss P: The good ended happily, and the bad unhappily. That is what Fiction means.

POETIC LICENSE: The liberty, usually limited to verse, taken by a poet in matters of word order, rhyme, use of archaic words, and figures of speech. Within the conventions of poetic form, license is granted so that the writer may be permitted to achieve certain effects. Not all practices, however, may be condoned as poetic license, for a poet may discover that, as a result of ineptitude, his license has been revoked.

POETIC PROSE: Elaborately wrought prose which makes use of the rhythms, figures, and other devices of verse. Many writers have adopted poetic prose for a short work or for passages of particular intensity in a longer one, as here in the description of the mermaid in Oscar Wilde's "The Fisherman and his Soul":

> Her hair was as a wet fleece of gold, and each separate hair as a thread of fine gold in a cup of glass. Her body was of white ivory, and her tail was of silver and pearl. Silver and pearl was her tail, and the green weeds of the sea coiled around it; and like sea shells were her ears, and her lips were like sea coral. The cold waves dashed over her cold breasts, and the salt glistened upon her eyelids.

POET LAUREATE: A title given to a poet appointed by the British sovereign. The poet laureate was generally expected to compose verse for state functions, but in modern times, his title has been chiefly a distinction.

From primitive times, poets have traditionally functioned as singers at the courts of kings who wished to hear their virtues and victories extolled in verse. In the medieval universities, where recipients of academic degrees were customarily crowned with laurel, one who had attained distinction in Latin rhetoric was designated *poet laureate*. In 1341, the Italian poet Petrarch was honored with a crown of laurel by the Senate of Rome for his achievements.

In England, the first official poet laureate was John Dryden, who held the laureateship from 1670 to 1688, though other poets, such as Ben Jonson and William Davenant, had been "court poets" before him. Though some poets laureate have been writers of little distinction, others, such as Wordsworth and Tennyson, have dignified the office. Since 1930, John Masefield has held the post.

POETRY: Though poetry is sometimes defined as any metrical composition, for the most part a distinction is made between it and verse. Sir Philip Sydney, saying that verse is "but an ornament and no cause to Poetry," expressed the attitude that is commonly, though not universally, accepted. If metrical form is disregarded as a basis for a definition of poetry, a different basis must be found. Wordsworth said that the opposite of poetry was factual or scientific writing, and modern theoreticians tend to agree with him. The meanings of a piece of prose, especially scientific prose, these critics feel, can be stated as intellectual concepts, but those of poetry cannot. By making wide use of the connotations and interrelations of words, poetry presents much that is beyond the expressive ability of prose. Though some critics have maintained that the aim of poetry is to produce pleasure and others that it is to give a unique sort of knowledge, there is considerable agreement that poetry presents an emotional and intellectual experience rather than an abstraction from experience.

POINT OF ATTACK: A term, sometimes limited to the drama, designating the point in a story at which the writer begins his action. The point of attack does not usually coincide with the beginning of the story. Easy changes of scene permit a playwright to present most of his story directly; in *Macbeth,* for example, the point of attack is near the beginning of the story, but in such modern plays as Ibsen's *Ghosts,* the conventions of the realistic theater tend to force the playwright to set the point of attack almost immediately before the catastrophe and to tell most of his story through exposition.

POINT OF VIEW: The point from which a story is seen or told. Though there are numerous possible arrangements, three principal points of view are most commonly employed: 1) the omniscient, which enables the writer to present the inner thoughts and feelings of his characters. Godlike, he may survey from his Olympian position past and present so that the reader may come to know more of his imaginative world than any single character in it. In *Ulysses,* for example, a work that employs shifting points of view, Joyce reveals the inner thoughts of his three major characters through the stream of consciousness (*q.v.*) and presents actions, unknown to the individual characters, going on in various parts of Dublin. Moreover, the omniscient author may sometimes openly comment on the behavior of his characters, as in Thackeray's *Vanity Fair;* 2) the point of view of a single character who is used by the author as a central observer or participant in the action. Utilizing this device, the writer may, in the third-person narrative, limit the knowledge available to the reader. Detective stories often employ this point of view. It may also be seen in Joyce's *Portrait of the Artist as a Young Man,* in which Stephen Dedalus' consciousness is all the reader knows; 3) the first-person narrative, in which the point of view is solely that of the character telling the story. He may be the central character, as in Defoe's *Robinson Crusoe,* or a minor figure who either observes or participates in the action, as in Conrad's *Heart of Darkness,* in which Marlow does both. This device, the furthest removed from the omniscient point of view, eliminates the presence of the author completely.

POLEMIC: A work, argumentative in nature, which presents the writer's viewpoint on a controversial subject. Many English authors such as Swift and Milton have written polemical works, of which Milton's *Areopagitica* is perhaps the most famous.

POLYPHONIC PROSE: Prose which has the qualities and elements of verse. As developed by Amy Lowell (1874-1925) from the nineteenth-century poet Paul Fort, who wrote verse which was printed as prose, polyphonic prose was a fusion of meter, alliteration, assonance, free verse, rhyme, and recurrence of significant images. Amy Lowell's *Can Grande's Castle* (1918) is the most notable example of this kind of writing. John Gould Fletcher, an associate of Amy Lowell, has been credited with giving the name to this prose and, in fact, made use of it himself.

PORTMANTEAU WORD: A word formed by combining two or more words. In *Through the Looking Glass,* Lewis Carroll referred to his own inventions in the poem "Jabberwocky" as "portmanteau words": "You see," says Humpty Dumpty, explaining to Alice that *slithy* combines *lithe* and *slimy,* "it's like a portmanteau—there are two meanings packed up in one word." James Joyce made extensive use of portmanteau words in *Finnegans Wake,* as, for example, "bisexcycle."

POTBOILER: A literary work produced for the sole purpose of providing the author with money. Generally, potboilers are of inferior literary merit, but occasionally they may have considerable distinction, as in the case of Dr. Johnson's prose tale

Rasselas, which was written in a week to pay his mother's funeral expenses.

POULTER'S MEASURE: The alternation of the alexandrine (or iambic hexameter) and the fourteener (or iambic heptameter) used widely in the sixteenth century. The term derives from the poulterer's practice of giving customers twelve eggs in the first dozen bought and fourteen in the second dozen. Poulter's measure is now rarely used; however, a modification may take the form of a stanza containing iambic trimeter in the first, second, and fourth lines and tetrameter in the third. See SHORT MEASURE.

PRECIS: A concise summary or abstract of a work.

PREFACE: A brief introduction to a work, stating the author's intention or commenting on the contents. Shaw's prefaces to his plays are notable examples of how such introductions may be extended into significant essays.

PRE-RAPHAELITES: Established in 1848 by Dante Gabriel Rossetti, Holman, Hunt, John Everett Millais, and other artists, the pre-Raphaelite Brotherhood challenged the dominant style of painting and extolled the purity and simplicity of the Italian "primitives," those painters preceding Raphael. In rejecting Renaissance and post-Renaissance art, which tended to idealize man and nature, the pre-Raphaelites attempted to introduce fidelity of detail into their painting. In time, however, Rossetti made pre-Raphaelitism over in his own image. Turning from the naturalism of Hunt and Millais, Rossetti and his followers filled their canvases with a subjective pseudo-medievalism. Opposed to the crassness of the contemporary industrial world, they sought to create beauty.

As a literary phenomenon, pre-Raphaelitism refers chiefly to the verse of Dante Rossetti, his sister Christina, and William Morris. When applied to their verse, the term *pre-Raphaelite* suggests pictorialism, symbolism, medievalism, archaic diction, and sensuousness. (It was this sensuousness that caused Rossetti and his disciples to be labeled the "fleshly school of poetry.") The themes of death and decay recur in their verse with some frequency. Pre-Raphaelite verse and attitudes had a considerable influence on later aesthetes who worshiped beauty and disdained the growing materialism of the age.

PRIMARY AND SECONDARY ACCENT: Primary accent is the stress given to the principal syllable of a word, as in *aés/thete* or *bál/ance*. Secondary accent, on the other hand, is the stress given a syllable less heavily emphasized than the principal one, as in *él/e/và/tor*, the primary accent, in the pronunciation of the word, occurring on the first syllable, the secondary on the third.

PRINTING: See EDITION.

PROBLEM PLAY: See THESIS PLAY.

PROEM: A preamble or introduction, especially to a speech.

PROLEGOMENON: See INTRODUCTION.

PROLEPSIS: A figure of speech in which an anticipated event is referred to as though it had already happened. A notable example occurs when Hamlet, lying wounded, says to his friend, "Horatio, I am dead."

PROLETARIAN NOVEL: See THESIS NOVEL.

PROLOGOS: See GREEK TRAGEDY, STRUCTURE OF.

PROLOGUE: An opening section of a longer work. The prologue may perform a number of functions. The prologue to Chaucer's *Canterbury Tales,* for example, establishes the situation in which the tales will be told. In many plays of the seventeenth and eighteenth centuries, a prologue, usually in verse, states a moral point or anticipates the theme and action. For a more restricted use of this term, see GREEK TRAGEDY, STRUCTURE OF.

PROPAGANDA NOVEL: See THESIS NOVEL.

PROPAGANDA PLAY: See THESIS PLAY.

PROSE: Literary expression not marked by rhyme or by metrical regularity. Prose is the type of language used in novels, short stories, articles, etc. See POETRY.

PROSE POEM: A brief composition printed as prose but containing the elements of poetry: carefully designed rhythms, alliteration, assonance, rhyme, figures of speech, and recurrent images. The prose poem as a distinct genre first appeared in Aloysius Bertrand's *Gaspard of the Night* (1836). Baudelaire, influenced by this work, wrote *Little Poems in Prose* (1862). Later writers, such as Oscar Wilde and Amy Lowell, have written such "poems."

PROSODIC SYMBOLS: See the page "Symbols and Abbreviations" at the beginning of this volume.

PROSODY: The theory of versification, dealing with such matters as meter, rhyme, stanzaic patterns, etc.

PROSOPOPOEIA: See PERSONIFICATION.

PROTAGONIST: In Greek drama, the first actor, who played the leading part and doubled in some minor roles. The term now refers to the most important character, usually the hero, in a play or story. See ANTAGONIST, DEUTERAGONIST, TRITAGONIST.

PROTASIS: That part of a Classical play in which the characters were introduced and the situation explained. Today, the term *protatic character* designates one who is brought on by the author only to assist in the exposition. In Pinero's *The Second Mrs. Tanqueray*, Misquith and Jayne, both of whom disappear after the first scene, are protatic characters.

PROTHALAMION: A song heralding a marriage. The term was invented by the sixteenth-century poet Edmund Spenser and used as the title of one of his poems. See EPITHALAMION.

PROVERB: A short popular saying, generally an observation or a piece of advice. Though it may be attributed to an individual, as some of the Biblical proverbs are attributed to Solomon and others, most proverbs are anonymous products of the folk.

PROVERBE DRAMATIQUE: A term applied by Alfred de Musset (1810-1857) to certain of his plays, both one-act and full-length. Each play illustrates an aphorism which forms its title. Among the best-known of these are *Il ne faut jurer de rien* (*One Should not Swear to Anything*) and *On ne badine pas avec l'amour* (*One Does not Jest with Love*).

PSALM: A song of praise to God, especially one in the Old Testament book of *Psalms*.

PSEUDO-STATEMENT: A term originated by I. A. Richards to distinguish scientific from poetic "truth." By the term *statement* Richards designates scientifically verifiable expressions of fact. Pseudo-statements, on the other hand, the kind made in poetry, are not, of necessity, verifiably true or even logically coherent; they serve, rather, to order, or organize, the reader's attitudes and emotional impulses. Such statements, Richards says, cut free of the belief we accord scientifically verifiable ones, are valuable for the psychological function they perform. In recent years, Richards has come nearer the views of those critics who believe that poetry conveys a special kind of knowledge not available elsewhere.

PSYCHIC DISTANCE: See ASTHETIC DISTANCE.

PSYCHOLOGICAL NOVEL: A novel which is concerned primarily with the mental and emotional lives of its characters rather than the external events of its plot. Although there have been through the history of literature many works which have analyzed with great subtlety the internal lives of their characters (*Hamlet,* for example), Romantic subjectivity, later reinforced by the psychological researches of Freud and his successors, has led many modern writers to concentrate not so much on the ethical consequences of an action as on the motives that impelled a character to perform it. This term *psychological novel* is descriptive of content rather than form or technique and is applied to work as formally conventional as the novels of C. P. Snow and as unconventional as those of James Joyce.

PUFFERY: Criticism by clique or coterie. A critic may "puff," *i.e.,* overpraise, the work of a friend or someone to whom he is obligated in the expectation of receiving some suitable favor, such as similar praise of his own work, in return. The false critic of R. B. Sheridan's play *The Critic* is appropriately named Mr. Puff.

PUN (PARONOMASIA): Word play involving 1) the use of a word with two different meanings; 2) the similarity of meanings in two words spelled differently but pronounced the same; or 3) two words pronounced and spelled somewhat the same but containing different meanings. Though puns have been called "the lowest form of humor" by many, they have been used for serious purposes, as in John Donne's "Hymn to God the Father." In the poem, the word *done* is a pun on Donne's own name; in addition, there is a pun on *Son,* meaning both Christ and the sun:

I have a sin of fear, that when I have spun
My last thread, I shall perish on the shore;
But swear by Thy self, that at my death Thy Son
Shall shine as he shines now, and heretofore;
And, having done that, Thou hast done;
I fear no more.

PURPLE PATCH: A heavily ornate passage which stands out from the writing around it. The term is regularly derogatory, implying a lack of taste in the author. For an example, see the speech in Oscar Wilde's *Salomé,* in which Herod describes his treasures.

PYRRHIC (DIBRACH): A metrical foot of two unstressed syllables. The pyrrhic foot is rarely recognized in modern scansion.

Q

QUADRIVIUM: See SEVEN ARTS, THE.

QUANTITATIVE VERSE: Verse, such as Classical Latin, based on quantity (*q.v.*) rather than stress. There have been attempts to write quantitative verse in English, but few have been successful.

QUANTITY: The time needed for the pronunciation of a syllable. In Classical verse, which is based on syllable length, or quantity, rather than stress, as English verse is, a long syllable was one which contained a long vowel or a short plus two or more consonants. A long syllable was considered equal to two short ones; this relationship formed the basis of substitution (*q.v.*) in Classical metrics. Whether or not this regularity was characteristic of these languages as spoken is not known. Long and short syllables exist in English (compare *file* and *bet*) though our system of scanning verse does not take account of them. Just as there are various degrees of stress (we have terms for only two, primary and secondary [*qq.v.*]), so there are in fact various degrees of length. It is the interactions of these various stresses and syllable lengths that make up the complexity of metrical rhythm.

QUART D'HEURE: French: "a quarter of an hour." In the French theater a brief one-act play, usually a curtain-raiser.

QUARTO: (Abbr. 4to or 4°) 1. A book made from printer's sheets which have been folded twice to form four leaves, or eight pages. See FOLIO.

2. The term also refers to the form in which many of Shakespeare's plays were printed. The size of the quarto page at that time was about 9 x 7 inches. The quarto editions of *Hamlet,* for example, published between 1603 and 1637, are referred to as *First Quarto, Second Quarto,* etc., or simply *Q1, Q2,* etc.

QUATORZAIN: A fourteen-line poem which does not follow the strict form of the sonnet (*q.v.*).

QUATRAIN: A stanza consisting of four lines which may follow a variety of rhyme schemes. The quatrain is the commonest stanza form in English verse:

> Oh, Moon! when I look on thy beautiful face
> Careering along through the boundaries of space,
> The question has frequently come to my mind,
> If ever I'll gaze on thy glorious behind.
> *Anonymous*

QUIPROQUO: Latin: *quid pro quo,* "something for something." A term, usually limited to the drama, referring to a misunderstanding on the part of two or more characters. The misunderstanding depends upon a misinterpretation of a word or situation, the two characters involved believing that their intrepretations are similar. Oliver Goldsmith's *She Stoops to Conquer,* for example, begins in Act II with a *quiproquo:* Marlow, invited to Mr. Hardcastle's home to meet his prospective bride, arrives thinking that it is an inn and Mr. Hardcastle an innkeeper. From that point on, a series of misunderstandings motivates the action.

R

RAISONNEUR: A character in a play, usually somewhat detached from the action, who acts as the author's spokesman. The *raisonneur,* though he may assist in resolving the plot, is not usually a central figure. He observes the other characters, regularly delivering one or more speeches in which he comments on the action and expresses the writer's views. Most commonly, he is found in

such nineteenth-century well-made plays (*q.v.*) as Oscar Wilde's
An Ideal Husband, in which the aristocratic Lord Goring is the
raisonneur.

REALISM: Refers to the subject matter of as well as the technique
by which a literary work has been created. In theory, the realist,
wishing to record life as it is, refrains from imposing a predetermined pattern (based perhaps on a philosophic orientation)
upon his materials. He allows the story "to tell itself," for truth,
he feels, resides in the events themselves rather than in his imagination. Free of romantic subjectivity, realistic writing emphasizes truthfulness of detail. This "theory" of realism, however, is
not to be taken without reservations, for any artist must shape
the materials of his art into a form which derives from his personal vision of reality.

As a technique, realism may logically handle any subject matter, but it has chiefly been concerned with the commonplaces
of everyday life and the middle and lower social classes. The
American novelist and critic William Dean Howells conceived
of realism as a device for depicting simple, everyday people with
"work-worn, brave, kindly faces," but other realists have strenu-
ously avoided such material in favor of more earthy narratives.

From the beginning of the "realistic movement," which dates
from the mid-nineteenth century, there has been no universally
accepted set of principles governing the manner or content of
so-called realistic works. In French literature, the realism in the
fiction of Flaubert, Balzac, and Maupassant is as different as it
is in such American authors as Sherwood Anderson and John
Steinbeck.

As a term, *realism* is not, of course, limited to the nineteenth
and twentieth centuries, for elements may be found in such
earlier works as Defoe's *Moll Flanders* and Ben Jonson's *Bar-
tholomew Fair.* Generally, however, "realistic" handling in past
works refers to the accuracy of speech and behavior with which
a writer has endowed his "low" characters.

In recent years, realists have turned from their concern with
accuracy of external detail to the complex workings of the mind.
The device of the stream of consciousness (*q.v.*), with its fidelity
to the inner psychological processes of characters, has become

part of much modern fiction. Such writers as Virginia Woolf and James Joyce, though not strictly speaking writers of realistic novels, have reported the flow of consciousness of their characters with such faithfulness that some critics have attacked their psychological realism as lacking in artistic selection. See NATURALISM.

RECESSIVE ACCENT: In poetry, an accent which has been moved to the first syllable of a word for metrical convenience. In *Henry IV, Part I*, Hotspur, speaking of a battle, says, "But I remember when the fight was done,/When I was dry with rage and *éx*treme toil."

RECTO AND VERSO: The recto is a right-hand page in a book, the front of a leaf; the verso a left-hand page, the back of a leaf.

REDACTION: The editing or revising of a work for publication.

REDUNDANT VERSE: See ACATALECTIC.

REFERENTIAL LANGUAGE: See EMOTIVE LANGUAGE.

REFRAIN: A line or lines repeated at intervals during a poem, usually at the end of each stanza. A refrain serves many purposes aside from helping to establish the meter and tone of the poem. It may be simply a nonsense line which lets everyone join the song, as "Inky, dinky, parlez-vous." Or it may be a line which reestablishes the lyric atmosphere at the end of a stanza as in Spenser's "Prothalamion": "Sweet Thames! run softly till I end my song." Sometimes a refrain becomes an ironic commentary, changing in tone as the stanzas change. Compare the first and last stanzas of the tragic ballad "The Cruel Brother," in which the refrain first reflects the gaiety of the courtship and then con-trasts with the mournful lines describing the murdered sister:

> A gentleman came oure the sea,
> Fine flowers in the valley
> And he has courted ladies three.
> With the light green and the yellow
>
> . . . .
>
> Now does she neither sigh nor groan:
> Fine flowers in the valley
> She lies aneath yon marble stone
> With the light green and the yellow.

See INCREMENTAL REPETITION, REPETEND.

REGIONALISM: The representation in a body of literature, created either by a single writer or by a group, of a particular locale. In regional literature, this locale is conceived of as a subject of interest in itself, and much attention is devoted to its description. It may, in fact, become so important as to play a role in the story and influence the lives of the characters. Regional literature is generally realistic and is likely to concern itself with life in rural areas or small towns rather than urban centers. The Five Towns novels of Arnold Bennett are examples of regional literature as are those novels of Thomas Hardy, such as *Return of the Native* and *The Mayor of Casterbridge,* which are set in the countryside he called Wessex.

REPETEND: Any repeated element in a poem. Sometimes this term is used as a synonym for *refrain,* but the two are usually distinguished. Where a refrain appears without alteration at regular intervals, a repetend is often varied and does not appear at any predetermined point. Coleridge uses repetends throughout *The Rime of the Ancient Mariner.* For example, he introduces the mariner's "glittering eye" and "skinny hand" at the beginning of the poem, and then works them into a new pattern in Part IV:

> "I fear thee, ancient Mariner!
> I fear thy skinny hand!
> And thou art long, and lank, and brown,
> As is the ribbed sea sand.
>
> I fear thee and thy glittering eye,
> And thy skinny hand, so brown."—
> Fear not, fear not, thou Wedding Guest!
> This body dropt not down.

REPETITION: One of the fundamental devices of art. Just as a composer repeats his themes after their development and a painter echoes the line of a figure in another part of his composition, so a writer re-uses various elements within his work, for to be satisfied, the mind demands not only the revelation of the new but also the recognition of the familiar. A sequence of novelties inevitably seems formless; it is the reappearance of something known which the mind requires before it can accept a work as a unified whole, as in fact, a work of art. The repetitive nature of some devices, such as the refrain and the repetend (*qq.v.*) is obvious at once, but many others—assonance, consonance, alliteration (*qq.v.*), for example—are also based on repetition, as are indeed the rhythmical patterns of both verse and prose.

RESOLUTION: The events following the climax of a play or story; the term is used synonymously with *falling action*.

RESTORATION COMEDY: English comedy as practiced from the restoration of the monarchy (1660) to the rise of the sentimental comedy of the early eighteenth century. Restoration comedies are graceful, elaborately witty, and regularly concerned with sexuality. Set in the aristocratic Restoration world of elegant licentiousness, they usually describe the courtship and marriage of a witty heiress and a town rake. There is much raillery at the expense of age, cuckoldry, rusticity, and persons, such as the fops, who vainly attempt to imitate the manners of the charmed inner circle of true wits. In Wycherley, Restoration comedy produced a satirist of moral force, and in Congreve, a stylist of extraordinary grace. Among its other practitioners are Etherege, Vanbrugh, and Farquhar.

REVENGE TRAGEDY: In the Elizabethan period, a type of drama in which revenge is the central motive. The plays of the Roman dramatist Seneca, emphasizing bloodshed and vengeance, were the models of the Elizabethans. In *The Spanish Tragedy* (*ca.* 1586), Thomas Kyd established the genre of the revenge tragedy in English. Perhaps the most popular play of its time, *The Spanish Tragedy* utilizes some of the devices of Senecan tragedy such as the revenge-seeking ghost and sensationalism of incident, though Seneca, following the decorum of the Classical theater, has messengers merely report catastrophic events. Generally, Elizabethan revenge tragedy contains such lurid incidents as incest, adultery, rape, infanticide, or suicide. The revenger himself is sometimes the instrument of purgation in a corrupt court, assuming a disguise (as in Marston's *The Malcontent*) or madness (as in *Hamlet*) to bewilder his enemies.

The action of *The Spanish Tragedy* contains many of the features of a typical revenge tragedy. The play opens by introducing us to a ghost, which seeks its own revenge, and the character of Revenge. While functioning as a chorus, they observe the elaborate intrigue involving Hieronomo, a Spanish nobleman who desires revenge for his murdered son. During the action, Hieronomo feigns madness and presents a play at court, devices later used by Hamlet. The conclusion is characteristically bloody.

Some other notable revenge plays of the period are Marlowe's *Jew of Malta,* Marston's *Antonio's Revenge,* and Tourneur's *The Revenger's Tragedy.*

REVIEW: 1. A brief account in which the writer gives his reactions to a book, movie, play, or musical performance. Noted authors, such as Bernard Shaw and W. H. Auden, at times have been reviewers for newspapers or periodicals.

2. A journal containing articles on subjects of a philosophical, scholarly, or critical nature, as *The Edinburgh Review* and the *Partisan Review.*

REVUE: A theatrical presentation which, devoid of plot, consists of sketches, dances, and songs designed for amusement and frequently containing satirical commentaries on the personalities and events of the day.

RHETORIC: In its most general meaning, the principles governing the use of language for effective speaking and writing. To the Classical theoreticians, the study of rhetoric was essential for effective oratory. To this end, such writers as Aristotle, Quintilian, and Longinus codified the theories of rhetoric, which, along with logic and grammar, became, during the Middle Ages, one of the basic studies of the trivium. (See SEVEN ARTS, THE).

The Greek Sophists at one time made rhetoric a tool for effective argumentation, regardless of the truth or validity of the viewpoint. Plato reported Socrates as saying that he thought rhetoric a superficial art, and in the dialogue *Protagoras,* he reveals how the clever Sophist Protagoras argues with the aid of rhetorical devices. Because rhetoric may be used in such a manner, the term sometimes carries pejorative connotations.

RHETORICAL ACCENT: See ACCENT.

RHETORICAL FIGURE: In general, a specific arrangement of words for rhetorical emphasis. Unlike figures of speech, such as metaphors and personifications (*qq.v.*), rhetorical figures do not alter the meanings of the words employed. For individual definitions and illustrations of some rhetorical figures, see APOSTROPHE, CHIASMUS, INVOCATION, RHETORICAL QUESTION, and ZEUGMA.

RHETORICAL IRONY: See IRONY.

RHETORICAL QUESTION: A question asked, not to elicit information, but to achieve a stylistic effect. Often a writer or speaker adds emphasis to a point by putting it in a question, the answer to which supports his argument. In *The Merchant of Venice,* Shylock uses this device in a speech defending his conduct:

> Hath not a Jew eyes? hath not a Jew hands, organs, dimensions, senses, affections, passions? . . . If you prick us, do we not bleed? If you tickle us, do we not laugh? If you poison us, do we not die? and if you wrong us, shall we not revenge?

Since "Yes, of course" is the answer to all of the questions preceding the climactic one, the same answer is imposed upon it by the pattern, and the speaker's point is confirmed.

RHYME: The repetition of similar or duplicate sounds at regular intervals, usually the repetition of the terminal sounds of words at the ends of lines of verse. (Since the spelling *rhyme* derives by association from *rhythm,* many prefer to use the older spelling, *rime.*) Verse has not always made use of rhyme, and some poets (*e.g.,* Milton) have spoken against it; nevertheless, rhyme is one of the most persistent of poetic devices. It calls attention to the word as sound, which we enjoy for its own sake, as opposed to the word as conveyer of meaning. It also functions as a marker, signaling the end of a rhythmical unit. When a rhythmical and a rhetorical unit coincide, the rhyme reinforces their correspondence; when they do not, the rhyme establishes, in the mind of the reader, an interaction between them. When regularly arranged, rhymes also serve to help mark stanzaic structure.

Of the various types of rhymes, some are distinguished by position, such as end rhyme—one which comes at the end of a line of verse—internal rhyme, and leonine rhyme (*qq.v.*), but most are marked by different relationships between sounds. Eye rhymes, however, such as *weak* and *break* depend on spelling.

An eye rhyme which was once a true ear rhyme is called a historical rhyme. Some of the commonest rhyme types are listed below:

The most usual English rhyme is variously called true, full, perfect, complete, or *rime suffisante*. In it, the final accented vowels of the rhyming words and all succeeding sounds are identical while preceding sounds are different, as in *bake-rake, heaven-seven*.

Rhymes that are not true rhymes may result either from the poet's ineptitude or from his desire to create a particular effect. Among the many names applied to such rhymes are *near, slant, oblique, approximate, half,* and *imperfect*.

Analyzed rhyme is a complex arrangement of near rhymes in the four lines of a quatrain ending, for example, thus: *pass, relief, laugh, peace.* Rhymes 1-4 and 2-3 exhibit consonance (*q.v.*) while rhymes 1-3 and 2-4 exhibit assonance (*q.v.*). Both of these phenomena, along with alliteration (*q.v.*), are sometimes considered types of rhyme.

Apocapated rhyme is one in which the end of a word is discounted, as in *rope-hopeless*.

In broken rhyme, one of the rhyme words extends over two lines.

Identical rhyme is the recurrence of two words which have exactly the same sound but are spelled differently and carry different meanings; also called *rime riche*. In the prologue to *The Canterbury Tales,* Chaucer, using identical rhyme, describes the pilgrims:

> And specially from every shires ende
> Of Engelond to Caunterbury they wende,
> The hooly blisful martir for to *seke,*
> That hem hath holpen when that they were *seeke.*

The term *identical rhyme* also designates the use of the same word in the rhyme position two or more times, as in the limericks of Edward Lear.

Linked rhyme, a device from early Welsh verse, is formed by joining a final syllable in one line to the first sound of the following line. In these lines from *The Wreck of the Deutschland,*

Gerard Manley Hopkins makes use of it by "joining" the word
door to the initial consonant of the word *drowned* to form a
rhyme with *Reward:*

> Dame, at our door
> Drowned, and among our shoals,
> Remember us in the roads, the heaven-haven of the
>   Reward . . .

In pararhyme, the consonants both before and after differing
vowels are identical, as in *look-luck. Cf.* CONSONANCE.

RHYME ROYAL: A seven-line stanza in iambic pentameter with the
rhyme scheme *ababbcc.* The term has been associated with King
James I of England, who himself used this stanza form. Others,
however, had used it before him, among them Chaucer in the
Parliament of Fowls, the "Clerk's Tale" in the *Canterbury
Tales,* and in *Troilus and Criseyde.* Sometimes this stanzaic
form is called the Chaucerian stanza:

> The double sorwe of Troilus to tellen,
> That was the King Priamus sone of Troye
> In lovynge, how his aventures fallen
> Fro wo to wele, and after out of joie,
> My purpos is, er that I parte fro ye.
> Thesiphone, thow help me for t'endite
> Thise woful vers, that wepen as I write.

Other poets who have used this form are Wyatt and Shakespeare, in modern times William Morris and John Masefield.

RHYME SCHEME: The arrangement of rhymes in a unit of verse.
The four-line stanza, or quatrain, for example, frequently has
a rhyme scheme of *abab* (that is, the first and third lines and the
second and fourth lines rhyme), though it may have such variations as *aabb* or *abcb* or *abba.* Some rhyme schemes in longer
units of verse are complex, as in the Petrarchan sonnet (*q.v.*).

RHYTHM: In language, the sense of movement attributable to the
pattern of stressed and unstressed syllables in a line of prose or
poetry or to the lengths of sounds in quantitative verse (*q.v.*). In
verse, the rhythm is determined by the metrical pattern, whereas
in prose or free verse (*q.v.*), it is the effect of an arrangement of

words more nearly approximating natural speech. A careful writer arranges his rhythms so that they intensify the expression of what is said. For different kinds of rhythm, see FALLING RHYTHM, RISING RHYTHM, SPRUNG RHYTHM, and METER.

RIDDLE: A puzzle generally in the form of a question, a statement involving a partial description of an object, or a comparison between two things in which only one is given. Riddles were a popular literary form in the Middle Ages and the Renaissance. Perhaps the most famous of all riddles is the one which the Sphinx presents to Oedipus: "What moves on four feet in the morning, on two at noon, and on three in the evening?" The answer, Oedipus replies, is Man: "As a child, he crawls on hands and knees; as an adult, he walks erect; and as an old man, he walks with a stick."

Riddles have always been a source of delight, and even such notable writers as Swift and Goethe have composed them.

RIME COUEE: See TAIL-RHYME STANZA.

RIME RICHE: See IDENTICAL RHYME.

RISING ACTION: See FREYTAG'S PYRAMID.

RISING RHYTHM: Occurs when the stress falls on the last syllable of a foot, as in the iamb and the anapest (*qq.v.*). Most English verse is written in rising rhythm, as is the following stanza from Lewis Carroll:

> He thought / he saw / an El / ephant,
>   That practiced on a fife:
> He looked again and found it was
>   A letter from his wife.
> "At length I realize," he said,
>   "The bitterness of life!"

ROCKING RHYTHM: Occurs when the stressed syllable in a foot of verse falls between two unstressed syllables:

> Believe me, if all those endearing young charms,
>   Which I gaze on so fondly today,
> Were to change by tomorrow, and fleet in my arms,
>   Like fairy-gifts fading away . . .
> > > *Thomas Moore*

RODOMONTADE: Vainglorious boasting, empty bragging. The term is derived from the character Rodomonte, a boastful Saracen king in Ariosto's *Orlando Furioso*.

ROMAN A CLEF: A novel, often satirical, in which actual persons appear under fictitious names. Oscar Wilde and Alfred Douglas were caricatured in Robert Hichens' *roman à clef, The Green Carnation* (1894).

ROMANCE: See MEDIEVAL ROMANCE.

ROMANTIC COMEDY: A play in which love is the central motive of an action which leads to a happy ending. Though the term is frequently applied to such Elizabethan plays as Shakespeare's *As You Like It,* it may with equal justification be applied to any modern play containing similar features.

ROMANTIC IRONY: See IRONY.

ROMANTICISM: Because the term *Romanticism* designates a phenomenon of immense scope, embracing not only literature but politics, philosophy, and the arts generally, there has been little agreement and much confusion as to what the word means. It has, in fact, been used in so many different ways that some scholars have, in despair, suggested that it be abandoned. However, the phenomenon would not become less complex with the abandonment of the term, and there is no reason to suppose that its successor would be any clearer.

Originally, *Romanticism* referred to the characteristics of romances, or fanciful stories, and carried pejorative connotations. In the eighteenth century, a Romantic landscape was not only an exotic one but one which evoked feelings of pleasing melancholy. It was the German critic Friedrich Schlegel, who, around the turn of the century, first used the term *Romantic* to designate a school of literature opposed to the Classic. From Germany, this meaning was carried to England and France.

Since individual Romantics are often in conflict and since no single figure or literary school displays all the characteristics labeled "Romantic," general definitions tend to be imprecise. In addition, these "Romantic" characteristics are often discerned in men and movements not usually so designated. They are not, in fact, the exclusive property of the Romantic period, the end of the eighteenth and beginning of the nineteenth centuries, but it is here that they are dominant and give identity to an era. A discussion of these characteristics will perhaps be more helpful than a strict definition.

One of the fundamentals of Romanticism is the belief in the natural goodness of man, the idea that man in a "state of nature" would behave well but is corrupted by civilization. From this belief springs not only the Romantic admiration for the primitive and for the child, but the Romantic faith in the emotions. If man is inherently sinful, reason must restrain his passions; but if he is naturally good, then his emotions can be trusted. They may, indeed, lead him correctly when reason fails. Romantic individualism is reinforced by this belief, for a man may properly express his unique emotional self if its essence is good. From this individualism stems the Romantic delight in self-analysis, the intricate examination and full exposure of the soul.

A belief closely linked to natural goodness is that of the perfectability of man, the idea that moral as well as mechanical progress is possible. Analogous is the Faustian striving after the sublime and the wonderful, that which transcends the mundane. In general, the Romantics admire change, flux rather than stasis. Commonly in opposition to the established order, they advocate not only moral change but radical political change as well. The Romantic often sees as his enemy the successful bourgeois, the insensitive Philistine, who has a vested interest in the stable, respectable institutions of society.

But the Romantic is not always a political revolutionary. His admiration for the natural, the organic, which in art leads to the overthrow of the classical rules and the development of a unique form for each work, in politics may lead him to subordinate the individual to the state and insist that the needs of the whole govern the activities of the parts.

To these characteristics, many more could be added without coming to a final definition. Romanticism is too diverse and too contradictory to be characterized in a way that is both simple and accurate. If an attempt is to be made, a Romantic may be described as one who seeks not the clarity and limitation of classicism but the mystery and aspiration which he sees in medievalism.

RONDEAU: One of the French fixed verse forms which is, along with the rondel and roundel (*qq.v.*), characterized by a refrain and the use of only two rhymes. In the rondeau, there are thirteen lines (fifteen if the refrains are counted as lines), usually of eight syllables, arranged in two five-line stanzas separated by a three-line stanza. The refrain, which is the first half of the opening line, is repeated at the ends of the second and third stanzas. The rhyme scheme, with "R" as refrain, is *aabba aabR aabbaR*.

> "To Ethel"
> (Who wishes she had lived—
> "In teacup-times of hood and hoop,
> Or while the patch was worn.")
>
> "In teacup-times!" The style of dress
>   Would suit your beauty, I confess;
> BELINDA-like, the patch you'd wear;
> I picture you with powdered hair,—
> You'd make a charming Shepherdess!
>
> And I—no doubt—could well express
> SIR PLUME's complete conceitedness,—
>   Could poise a clouded cane with care
>   "In tea-cup times!"
>
> The parts would fit precisely—yes:
> We should achieve a huge success!
>   You should disdain, and I despair,
>   With quite the true Augustan air
> But . . . could I love you more, or less,—
>   "In teacup-times"?
>   *Austin Dobson*

RONDEAU REDOUBLE: A fixed form of verse more complex than the ordinary rondeau (see above). It consists of six quatrains on two rhymes. Each line of the first quatrain is used in order as the final line of the four succeeding quatrains. The last quatrain is followed by a refrain which consists of the first half of the opening line: *abab, baba, abab, baba, abab, babaR.*

RONDEL: One of the French fixed forms of verse, the rondel consists of thirteen lines (fourteen if the second line of the refrain is repeated at the end) divided into three stanzas. The first two lines are the same as the seventh and eighth and are duplicated again in the thirteenth and fourteenth (if it appears). The scheme is *abba, abab, abbaa*(b).

> Beside the idle summer sea
> And in the vacant summer days,
> Light Love came fluting down the ways,
> Where you were loitering with me.
>
> Who has not welcomed, even as we,
> That jocund minstrel and his lays
> Beside the idle summer sea
> And in the vacant summer days?
>
> We listened, we were fancy-free;
> And lo! in terror and amaze
> We stood alone—alone at gaze
> With an implacable memory
> Beside the idle summer sea.
>
> *W. E. Henley.*

RONDELET: A brief poem in a fixed form, consisting of five lines on two rhymes in a single stanza. After the second and fifth lines, the first part of the opening lines appears as a refrain, thus: *abRabbR.*

ROUND CHARACTER: See FLAT AND ROUND CHARACTERS.

ROUNDEL: Although this term is sometimes used as a synonym for both rondeau and rondel (*qq.v.*), it is often limited to a variation on the rondeau developed by Swinburne. The Swinburne roundel consists of three stanzas of three lines each on two rhymes. At the end of the first and third stanzas is a refrain consisting of the first part of the first line, which may rhyme with the second line. The arrangement of rhymes is *abaR bab abaR* ("R" is the refrain). In describing it Swinburne used the form of the roundel itself:

A roundel is wrought as a ring or a starbright sphere,
With craft of delight and with cunning of sound unsought,
That the heart of the hearer may smile if to pleasure his ear
    A roundel is wrought.

Its jewel of music is carven of all or of aught—
Love, laughter, or mourning—remembrance of rapture or fear—
That fancy may fashion to hang in the ear of thought.

As a bird's quick song runs round, and the hearts in us hear
Pause answer to pause, and again the same strain caught,
So moves the device whence, round as a pearl or tear,
    A roundel is wrought.

ROUNDELAY: 1. A short, simple song with a refrain; also the musical setting of such a song or a dance based on it.

    2. Loosely, any of the fixed forms using a refrain, such as the
rondeau, rondel, etc.

RUBAIYAT: From Arabic: *rubai,* "quatrain." A collection of four-
line stanzas, or quatrains, as in Fitzgerald's translation of the
Rubáiyát of Omar Khayyám.

RUNE: 1. From Anglo-Saxon: *rūn,* "secret" or "mystery." A letter
of the ancient Germanic alphabet, based perhaps on the Greek
or Roman, dating from the third century A.D. Carved on horns,
weapons, and amulets, runes acquired magical power and were
used in incantations and in healing. Runic writing may be seen
in the verse of the Anglo-Saxon poet Cynewulf, who placed in
certain of his poems a series of words in runic characters, the
first letters of which spelled out his own name. Thus, a rune has
meant secret writing.

    2. A Finnish or, loosely, an ancient Scandinavian poem. (From
runco, "poem" or "canto.")

RUNNING RHYTHM: Used by Gerard Manley Hopkins in the
preface to *Poems* (1930), the term *running rhythm* refers to a
rhythm measured by feet of two or three syllables, aside from
imperfect feet at the beginning or end of the line. Each foot
contains a principal accent or stress, the remaining part consisting of one or two unaccented syllables called "the slack." The
term *running rhythm* is synonymous with *common rhythm,* the

usual rhythm of English verse, as opposed to sprung rhythm
(*q.v.*). See FALLING RHYTHM, RISING RHYTHM, ROCKING RHYTHM.

RUN-ON LINE: A line of verse which continues into the following
line without a grammatical break. *Enjambement,* the running
on of such lines, is encountered frequently in English poetry.
Byron, utilizing the run-on line, defended himself in the following couplet:

> I say no more than hath been said in Dante's
> Verse, and by Solomon and by Cervantes.

S

SAGA: A medieval Icelandic or Scandinavian prose narrative involving a famous hero or family or the heroic exploits of kings
and warriors. Until the twelfth century, sagas were transmitted
orally; in those extant, the authorship is often unknown, the
style simple and impersonal. Later writers have attempted at
times to imitate the narrative form of the saga. For the *Saga of
King Olaf,* for example, Longfellow derived material from the
notable saga *Heimskringla.*

SAGA NOVEL: A narrative portraying the life of a family. Usually
the story is continuous through a series of novels, as in Gals-
worthy's *The Forsyte Saga.*

SAPPHIC ODE: As practiced by Sappho, an ode written in regular
stanzas. The term is sometimes used synonymously with *Horatian Ode* (*q.v.*).

SAPPHICS: A quatrain utilizing a meter derived from the Greek
poet Sappho. There are eleven syllables in the first three verses
and five in the fourth. The verse pattern of the first three lines,
in which the fourth and eleventh syllables may be long or short,
is ‿|‒≃|‒‿‿|‒‿|‒≃; that of the fourth, which admits varia-
tion in the final syllable, is ‒‿‿|‒≃. An example of a Sapphic
stanza is taken from Swinburne's poem "Sapphics":

> All the night sleep came not upon my eyelids,
> Shed not dew, nor shock nor unclosed a feather,
> Yet with lips shut close and with eyes of iron
> Stood and beheld me.

SARCASM: Bitter, derisive expression, frequently involving irony as a device, whereby what is stated is the opposite of what is actually meant. In such a statement as "Oh, Hotchkiss, you're unquestionably a genius," the speaker can, by employing the proper intonation, indicate that in reality Hotchkiss is a fool. See IRONY.

SATIRE: Ridicule of an idea, a person or type of person, or even mankind. Satire has been used from Classical times to mock human vices and frailties. In his verse satires, the Roman writer Horace, scoffing gently at man's foibles, is amused rather than sternly indignant, whereas Juvenal, severe in his reaction to man's vices, expresses his moral displeasure with trenchant force. The former type of satire has come to be known as Horatian, the latter as Juvenalian. Most of Swift's writings (*e.g.*, "A Modest Proposal," *A Tale of a Tub, Gulliver's Travels*) are Juvenalian in character; in Shakespeare's plays, on the other hand, certain characters, such as Falstaff, are satirized gently for comic rather than moral purposes.

In the poem quoted below, Thackeray ridicules the emotional excesses of the hero of Goethe's novel *The Sorrows of Young Werther:*

> Werther had a love for Charlotte
>   Such as words could never utter;
> Would you know how first he met her?
>   She was cutting bread and butter.
>
> Charlotte was a married lady,
>   And a moral man was Werther,
> And for all the wealth of Indies,
>   Would do nothing for to hurt her.
>
> So he sigh'd and pined and ogled,
>   And his passion boil'd and bubbled,
> Till he blew his silly brains out,
>   And no more was by it troubled.
>
> Charlotte, having seen his body
>   Borne before her on a shutter,

Like a well-conducted person,
   Went on cutting bread and butter.
                          "The Sorrows of Werther"

SATYR-PLAY: In Greek drama, a comic afterpiece concerned with animals or satyrs, creatures half-man and half-goat. The satyr-play developed from phallic celebrations in honor of Dionysus. In the great age of Greek tragedy, the satyr-play, the fourth play of a tetralogy, provided comic relief after the seriousness of the preceding three tragedies. Eventually, retained only by convention, it was transferred to the beginning of the performance. The only extant satyr-play is Euripides' *Cyclops*.

SCALD: An ancient Scandinavian bard or court singer. *Cf.* SCOP.

SCANSION: The analysis of the metrical patterns of verse. Scansion includes the arrangement of accented and unaccented syllables into metrical feet and the grouping of lines according to the number of feet. It also includes the classifying of stanzas according to their rhyme schemes and the number of lines they contain. When a line deviates awkwardly from the basic metrical scheme of a poem, we say that it does not scan. However, a poem in which all lines adhere strictly to a theoretical metrical scheme is rare, for strict metrical regularity is monotonous, and a system of scansion simple enough for practical use cannot adequately reflect the subtleties of verse rhythm. Below is a stanza from Lewis Carroll's "Father William," with the scansion marked.

  "You are old, / Father Wil / liam," the young / man said,

    "And your hair / has become / very white;

  And yet / you inces / santly stand / on your head—

    Do you think / at your age, / it is right?"

The rhythm of the quatrain is anapestic with iambs at the end of the first line and the beginning of the third. Tetrameters alternate with trimeters thus: $a^4b^3a^4b^3$. Scansion is sometimes a matter of individual judgment, but these lines present no special difficulty. See METER, PROSODIC SYMBOLS (at the beginning of this volume).

SCENARIO: A plot outline of a theatrical work, giving the order of scenes and the characters involved.

SCENE: Usually limited to drama, the term *scene* refers to a division of the action within an act, though in some plays only scene divisions are indicated. Various conventions have determined the marking of scenes. The French classical playwrights, for instance, began and concluded scenes by the entrances and exits of characters. The Elizabethans, on the other hand, inconsistent in their practice of marking acts and scenes, sometimes omitted all divisions or, like Ben Jonson, indicated new scenes when there was a new grouping of characters. Many editors of Shakespeare's plays have indicated new scenes with successive changes in a play's locale. (It should be noted that at times the change of locale is assumed, for the text may not indicate a setting for the action.)

In the modern theatrical performance scene divisions are marked by the use of the curtain, which is lowered at the conclusion of the scene to indicate a change either in time or locale.

SCENE A FAIRE: French for *obligatory scene* (*q.v.*).

SCHOOL OF NIGHT: So called by Shakespeare in *Love's Labour's Lost* (Act IV, Scene iii), the School of Night was a group of Elizabethan intellectuals which centered around Sir Walter Raleigh. The Earls of Derby and Northumberland are believed to have been part of the group, which included the poets Marlowe, Chapman, Matthew Roydon, and William Warner. Its leading scholar was the mathematician Thomas Harriot. The group studied astronomy, geography, chemistry, theology, and philosophy. Though the members are not known to have held any central doctrine, they were widely suspected of being atheists. Shakespeare, in his play, satirizes what is believed to have been an antifeminist attitude held by some of the group.

SCHOOL PLAYS: Plays influenced by Roman comedy, performed in schools and colleges during the early sixteenth century in England. As part of the revival of interest in Roman drama, English secondary schools and colleges presented for their own enlightenment and enjoyment the comedies of Terence and Plautus. Occasionally, the Court or eminent persons might invite the school to perform before them. Soon, original plays, based on Classical models, appeared in English and Latin. The earliest extant school play in English, *Roister Doister,* written by Nicholas Udall while headmaster of Eton (1534-41), follows its Roman predecessors in division of acts and scenes, unities of time and place (*q.v.*), dramatic motivation, and organization of plot.

Some critics have suggested that the techniques of Senecan tragedy and Roman comedy were important influences on later Elizabethan writers who, as students, had been acquainted with Classical drama in the schools.

SCIENCE FICTION: Novels and stories dealing, usually in a speculative manner, with the achievements of science. At its simplest, science fiction consists of tales of adventure set on the planets instead of more conventional locales, but at its subtlest, it can serve as the medium for social comment, as in Aldous Huxley's *Brave New World,* or theological speculation, as in C. S. Lewis' *Out of the Silent Planet.* Among the "classic" writers of science fiction are Jules Verne and H. G. Wells.

SCOP: An Anglo-Saxon minstrel. His function was to entertain at the court with songs, either traditional or composed by himself, of heroic deeds.

SECENTISMO: A term used to characterize the bombastic, flamboyant style of the seventeenth-century Italian poet Marino and his followers; used synonymously with Marinism (*q.v.*). See GONGORISM.

SECONDARY ACCENT: See PRIMARY ACCENT.

SEER: See VATES.

SEMANTICS: 1. That branch of linguistics which deals with the meanings of words and especially with historical changes in those meanings.

2. The study of the relations between signs (and especially words, or verbal symbols), their meanings, and the actions—both mental and physical—evoked by them. Originally, semantics was concerned with the scientific rather than the imaginative use of language, but some theories of literature as a type of symbolic activity have been based on or influenced by semantics. One of the most notable of these is found in I. A. Richards' *Principles of Literary Criticism* (1925).

SENSE: See FOUR MEANINGS OF A POEM.

SENSIBILITY: For most of the eighteenth century, a man of sensibility, a quality supposed to be characteristic of all persons of virtue and breeding, was one who possessed a sympathetic heart, a quick responsiveness to the joys and sorrows of others, and a propensity towards the shedding of compassionate tears. The doctrine of sensibility, a reaction against the seventeenth-century emphasis on reason and the Hobbesian theory of the innate selfishness of man, was founded on the concept of man as inherently benevolent and sympathetic. Many of its manifestations, which would today be described as expressions of sentimentality (q.v.), were criticized in their own time (See Jane Austen's *Sense and Sensibility*). Sensibility carried to excess is sometimes distinguished by the term *sentimentalism*.

Today the term *sensibility* suggests highly developed emotional and intellectual apprehension and particularly a responsiveness to aesthetic phenomena. With varying shades of meaning, this word has been used by a number of the New Critics (q.v.) to describe qualities of the temperaments which produce or appreciate poetry. See DISSOCIATION OF SENSIBILITY, SENTIMENTALITY, SENTIMENTAL COMEDY, SENTIMENTAL NOVEL.

SENTIMENTAL COMEDY: In the early eighteenth century in England, a type of play which emphasized the distresses of middle-class characters in order to evoke the audience's sympathies. Also called the drama of sensibility, it not only ends happily but depicts good and bad characters with extraordinary simplicity. The hero may, consequently, be absolutely magnanimous, always acting from a sense of honor, and acutely attuned to the sensibilities of others, including those on lower social levels. These specific elements of sentimental comedy developed from both theatrical and social changes at the end of the seventeenth century.

As part of a reaction to the "debauchery" of some Restoration drama (q.v.), Jeremy Collier's *Short View of the Immorality and Profaneness of the English Stage* (1698), a work which had considerable influence in bringing about changes in taste, attacked what Collier considered the moral improprieties of English drama in the previous age. Moreover, the rising middle class brought with it a new audience for the theaters. To cater to the respectable bourgeoisie, playwrights such as Richard Steele and later Hugh Kelley (*False Delicacy*, 1768) and Richard Cumberland (*The West Indian*, 1771) composed plays which stimulated the tears of its spectators by portraying virtue, first in distress but eventually triumphant. See SENSIBILITY.

SENTIMENTALITY: "That man has no soul," said Oscar Wilde, "who can read of the death of Little Nell without laughing." To the critical intelligence, the tears induced by the demise of the angelic child of *The Old Curiosity Shop* seem excessive, although sorrow, and even tears, at the actual death of a beloved child are hardly inappropriate. The emotion evoked by Little Nell's death, however, appears uncalled for because she is not a child at all; she is so perfect, so angelic, so impossibly good as to be unreal, mechanical rather than human. The critical reader is thus presented with the absurd spectacle of an adult weeping over the death of a doll.

The suspension of the activities of the intelligence, of the powers of ethical and intellectual judgment, is the basis of sentimentality. With these powers in suspension, the reader accepts the sentimentalist's simplified view, usually one in which humanity appears as essentially virtuous (see SENSIBILITY), and consequently luxuriates in an outpouring of emotion unimpeded by thought.

When, however, a writer presents a sentimental character in a work not designed to elicit floods of emotion, he may wish to evoke in his reader an ethical judgment. In Shakespeare's *Richard II*, Richard, luxuriating in the sensations of the moment, is sentimental, but the play is not, for the spectacle of a weak, ineffectual monarch surrounded by forces he cannot cope with evokes not tears but judgment. Richard is not without sympathy, but it comes about not through an appeal to the spectator's shallow, uncomplicated emotions but is due rather to an appreciation of Richard's eloquence and sensitivity. He engages the spectator's feelings but does not escape his censure.

In eighteenth-century England, when sentimental comedy and the sentimental novel (*qq.v.*) stimulated the tears of their spectators and readers, emotional expression was considered a manifestation of benevolence. To some extent, sentimentality is today still considered an indication of gentleness, though the term itself has acquired pejorative connotations. In many motion pictures, radio and television "soap operas," and much popular fiction, sentimentality is an important ingredient for those who enjoy the self-indulgence of unwarranted emotionalism.

SENTIMENTAL NOVEL: In eighteenth-century England, a narrative designed to evoke the sympathies of the reader by demonstrating that unflagging adherence to morality and honor lead to rewards and that a flood of emotion indicates a kind heart. Like sentimental comedy (q.v.), the sentimental novel appealed to the new middle classes who believed that expression of feeling was a manifestation of virtue. Sensitive to what his readers desired, Samuel Richardson, in *Pamela, or Virtue Rewarded* (1740), portrayed the struggles of a servant girl to remain virtuous in the face of repeated attempts on her honor. Other notable novels of sensibility, as they are also called, are Goldsmith's *The Vicar of Wakefield* (1766) and Henry MacKenzie's *The Man of Feeling* (1771). See SENSIBILITY.

SEPTENARY: A line of seven metrical feet, so called from a verse in Latin prosody. See FOURTEENER, HEPTAMETER.

SEPTET: A poem or stanza of seven lines. The most common seven-line stanza form is the rhyme royal (q.v.).

SERENADE: A song written to be sung at night beneath a lady's window and, by extension, a poem in imitation of such a song, as Shelley's "Indian Serenade."

SESTET (SEXTET): A poem or stanza of six lines. The term is often used to designate the second part of the Petrarchan sonnet (q.v.).

SESTINA: One of the more complicated of the French fixed forms of verse, the sestina originated in medieval Provence. It has six unrhymed stanzas, in which the terminal words of each line are repeated in varying orders, followed by a tercet (a unit of three lines) which may include three of the terminal words or all six, used two to a line. In the diagram below, each letter represents the terminal word of a verse and each line a stanza:

```
a b c d e f
f a e b d c
c f d a b e
e c b f a d
d e a c f b
b d f e c a
  e c a
```

The form has been used by Dante and Petrarch and in English by such poets as Swinburne (who introduced rhyme and varied the word order), Kipling, Pound, and Auden.

SETTING: The time and place in which the action of a story or play occurs. In the theater, the word *setting* may refer to the physical appurtenances of a production, the scenery and properties, or it may refer to the scenery alone.

SEVEN ARTS, THE: In the Middle Ages, the seven liberal arts consisted of three studies—Latin grammar, logic, and rhetoric (including oratory)—called the Trivium, which led to the A.B. degree in four years; and the Quadrivium, consisting of four studies—arithmetic, geometry, astronomy, and music—which led to the M.A. degree in three years.

SEXTET: See SESTET.

SHAKESPEAREAN SONNET: A poem of fourteen lines in iambic pentameter divided into three quatrains and a concluding couplet. Also called the English sonnet, it is a variation of the Petrarchan sonnet (*q.v.*). The rhyme scheme is generally *abab, cdcd, efef, gg,* or *abba, cddc, effe, gg.* Developed by Sir Thomas Wyatt and the Earl of Surrey during the first half of the sixteenth century, the Shakespearean sonnet derives its name from its greatest practitioner. Like many other English sonneteers, Shakespeare used the final couplet to express the central theme of the poem:

> Weary with toil, I haste me to my bed,
> The dear repose for limbs with travel tired;
> But then begins a journey in my head
> To work my mind, when body's work's expir'd:
> For then my thoughts—from far where I abide—
> Intend a zealous pilgrimage to thee,
> And keep my drooping eyelids open wide,

Looking on darkness which the blind do see:
Save that my soul's imaginary sight
Presents thy shadow to my sightless view,
Which, like a jewel hung in ghastly night,
Makes black night beauteous and her old face new.
Lo! thus, by day my limbs, by night my mind,
For thee, and for myself no quiet find.

SHORT COUPLET: A tetrameter couplet, usually either iambic or trochaic, such as the following:

The rabbit has a charming face:
Its private life is a disgrace.
I really dare not name to you
The awful things that rabbits do.

Anonymous

Couplets, such as these, which contain eight syllables to the line may also be called octosyllabic couplets.

SHORT MEASURE (S.M.): A quatrain, rhyming either *abab* or *abcb,* in which the first, second and fourth lines are iambic trimeter and the third iambic tetrameter. The short measure may be formed as a variation on the hymnal stanza (*q.v.*) or by the poulter's measure (*q.v.*) written as a quatrain.

SHORT NOVEL: A narrative briefer than the novel but longer than the short story. Also called *novelette,* the form has been used by such noted writers as Henry James (*Turn of the Screw, Aspern Papers*) and Joseph Conrad (*Heart of Darkness*).

SHORT SHORT STORY: A term which may be applied to any particularly brief short story but which is usually used to designate a sketch of a character or incident which is both short in length and simple in form.

SHORT STORY: A prose narrative briefer than the short novel, more restricted in characters and situations, and usually concerned with a single effect. Unlike longer forms of fiction, the short story does not develop character fully; generally, a single aspect of personality undergoes change or is revealed as the result of conflict. Within this restricted form, there is frequently concentration on a single character involved in a single episode. The climax may occur at the very end and need not involve a dénouement (*q.v.*), though many other arrangements are possible. Because of limited length, the background against which the characters move is generally sketched lightly.

American writers since Poe, who first theorized on the structure and purpose of the short story, have paid considerable attention to the form. O. Henry, for example, popularized the type of climax called the surprise ending, involving an ironic reversal of expectation. Other writers of short stories, particularly those influenced by late nineteenth-century naturalism (*q.v.*) have emphasized the sleazy realities and sordid truths of life. In some later works, interest in the inner psychological processes of character has reduced action to a minimum. Many distinguished writers such as D. H. Lawrence, Katherine Mansfield, and Ernest Hemingway have made considerable reputations as short-story writers.

SIGNATURE: In printing, the original printer's sheet with four or more pages printed on it. When folded and bound, this forms a section of a book. The term *signature* can also refer to a mark placed so that it will appear at the bottom of the first of the pages formed from a single sheet and constitute a guide to the bookbinder as to the order in which these sections, or signatures, are to be bound.

SIMILE: An expressed comparison between two unlike objects, usually using *like* or *as*. "Tom is as ugly as Bill" is a simple comparison, but "Tom is as ugly as sin" is a simile. This stanza from Burns is built around a pair of similes:

> O, my luve is like a red, red rose
> That's newly sprung in June.
> O, my luve is like the melodie
> That's sweetly played in tune.

See EPIC SIMILE, METAPHOR.

SIMILITUDE: Used synonymously with *parable* and *allegory* (*qq.v.*), though the two forms differ in technique. On the title page of John Bunyan's allegory, *Pilgrim's Progress,* there appears: "Delivered under the similitude of a dream." Bunyan also quotes from Hosea, xii:10: "I have used similitudes." Sometimes the term is used interchangeably with *simile* (*q.v.*).

SIRVENTES: A type of Provençal lyric verse written to satirize political figures, personal foes, or to instruct readers morally. It had no fixed form.

SKELTONIC VERSE: A rough, doggerel-like verse by, or in the manner of, John Skelton (ca. 1460-1529). Skelton's verse, called "tumbling verse" by James VI of Scotland, is composed, for the most part, in short lines with two or three accents and an indefinite number of syllables. These lines rhymed in irregular groups. Below is part of Skelton's "To Mistress Margaret Hussey":

> Merry Margaret, as midsummer flower,
> Gentle as falcon or hawk of the tower,
> With solace and gladness,
> Much mirth and no madness,
> All good and no badness;
> So joyously,
> So maidenly,
> So womanly,
> Her demeaning;
> In every thing
> Far far passing
> That I can indite
> Or suffice to write
> Of merry Margaret, as midsummer flower,
> Gentle as falcon or hawk of the tower.

SKETCH: A brief story, play, or essay not as fully developed as the typical examples of these genres. Among the commonest types are the character sketch, a short description of an interesting personality, and the sketch composed for a revue, a simple playlet satirizing some topical trend or event. A group of short pieces by Dickens are collected under the title *Sketches by Boz*.

SLACK, THE: In a foot of verse, the unaccented syllable or syllables. In an anapest such as $\breve{con}\breve{tra}\acute{dict}$, the slack consists of the first two syllables.

SLANT RHYME: See RHYME.

SLAPSTICK: Low comedy characterized by physical action, such as the throwing of custard pies. Originally, a slap-stick was a cudgel made of two flat pieces of wood attached to a handle so that when a comedian, such as Harlequin of the *commedia dell' arte* (*q.v.*), used it on the buttocks of one of his fellows, a sharp report was heard.

SLICE OF LIFE: (French: *tranche de vie*) This phrase is used to describe the work of Zola and other practitioners of naturalism (*q.v.*). It implies that the writer has simply exhibited a chunk of life, raw and bleeding, without having made any effort to select his materials or arrange them. Since no works so composed exist, the term is better considered an appellation than a description.

S.M.: Abbreviation for short measure (*q.v.*).

SOCIOLOGICAL NOVEL: See THESIS NOVEL.

SOCK: See BUSKIN.

SOCRATIC IRONY: See IRONY.

SOLECISM: A substandard deviation from conventional usage in grammar or pronunciation. Such expressions as "I ain't got none" and "He don't" are typical solecisms. See BARBARISM.

SOLILOQUY: An extended speech in which a character alone on stage expresses his thoughts. A soliloquy may reveal the private emotions of the speaker, as, for example, Hamlet's "To be or not to be" and "How all occasions do inform against me"; or it may, often simultaneously, give information and display character, as does Richard III's opening speech "Now is the winter of our discontent." In the Greek and Roman drama, the soliloquy, though it occurs, is not common. The playwrights of the Elizabethan theater used it regularly and brought the device to its expressive height. Although the modern theater, limited for the most part by the conventions of realism, has made little use of the soliloquy, an example may be found at the opening of W. H. Auden's *The Ascent of F6*.

SONG: Any poem, even though there is no intention of its being set to music, may be called a song. (See, for example, Kipling's "Song of the Galley-Slaves.") However, this term, which may also designate poetry in general, usually refers to a poem in a regular metrical pattern designed to be sung. Many of the finest English lyrics were composed originally as songs, such as this one by Shakespeare:

Take, O take those lips away,
That so sweetly were forsworn,
And those eyes, the break of day,
Lights that do mislead the morn;
But my kisses bring again,
Bring again,
Seals of love, but sealed in vain,
Sealed in vain.

from *Measure for Measure*

SONNET: A verse form containing fourteen lines, in English usually iambic pentameter, and a complicated rhyme scheme. The sonnet, developed in Italy in the early thirteenth century, was one of the favorite forms of Dante (*Vita Nuova*) and Petrarch, whose sequence of sonnets to the lady whom he called Laura established the conventions of much Renaissance love poetry. In the first part of the sixteenth century, the form appeared in English in the work of Sir Thomas Wyatt. Later developed by the Earl of Surrey, it was used by most of the major Elizabethan poets such as Spenser, Sidney, Daniel, Drayton, and Shakespeare. After Milton, the form ceased for a time to be popular but was revived by the Romantics and has been much used since. For discussions of various sonnet types, see MILTONIC, PETRARCHAN, SHAKESPEAREAN, and SPENSERIAN SONNET.

SONNET SEQUENCE: A group of sonnets by a single author among which there is a thematic link. The sonnets of such a group are usually love poems which reflect the progress of an attachment or analyze the feelings of the writer. Shakespeare's sonnets are usually considered to constitute such a sequence. Other examples are Sidney's *Astrophel and Stella* and Elizabeth Browning's *Sonnets from the Portuguese*.

SOTIE: A type of farcical drama popular during the Middle Ages in France.

SPEECH, DIVISIONS OF A: In setting down the divisions of an oration, the Classical rhetoricians, by no means in complete agreement, named these parts as follows: 1) Introduction, also called the Proem or Exordium; 2) Statement of the case; 3) Argument or Agon; 4) Conclusion, also called the Epilogue or Peroration.

Some writers have subdivided the second part into a) agreed-upon points; b) the issues involved; and c) what the speaker intends to establish. Similarly, the third section has been divided into a) Proof and b) Refutation of the opponent's argument. In general, modern rhetoricians have retained most of these divisions.

SPENSERIAN SONNET: A sonnet whose rhyme is *abab bcbc cdcd ee.* Developed by the Elizabethan poet Edmund Spenser and also called the link sonnet, it has the epigrammatic final couplet of the usual Shakespearean sonnet (*q.v.*), and often contains no break between the octave and sestet. Below is one of Spenser's *Amoretti:*

> One day I wrote her name upon the strand,
> But came the waves and washed it away:
> Agayne I wrote it with a second hand,
> But came the tyde, and made my payne his pray.
> Vayne man, sayd she, that dost in vaine assay
> A mortall thing so to immortalize!
> For I my selve shall lyke to this decay,
> And eek my name bee wyped out lykewise.
> Not so, quod I, let baser things devize
> To dy in dust, but you shall live by fame:
> My verse your vertues rare shall eternize,
> And in the hevens wryte your glorious name;
> Where, whenas death shall all the world subdew,
> Our love shall live, and later life renew.

SPENSERIAN STANZA: A stanza of nine lines rhymed $abab bcb^5 c^6$; in the final line, an alexandrine (*q.v.*) is added to the ten-syllable lines of the *ottava rima* (*q.v.*). First used by Spenser in *The Faerie Queene,* the Spenserian stanza appears in such works as Byron's *Childe Harold's Pilgrimage,* Keats' *Eve of St. Agnes,* and Shelley's *Adonais.*

SPONDEE: A metrical foot consisting of two long or accented syllables. In English, spondees are introduced for variety but never form the basis of a rhythm. The following contains a number of such feet:

> One, two,
> Buckle my shoe;

Three, four,
Knock at the door;
Five, six,
Pick up sticks . . .

Anonymous

SPOONERISM: The accidental reversal of sounds, especially initial sounds, of words, as in "poured with rain" for "roared with pain." The term has immortalized the Rev. W. A. Spooner of New College, Oxford, who was much given to such slips.

SPRUNG RHYTHM: As described by Gerard Manley Hopkins in his Preface to *Poems* (1876-1889), sprung rhythm is measured by feet consisting of from one to four syllables; however, any number of unaccented syllables may be used for special effect. In a foot of sprung rhythm, there is, regardless of the number of syllables, only one stress, which occurs on the initial syllable. Four kinds of feet are possible: a monosyllable, a trochee, a dactyl, and a first pæon (*qq.v.*). These are mixed, any one foot following any other in no prescribed order. Unlike running rhythm (*q.v.*), the common form of English meter, sprung rhythm may contain two stresses which may follow one another (each a monosyllabic foot) or which may be divided by one, two, or three unaccented syllables. In addition, Hopkins states, lines in sprung rhythm are "rove over," the scansion of one line being carried over from a previous line; if one ends with one or more unstressed syllables, the following has that many less at the beginning. Consequently, scansion is not limited to the individual lines of a stanza but runs through it to the end.

In the Preface to his poems, Hopkins points out that sprung rhythm is that of common speech and written prose as well as most music. Moreover, it is found in nursery rhymes, as in the following:

Old Mother Twitchett has but one eye
And a long tail which she can let fly.
And every time she goes over a gap,
She leaves a bit of her tail in a trap.

STAGE DIRECTION: Information not part of the dialogue of a play given to the actor, director, or reader. This information may be a description of an action or a setting. Further, the writer may describe a character or analyze his personality. Stage directions range from such laconic instructions as "Exit, pursued by a bear" to the lengthy elucidations which Shaw inserted into the published versions of his plays.

STAND: A synonym for *epode*. See ODE.

STANZA: A group of lines which form a division of a poem. A stanza pattern is determined by the number of lines, the number of feet per line, the meter, and the rhyme scheme. Usually, a stanza pattern once established remains unaltered, but slight variations are sometimes introduced, as in Coleridge's *Rime of the Ancient Mariner*. For descriptions of some of the commonly recognized stanza forms, see OTTAVA RIMA, QUATRAIN, RHYME ROYAL, SPENSERIAN STANZA. See also VERSE PARAGRAPH.

STASIMON: See GREEK TRAGEDY, STRUCTURE OF.

STATEMENT: 1. A term used by I. A. Richards in his literary criticism to indicate scientifically verifiable discourse. See PSEUDO-STATEMENT.

2. A division of a speech (*q.v.*).

STAVE: A synonym for *stanza* (*q.v.*).

STICHOMYTHIA: Greek: *stichos,* "a line"; *mythos,* "speech." In drama, dialogue consisting of single lines spoken alternately by two characters. Generally a verbal duel, stichomythia is characterized by repetitive patterns and antithesis, as in these lines from *Hamlet,* Act III, Scene iv:

> Hamlet: Now, mother, what's the matter?
> Queen: Hamlet, thou hast thy father much offended.
> Hamlet: Mother, you have my father much offended.
> Queen: Come, come, you answer with an idle tongue.
> Hamlet: Go, go, you question with a wicked tongue.

Used in Classical drama, stichomythia was also employed by the Elizabethan dramatists with some frequency.

STILNOVISM: See DOLCE STIL NUOVO.

STOCK AND TYPE CHARACTER: A stock character is a familiar figure who appears regularly in certain literary forms. Among the most familiar stock characters of contemporary folklore are the hard-boiled private eye, whose achievements with small arms and susceptible ladies are legend, and the strong, silent man of the West, who rides out of the dawn, rights a wrong, and rides into the sunset. Equally familiar are the stock characters of nineteenth-century melodrama, the imperiled heroine, her gallant savior, and the mustache-twirling villain, whose destiny is perpetual frustration. A stock character, however, need not always be a result of the author's ineptitude. Shakespeare's Falstaff, a variation on one of the classic stock characters, the *miles gloriosus* or braggart soldier, is notable for his individuality; as is Beaumarchais' Figaro, a later version of the clever servant of Classical comedy.

The term *type character,* though often used synonymously with *stock character,* is sometimes distinguished from it. A stock character, though familiar, need not be typical of a group; a type character is a representative of a general class of people. The braggart, consequently, is a type character, whereas the braggart soldier is a stock character.

STOCK RESPONSE: A reaction on the part of the reader or spectator which follows a standard pattern, as when the appearance of a mother evokes feelings of reverence no matter what her character may be. The stock response involves a lack of critical judgment which, in melodrama for instance, leads the unsophisticated reader to react with terror to the exaggerated perils facing the virtuous heroine, whereas laughter may be appropriate to the unreality of the situation.

STOCK SITUATION: A frequently recurring pattern or incident in drama or fiction. The situation involving mistaken identity, for example, has been used from Classical comedy to the present; similarly, the love triangle involving two men in pursuit of one woman or vice versa has appeared frequently in both comedy and tragedy. A stock situation, though often unimaginative, may be developed with such skill as to give it new effectiveness. The triangle of lovers in Shakespeare's *Twelfth Night,* for example, while a stock situation, is so adroitly handled that it acquires its own character.

STORM AND STRESS: See STURM UND DRANG.

STORY WITHIN A STORY: A narrative enclosed within another upon which equal or primary interest is centered. Examples are the short tales which, from time to time, are interspersed among the adventures of Mr. Pickwick and his friends. Certain stories in *The Thousand and One Nights* are interrupted by other stories and only concluded after the new story has been told. *The Thousand and One Nights* also illustrates the techniques of the frame story, a narrative which serves to connect a series of otherwise disparate tales. The frame story is also exemplified by Boccaccio's *Decameron* and Chaucer's *Canterbury Tales*.

STREAM OF CONSCIOUSNESS: Coined by William James in *Principles of Psychology* (1890) to refer to the flow of inner experiences, the term *stream of consciousness* in literature designates a technique for the depiction of the thoughts and feelings which flow, with no apparent logic, through the mind of a character. To create the illusion of the chaotic stream, which we recognize in reality, the writer presents the seemingly random impressions and feelings which the character has at a specific time. Since, however, the writer is concerned with artistic form rather than absolute fidelity to life, only those elements in the stream are selected which are relevant to the narrative.

In Joyce's *Ulysses*, for example, the reader may be confused because the stream of consciousness frequently begins and ends abruptly, but this phenomenon demonstrates that inner consciousness and external reality are intimately related. In the passage below, Joyce describes an action of Mr. Bloom objectively, then abruptly presents his character's inner feelings and thoughts, which are centered on Blazes Boylan, his wife's lover, whom he has just seen:

> Mr. Bloom reviewed the nails of his left hand, then those of his right hand. The nails, yes. Is there anything more in him that they she sees? Fascination. Worst man in Dublin. That keeps him alive.

Attempting to give the illusion of the flux, Joyce, like other practitioners of this technique, reduced his sentences to apparently dissociated fragments. Freed of linguistic logic but held together by psychological association, the stream may become an effective artistic device for realistic characterization.

First developed by the French novelist Edouard Dujardin in *Les lauriers sont coupés* (1888), the stream-of-consciousness technique has been widely influential. Virginia Woolf and William Faulkner have used it, as have many lesser figures.

STRESS: A term sometimes limited to the emphasis placed on a syllable in a word as opposed to the emphasis demanded by a metrical pattern, it is usually a general synonym for *accent* (*q.v.*). See ICTUS, PRIMARY and SECONDARY ACCENT.

STROPHE: In Greek prosody, a group of lines of varying lengths constituting the first part of an ode (*q.v.*). Since this term is sometimes used as a synonym for *stanza,* a poem whose stanzaic structure does not vary is called monostrophic. In free verse (*q.v.*), the word *strophe* is sometimes used to describe a group of lines which constitute a unit, or verse paragraph (*q.v.*).

STRUCTURE: 1. In the work of John Crowe Ransom, the explicit argument or paraphrasable statement made in a poem, opposed to the texture, which is, briefly, everything else—the phonetic pattern, the sequence of images, the meanings suggested by the connotations of words, etc. The texture and structure, which together yield the complete meaning of the poem, combine to give it what Ransom calls its "ontology," the unique status which differentiates it from nonpoetic discourse.

2. In speaking of meter, Ransom uses the term *texture* to refer to the variations on the basic metrical pattern, or structure.

3. The inherent relationships among the elements of a work of art. *Structure* usually refers to the organization of elements other than words. For the latter, the term *style* (*q.v.*) is used. See FORM.

STURM UND DRANG: German: "storm and stress." A German literary movement of the latter part of the eighteenth century. In the 1770's, a group of young writers, impatient with the doctrines of the Enlightenment, especially as exemplified by French classicism, turned instead to the admiration and portrayal of turbulent emotion and forceful individualism. They preferred inspiration to reason and sought to model themselves on Shakespeare rather than the Graeco-Roman writers. Intensely nationalistic, they investigated and made use of folk literature. The young Goethe's *Götz von Berlichingen,* with its unconquerable

hero and its admiration for the medieval past, is a representative
Sturm und Drang work. Schiller's *Die Räuber* (*The Robbers*)
also shows the influence of the movement. Among the others
associated with it were Herder, Lenz, and Friedrich Klinger,
whose play *Wirrwarr, oder Sturm und Drang* gave the group its
name.

STYLE: The word *style* is used in at least two senses which should
be discriminated. If we say of a writer, "Hotchkiss' thought is
intelligent enough, but the poor fellow has no style," we are
assuming that style is an immutable quality found in some
writers and lacking in others. In this sense, sometimes called the
Platonic, style implies the perfect matching of the means with
their end. Thus, the term *style* may be used as a general synonym for *excellence,* or it may, more specifically, suggest that a
writer has found the unique verbal pattern that precisely expresses the meaning he wishes to convey.

In a second sense, the Aristotelian, style may classify rather
than evaluate. Thus, we speak of a satiric style, a Miltonic style,
an Italianate style, etc. A critic may not admire a particular
style or may consider its use in certain circumstances inappropriate, but distinguishing its presence in a writer serves merely
to classify, not to condemn him. When an analysis of a writer's
style is carried far enough, it ends in the man himself. The total
of the qualities which characterize an individual writer's style
(some of which may be too subtle ever to be discriminated)
constitutes his literary personality and reflects his psychological
one. The style, said Buffon, is the man.

SUBJECTIVITY: A quality of writing in which the expression of
personal feeling or experiences is primary. In autobiography,
for example, the writer, in presenting his private emotions and
memories, is generally subjective in his attitudes toward himself
and others. Similarly, in semi-autobiographical fiction, such as
Thomas Wolfe's novels or Samuel Butler's *The Way of All
Flesh,* the writer dramatizes feelings and incidents which are
derived from his own experiences. In general, Romanticism
(*q.v.*) has encouraged this kind of writing, for the expression of
personal feeling, to the Romantic, confirms his individualism.
In time, excessive concern with the inner life has given rise to

"private" expression of the sort evident in the poetry of Rimbaud and Dylan Thomas.

Subjectivity, however, may indicate the inner thoughts or feelings of the characters in a literary work rather than the author. In Browning's dramatic lyrics, for example, the central element is the revelation of the speaker's nature. In literary judgment, the term *subjectivity* refers to personal taste and response, particularly in the type of criticism called *impressionistic (q.v.).*

SUBLIME, THE: A quality possessed by a work which, as a result of the author's inspiration rather than his reasoned judgment, does not so much convince the reader as it thrills, or transports him. This idea was formulated by an anonymous Greek rhetorician writing in Rome in the first or second century A.D. Because he was confused with the third-century Greek Platonic philosopher and rhetorician Dionysius Cassius Longinus, he is often called the "pseudo-Longinus." The sublime was much admired by the Romantics, who often sought to achieve it in their own works.

SUBPLOT: A secondary action coincident with the main one in a story or play. The subplot may be largely unrelated to the main action (Middleton and Rowley's *The Changeling*) but it may also be a reflection of or variation on that action. It may then be called a *counterplot,* an important element in many of Shakespeare's plays (*Hamlet, King Lear, The Tempest,* etc.). The subplot or plots may be comic (*The Tempest*) or serious (*King Lear*) to contrast with the main plot or to reinforce its mood.

SUBSTITUTION: The use of a foot other than the one regularly demanded by the meter. In quantitative verse (*q.v.*), substitution is made on the basis of equivalence, the doctrine that two short syllables equal one long (a dactyl or anapest may be substituted for an iamb or trochee if the two short syllables are read at double speed). When a trochee is substituted for an iamb or a dactyl for an anapest (and vice versa), the result is an inverted foot, in stress prosody sometimes called *inverted stress* or *accent.* The commonest substitution in English verse is the use of a trochee for an iamb at the beginning of a line, as at the opening of Shakespeare's Sonnet XXVII:

Weáry / wĭth toíl / Ĭ háste / mĕ tó / mỹ béd.

SUMMARY: A short restatement of the main points of a book or chapter. A summary may appear as the concluding section of a work.

SURPRISE ENDING: A sudden and unexpected turn in the action at the end of a work, especially common in the short stories of O. Henry.

SURREALISM: A movement, originating in France in the 1920's, which attempted to express in art, primarily in literature and painting, the working of the unconscious. Although the term *Surrealism* was coined by Guillaume Apollinaire, the founder of the movement was the poet André Breton, who, in 1924, issued the first Surrealist manifesto, which explained that a higher reality could be captured by freeing the mind from logic and rational control. Earlier, Breton, influenced by the techniques of Freudian analysis, had been experimenting with automatic writing. The British critic Herbert Read has placed Surrealism in the tradition of Romanticism, a central concept of which has been the exploration of the mind.

Among the painters who have worked in the Surrealist manner are Chirico, Picasso, Tanguy, and Salvador Dali; among the poets, Aragon and Eluard. Both Joyce, especially in *Finnegans Wake,* and Dylan Thomas have been called Surrealists, but the element of conscious control in these writers makes the appellation doubtful.

SUSPENSE: In a literary work, an expectant uncertainty concerning the outcome of the plot. To hold his reader, the writer of a detective story, for example, may resort to sudden disappearances of key characters or the introduction of clues which implicate apparently innocent people, always keeping the final solution just out of sight. In Sophocles' *Oedipus Rex,* suspense is achieved through a withholding of the knowledge that Oedipus himself has killed Laius, his father. During the play, the spectators, aware that Oedipus will eventually make the discovery, share the hero's uncertainties and fears as he pursues the truth of his own past.

SYLLABIC VERSE: Is measured not by stress or quantity (*q.v.*) but by the number of syllables in each line. In English poetry,

Milton and Pope, among others, have written such verse. SYLLEPSIS: A rhetorical figure in which a word brings together two constructions, each of which has a different meaning in connection with the yoking word. Syllepsis may be the result of inept writing or may be used for humorous effect: "Hotchkiss spied on his wife with interest and a telescope." Here, the word *with* involves both accompaniment (*interest*) and means (*telescope*).

SYMBOL: Before a symbol can be defined it must be distinguished from a sign. An object that signifies something else, such as a red light which instructs the motorist to stop, is a sign. To be efficient, the sign must have only one meaning. A symbol, on the other hand, is more complex. In its simplest sense, it is also something that stands for something else. The cross, for example, is a symbol of Christianity, the hammer and sickle of Communism, John Bull of England, etc. Such symbols are more complicated than signs, however, for they sum up a large number of ideas and attitudes and can mean different things in different circumstances. The cross, standing for the whole complex of Christianity, is an object of reverence to some and of contempt to others. Nevertheless, such symbols are public and generally understood.

These symbols are used in literature as in ordinary discourse, but in literature we often find, in addition, symbols of a different sort. Such symbols do not have a publicly accepted meaning but take their significance from the total context in which they appear. (Symbols may also be taken from a special area of knowledge, such as Freudian psychology, or from a private system of the author's; however, the most powerful symbols are usually formed—or, if borrowed, modified—by the works in which they are found.) Thus, the white whale of Melville's *Moby Dick*, one of the most discussed of literary symbols, is simply the animal which Captain Ahab pursues but at the same time much more. As the novel proceeds, Melville associates so much meaning with Moby Dick that the reader accepts him as an object of great significance, as a "grand god": "Moby Dick moved on, still withholding from sight the full terrors of his submerged trunk, entirely hiding the wrenched hideousness of his jaw. But soon the fore part of him slowly rose from the water . . . and warningly waved his bannered flukes in the air, the grand god revealed himself, sounded, and went out of sight." Many critics have discussed the meaning of Moby Dick without final agreement, for such complex symbols do not admit of easy definition and are perhaps expressible only in terms of themselves.

Sometimes, not only an image but an entire work may be taken as a symbol. Thus, the journey of Coleridge's Ancient Mariner may symbolize the universal journey into the depths of despair and back to psychological and spiritual stability.

SYMBOLIC ACTION: In his critical writings, notably *Attitudes toward History* (1937) and *The Philosophy of Literary Form: Studies in Symbolic Action* (1941), Kenneth Burke uses the term *symbolic action* to designate the unconscious or conscious "ritual" which the writer undergoes in the creation of a literary work and which he embodies within it. For the creator, Burke states, the work of art is a "strategy" for handling or controlling his own problems. By disguising his identity, the writer, in the act of creation, performs a symbolic action, that "which a man does because he is interested in doing it exactly as he does it." These symbolic acts center on initiation, rebirth, purification, and other ancient collective ceremonies. Thus, T. S. Eliot's *Murder in the Cathedral* is a purification ritual and Thomas Mann's *Death in Venice* involves a scapegoat ritual, in which the immorality of the artist is punished by death.

Despite Burke's apparent emphasis on the relationship of the work to the artist, he does not slight the effect of the symbolic action on the reader, for he states that, though many of the things that the work does for the artist are not the same for the reader, "if we try to discover what the work is doing for the artist, we may discover a set of generalizations as to what works of art do for everybody."

SYMBOLISM: In *The Symbolist Movement in Literature* (1899), Arthur Symons said that Symbolism was seen "under one disguise or another, in every great imaginative writer." By this, Symons meant that these writers had apprehended and expressed "an unseen reality." Whether or not they did so, the work of many distinguished writers undoubtedly contains symbols and so provides some support for Symons' remark. The term *Symbolism*, however, is commonly used to designate a literary movement which began in France in the latter part of the nineteenth century. Before the movement was given a name, several writers had made conscious use of symbols. Influenced by Swedenborg, Baudelaire said in his sonnet *"Correspondences"* that the world was "a forest of symbols." The morbid images of Parisian life with which he filled his poems were intended not only as descriptions but as expressions of his own spiritual state. Among the other ancestors of the Symbolists were Verlaine, Rimbaud and Mallarmé, the last two visionaries like Baudelaire.

In the mid-1880's, they were discovered by a group of young poets associated with the magazine *Le Décadent*. These poets now called themselves "Symbolists," a word which was defined, or at least described, in a manifesto issued in 1886 by Jean Moréas, who said that the Symbolist poet attempted to express a "primordial Idea" not in itself but through concrete phenomena which were in fact appearances with "esoteric affinities" to it. Among the Symbolists, along with Moréas, were René Ghil, Gustave Khan, Stuart Merrill, and Emile Verhaeren. Other names associated with the movement are Maeterlinck, Villiers de l'Isle Adam, and Jules Laforgue. In England, the Symbolists were admired by George Moore, Symons, and Yeats. The Symbolist movement has influenced such modern poets as T. S. Eliot, Paul Valéry, and Dylan Thomas.

SYNAESTHESIA: The intermingling of sensations; the sensing, for example, of certain sounds through colors or odors. In the late eighteenth and in the nineteenth centuries, there was much interest in synaesthesia, and many attempts to mix the effects of the various arts were made. Baudelaire's sonnet *"Correspondences,"* in which he described certain perfumes as "soft as oboes, green as meadows" is probably the most widely known example. Another is the sonnet called *"Voyelles,"* in which Rimbaud associated a specific color with each of the vowel sounds. Among other writers who made use of the theory of synaesthesia were J. K. Huysmans and Oscar Wilde.

SYNALEPHA: See ELISION.

SYNCOPATION: The simultaneous occurrence in verse of two dif-
erent accentual patterns, one of the meter, the other of normal
speech. In "The Wife of Usher's Well," for example, the basic
meter is iambic. The final line of the second stanza would
normally be scanned thus:

> That her three sons were gane.

The normal speech rhythm, syncopated against the rigid metrical one, is as follows:

> That her three sons were gane.

The speech rhythm may also bring about syncopation by alter-
ing the number of stresses with which a line is read, as in the
second line of Shakespeare's sonnet, which begins:

> Farewell! thou art too dear for my possessing
>
> And like enough thou knowest thy estimate . . .

The scansion above reflects the regular metrical pattern. In fact,
that pattern contrasts with the actual speech pattern below:

> And like enough thou knowest thy estimate.

SYNCOPE: The omission of a letter or a syllable within a word, as
in *o'er* for *over*. See ELISION.

SYNECDOCHE: A figure of speech in which a part represents the
whole object or idea. In Sonnet LV, for example, Shakespeare,
expressing the idea that art is eternal, uses the word *rhyme* to
refer to the entire poem:

> Not marble, nor the gilded monuments
> Of princes, shall outlive this powerful rhyme . . .

SYNONYM: A word which has a meaning identical or closely related to that of another word in the same language. Thus, *king*
is synonymous with *sovereign*.

SYNOPSIS: A condensation of a work; used interchangeably with
the term *summary*.

T

TABLEAU: 1. A stationary, silent grouping of performers in a theatrical production (or sometimes on a float) for a special effect. In the final scene of Gogol's *The Inspector-General,* the announcement that the inspector-general has arrived results in a sudden freeze by the corrupt officials, who form a tableau as the curtain falls.

2. An elaborate stage presentation consisting of dance, pantomime, or ballet in impressive settings.

TAIL-RHYME STANZA: A unit of verse in which a short line, following a group of longer ones, rhymes with a preceding short line. Also called by the French term *rime couée,* the tail-rhyme stanza has a number of variants, but a common form is $aa^4b^3cc^4b^3$. Sometimes the tail-rhyme is used to connect succeeding stanzas. In Shelley's "To Night," the form of the tail-rhyme stanza is as follows:

> Wrap thy form in a mantle gray,
>   Star in-wrought!
> Blind with thine hair the eyes of Day;
> Kiss her until she be wearied out;
> Then wander o'er city and sea and land,
> Touching all with thine opiate wand—
>   Come, long sought.

TALE: In its simplest meaning, a narrative. The term has referred to such realistic stories as Chaucer's *Canterbury Tales* and to such bizarre ones as those written by Poe. Generally, the tale is loosely plotted, told by a narrator, and little concerned with development of character. The term, usually synonymous with *short story,* can refer to a novel, such as Dickens' *A Tale of Two Cities.* It is now frequently used to designate stories which are exotic or adventurous, as in James Michener's *Tales of the South Pacific.*

TALL TALE: A narrative containing extravagant occurrences which are discounted as false. The feats of Paul Bunyan or Mark Twain's story of the remarkable jumping frog are exaggerations worthy of the appellation *tall tale*.

TAUTOLOGY: A pointless repetition of a word or idea, as "Hotchkiss, unfortunately, did not confine his remarks to only one subject."

TELESTICH: See ACROSTIC.

TENOR: See METAPHOR.

TENSION: As used by Allen Tate, the term *tension* designates the totality of meaning in a poem. The term, Tate says, is not used as a general metaphor; it derives from the logical terms *extension* and *intension* (see MEANING) after the prefixes have been removed. According to Tate, a poem has at once literal meaning (extension) and metaphorical (intension). It is the simultaneous existence of these two sets of meaning that Tate refers to as *tension*. An additional meaning of the term involves what the New Critics call "conflict-structures," some of which Robert Penn Warren has listed as follows: ". . . tension between the rhythm of the poem and the rhythm of speech . . . between the formality of the rhythm and the informality of the language; between the particular and the general, the concrete and the abstract; between the elements of even the simplest metaphor; between the beautiful and the ugly; between ideas; between the elements involved in irony; between prosisms and poeticisms."

In the poem's ability to organize tensions, some of the New Critics find a basis upon which they make value judgments.

TERCET: In verse, three lines which constitute a unit. When used interchangeably with the term *triplet, tercet* designates a three-line stanza on a single rhyme. However, the word *tercet* may also be applied to half of the sestet of a Petrarchan sonnet (*q.v.*) and to the *terza rima* stanza (*q.v.*). The tercets (or triplets) below are from Thomas Carew's "Inscription on the Tomb of the Lady Mary Wentworth":

> And here the precious dust is laid;
> Whose purely-tempered clay was made
> So fine, that it the guest betrayed.

Else the soul grew so fast within,
It broke the outward shell of sin,
And so was hatched a cherubin.

TERZA RIMA: A series of interlocking tercets in which the second line of each one rhymes with the first and third lines of succeeding: *aba, bcb, cdc,* etc. Italian in origin, the form was used by Dante in *The Divine Comedy* as well as by Petrarch and Boccaccio. It was introduced into English by Sir Thomas Wyatt in the sixteenth century but, though used (with variations) by such poets as Shelley, Browning, and Auden, has not become genuinely popular. The most famous example of terza rima in English is Shelley's "Ode to the West Wind":

O wild West Wind, thou breath of Autumn's being,
Thou, from whose unseen presence the leaves dead
Are driven, like ghosts from an enchanter fleeing,

Yellow, and black and pale, and hectic red,
Pestilence-stricken multitudes: O thou
Who chariotest to their dark wintry bed

The wingèd seeds, where they lie cold and low,
Each like a corpse within its grave, until
Thine azure sister of the Spring shall blow

Her clarion o'er the dreaming earth, and fill
(Driving sweet buds like flocks to feed in air)
With live hues and odours plain and hill:
Wild Spirit, which art moving everywhere;
Destroyer and preserver; hear, oh, hear!

TETRALOGY: 1. Four works which constitute a group. Shakespeare's history plays are sometimes grouped into two tetralogies: the first consists of the three parts of *Henry VI* and *Richard III,* the second of *Richard II,* the two parts of *Henry IV* and *Henry V.*

2. The four plays submitted for the prize in tragedy in the competition at Athens in the fifth century B.C.—a trilogy of tragedies plus a satyr play (*q.v.*).

TETRAMETER: A line of four metrical feet. Though the following lines contain a variety of feet, they are all tetrameter:

Fe, / Fi, / Fo, / Fum!
I smell / the blood / of an Eng / lishman;
Be he / alive / or be / he dead,
I'll grind / his bones / to make / my bread.

Anonymous

TETRASTICH: A stanza of four lines; a term used synonymously with quatrain.

TEXTURE: See STRUCTURE.

THEME: Sometimes used to indicate the subject of a work, the term *theme* is more frequently employed to designate its central idea or thesis. A theme may be stated directly or indirectly. When not specifically given, it may be abstracted from the work. Keats' "Ode on a Grecian Urn," for example, embodies the themes of the permanence of art and the impermanence of life.

THESIS: 1. A proposition to be maintained, especially one laid down for formal defense or proof.

2. An essay presented by a candidate as partial fulfillment of the requirements for a university degree.

3. In Greek verse, *thesis* was "a putting down" and thus the lowering of the hand or foot on an accented syllable while beating time. By extension, *thesis* came to mean a stressed syllable, as opposed to *arsis* (raising), the unaccented part of a foot of verse. In Latin usage, however, *thesis* and *arsis* referred to the lowering and raising of the voice on unstressed and stressed syllables respectively, reversing the Greek usage. In modern prosody, the Latin usage is the one most commonly found; however, since the Greek is sometimes encountered, confusion, as Fowler has said, "is not unknown." Syllables are spoken of as being "in thesis" or "in arsis."

THESIS NOVEL: A narrative which treats a problem, generally social or political, in order to suggest a thesis. The brutality and senselessness of war, for example, is the thesis of Remarque's *All Quiet on the Western Front*. Used synonymously with *propaganda novel,* the term *thesis novel* indicates the broad category under which two other types may be subsumed. One of these, the sociological novel, emphasizes economic and social conditions and their effects on character. Such works as H. B. Stowe's *Uncle Tom's Cabin* and Steinbeck's *The Grapes of Wrath* are well-known examples. The proletarian novel, while not notably different from the sociological novel, portrays the distressing economic conditions of the working class.

THESIS PLAY: (French: *pièce à thèse*) A drama in which a social problem is illustrated and, usually, a solution suggested. This form originated in nineteenth-century France with such plays as Dumas *fils' Le Fils naturel*. Other examples are the plays of Eugène Brieux and such early plays of Shaw as *Widowers' Houses* and *Mrs. Warren's Profession*. Two other terms often used to characterize plays of this type are *problem play* and *propaganda play,* though the latter suggests more militant works such as Odets' *Waiting for Lefty.* The general type is sometimes called the *drama of ideas.*

THRENODY: From Greek: *threnos,* "lamentation"; *ode,* "song." A lyric lamenting someone's death. In Classical Greek poetry, the threnody was a choral dirge. See MONODY.

TIRADE: In a drama, the French term *tirade* designates a long, uninterrupted speech addressed to one or more characters on stage with the speaker.

TMESIS: The separation of a compound word by the insertion of another word between its two parts, as in "what person soever" for "whatsoever person."

TONE: In general, critics use the term *attitude* to refer to the author's relationship to his material or to his audience or both. These attitudes, as they appear in the work itself, constitute or determine its tone. A speaker indicates tone, at least in part, by changes in voice and manner, but a writer must rely on the verbal devices at his command. In the quatrains below, for example, both Marvell and Herrick handle the traditional *carpe diem* theme (*q.v.*), but the former's tone is one of passionate entreaty, the latter's of gentle persuasion:

> Let us roll all our strength and all
> Our sweetness up into one ball,
> And tear our pleasures with rough strife
> Through the iron gates of life.
>> Marvell, "To His Coy Mistress"

> Gather ye rosebuds while ye may,
> Old Time is still a-flying:

And this same flower that smiles to-day
     To-morrow will be dying.
                    Herrick,
                    "To the Virgins, to Make Much of Time"

For a more restricted use of the word *tone,* see FOUR MEANINGS
OF A POEM.

TOUR DE FORCE: A work offering a striking demonstration of the
author's virtuosity and skill. Such a work may be of considerable
literary distinction, as are Joyce's *Ulysses* and *Finnegans Wake.*
However, the term may also be used to characterize a vapid
presentation which has little quality except its technical skill.

TRACT: A brief essay, usually in the form of a pamphlet, on a
religious or political subject. The famous *Tracts for the Times*
(1833-1841), for example, were a series of papers presenting the
religious views of Newman and others in the Oxford Movement.

TRACTARIAN MOVEMENT: See OXFORD MOVEMENT.

TRAGEDY: Greek: *tragoidia,* "goat song." The term *tragedy* probably refers to an ancient totemic ritual, the sacrifice of a goat,
associated with the god of the fields and vineyards, Dionysus.
In time, contests in the writing of tragedies came to be held as
part of the ceremonies of the Great Dionysia at Athens, the
springtime festival of the death and resurrection of the god.
From these contests developed the body of literature called
Greek tragedy.

In his *Poetics,* written after the great age of Athenian tragedy
had passed, Aristotle defined tragedy as an imitation of an
action that is serious, complete in itself, and of a certain magnitude. He said also that this action roused pity and fear in the
spectators and then purged them of these emotions. The tragic
hero, a man neither villainous nor exceptionally virtuous, moves
from happiness to misery through frailty or some error in judgment.

These and other pronouncements by Aristotle applied well
enough to the body of literature with which he was acquainted,
but since his time many plays unlike those he described have
been called tragedies. The mingling of the serious and the comic
in Elizabethan tragedy, for example, is quite un-Aristotelian, as

is the selection of a character like Macbeth, a man dominated by evil, as tragic hero. In the eighteenth century, serious drama began to concern itself with a hero who was not, as he had been in the drama of the past, a king, aristocrat, or other person of high position, but an ordinary man of the middle classes. In modern drama, he may be a member of the proletariat and the cause of his downfall the evils of society rather than fate or a flaw within himself. When delving into their characters, in fact, modern playwrights find not moral flaws but psychological abnormalities.

Whether or not tragedy is possible in the modern theater is a question that has often been debated but never decided. Such playwrights as Eugene O'Neill and Arthur Miller have used some of the appurtenances of the Classical theater in an attempt to evoke tragic effects, but modern plays that can be described as tragedies are rare, or, perhaps, nonexistent.

See GREEK TRAGEDY, STRUCTURE OF; CATHARSIS; HAMARTIA; HUBRIS; UNITIES OF TIME, PLACE, AND ACTION.

TRAGEDY OF BLOOD: See REVENGE TRAGEDY.

TRAGIC FLAW: The defect in the tragic hero which leads to his downfall; a synonym for *hamartia* (*q.v.*).

TRAGIC IRONY: See IRONY.

TRAGICOMEDY: A play in which the action, though apparently leading to a catastrophe, is reversed to bring about a happy ending. The term is frequently associated with some of the plays of Beaumont and Fletcher, whose *Philaster, or Love Lies A-Bleeding* (ca. 1610) is an example of the form. The typical tragicomedy concerns noble characters involved in improbable situations. Love, frequently seen as a contrast of the pure and the sensual, is the central motive of the elaborate plot, in which both hero and heroine are rescued from imminent disaster so that the play may conclude happily.

Fletcher, defining the term *tragicomedy* in his preface to *The Faithful Shepherdess,* wrote: "A tragicomedy is not so called in respect to mirth and killing, but in respect it wants deaths, which is enough to make it no tragedy, yet brings some near it, which is enough to make it no comedy . . ." The term may be used to characterize such plays as Shakespeare's *Cymbeline* and

The Winter's Tale and, by extension, any play which involves a similar movement of plot.

TRANCHE DE VIE: See SLICE OF LIFE.

TRANSCENDENTALISM, NEW ENGLAND: A movement, most prominent from 1835 to 1845, which was essentially religious and which emphasized the primacy of the individual conscience. Influenced by nineteenth-century philosophical idealism and Christian mysticism, the Transcendentalists (a term first used by their opponents but later accepted by the group) never regarded themselves as a school; in fact, they prided themselves on their lack of accord in matters of doctrine. However, on some principles they were in tacit agreement.

Rejecting the authority of religious dogma, they believed that each man's inner consciousness embodied something divine. In nature, man could find God's moral law, and through his personal experiences with God reveal his own moral being. This idea was presented in Emerson's *Nature* (1836), the first extensive statement of New England Transcendentalism:

> We can foresee God in the coarse, and, as it were, distant phenomena of matter; but when we try to define and describe himself, both language and thought desert us, and we are as helpless as fools and savages. That essence refuses to be recorded in propositions, but when man has worshipped him intellectually, the noblest ministry of nature is to stand as the apparition of God. It is the organ through which the universal spirit speaks to the individual, and strives to lead back the individual to it.

The Transcendentalists believed that truth might be discovered by an intuitive process and morality guided by conscience. Similarly, inspiration could be trusted as a source for artistic creation.

For the most part, the Transcendentalists were social reformers, supporting such issues as temperance, public education, and women's rights. Anti-slavery sentiment among them continued up to the Civil War, by which time Transcendentalism had lost much of its force.

In addition to Emerson and Thoreau, some of the other members of the Transcendentalist group were Theodore Parker,

Bronson Alcott, Margaret Fuller, George Ripley, Orestes Brownson, and Ellery Channing.

TRANSFERRED EPITHET: An adjective used to describe a noun to which it does not normally apply. The transferred epithet is a common poetic device; some examples are "sad storm," "embalmed darkness," and "dreamy house."

TRANSLATION: *Traduttore, traditore* (translator, traitor). The Italian proverb embodies a painful truth: that a faithful translation is a contradiction in terms. In the work of a literary artist, effect, and indeed meaning, depend so precisely upon sound, rhythm, connotation, etc., that to alter any of these elements is to cause distortion and even destruction. From lyric poetry, for example, the translator can often extract little more than a metrical paraphrase. From most prose, narrative verse, or works with a strong intellectual content, however, enough can be salvaged so that the translation is at least a likeness of the original. A reader need not, therefore, ignore Chekov, Tolstoy, and Dostoevsky till he has mastered Russian. He may never learn Greek or Italian, but a readable translation of the *Iliad* or *The Divine Comedy* will give him something, though far from everything, of what is in those works. Occasionally a translation, such as the King James Bible, is so striking that, faithful to the original or not, it becomes a notable work in its own right.

TRAVESTY: See BURLESQUE.

TREATISE: A formal work in which conclusions are supported by the systematic examination of a body of evidence or principles.

TRIAD: The strophe, antistrophe, and epode of the Pindaric ode. See ODE.

TRIBRACH: A foot of three short or unstressed syllables; uncommon in English verse.

TRILOGY: 1. Any three works composed as a continuous story, such as the three parts of Shakespeare's *Henry VI* or John Dos Passos' *U.S.A.* (1930-36), consisting of *The 42nd Parallel, Nineteen-Nineteen,* and *The Big Money.*

2. In ancient Greek drama, the three tragedies which presented the development of a legend or myth. Such trilogies as Aeschylus' *Oresteia* (fifth century B.C.), dramatizing the Aga-

memnon—Orestes myth, were performed at religious festivals. See TETRALOGY.

TRIMETER: A line of verse consisting of three metrical feet, as in the first, second, and fifth lines of this limerick:

> There's a not / able clan / named Stein:
> There's Gertrude, there's Ep and there's Ein.
>   Gert's prose has no style,
>   Ep's statues are vile,
> And nobody understands Ein.
>
> *Anonymous*

TRIOLET: One of the French fixed forms of verse, used by English poets, especially the Parnassians (*q.v.*), in the late nineteenth century. Containing only two rhymes, the triolet has a total of eight lines: the first two are repeated as the last two; the fourth is the same as the first. The rhyme scheme is thus *abaaabab*.

TRIPLE METER: One with three syllables to the metrical foot.

TRIPLE RHYME: See FEMININE RHYME.

TRIPLE RHYTHM: A synonym for triple meter (*q.v.*).

TRIPLET: See TERCET.

TRISTICH: A stanza of three lines. See TERCET.

TRITAGONIST: In ancient Greek drama, the third actor, added by Sophocles. Generally, the three actors assumed various roles in the play by changing masks and costumes. See DEUTERAGONIST and PROTAGONIST.

TRIVIUM: See SEVEN ARTS, THE.

TROBAR CLUS: In the twelfth century, certain of the troubadour poets, such as Marcabru, Peire d'Auvergne, and Giraut de Bornelh, adopted a deliberately difficult, almost private style called the *trobar clus,* in which the complexity of phraseology made the poet's meaning difficult to ascertain. This style was opposed to the *trobar clar,* or "open" writing. It has been suggested that an English analogue which gives some idea of the nature and difficulty of the *trobar clus* style is Donne's "Nocturnal upon St. Lucy's Day."

TROCHEE: A foot of verse consisting of two syllables, the first stressed, the following unstressed, as in this example in which the first and third lines are trochaic:

Síng a̅ / sóng o̅f / síxpe̅nce
A pocket full of rye
Four and twenty blackbirds,
Baked in a pie.
Anonymous

TROPE: 1. Used in the eighteenth century to designate elaborate figurative language, the term *trope* (from Greek: "a turn") is less frequently employed in modern literary discussions. The term *figure of speech* is now more currently used to refer to language which departs from its literal meaning. Among the major tropes are metaphor, simile, hyperbole, personification, and metonomy (*qq.v.*). Some forms of irony (*q.v.*) are also considered tropes when the ironical expression involves the reverse of the literal meaning.

2. An interpolated amplification of phrases or passages in the services of the medieval church. See LITURGICAL DRAMA.

TROUBADOUR: A member of the class of lyric poets whose activities were centered in Southern France in the twelfth and thirteenth centuries. Though some of them lived in northern Italy and northeastern Spain, they wrote in *langue d'oc* (the dialects of southern France), loosely called Provençal.

The troubadour, writing of love and chivalry, often addressed his poems to a noble lady, usually married, whom he served and revered in the tradition of courtly love (*q.v.*). Interest in metrical technique led to the development of many intricate fixed forms. Among the most famous Provençal poets were William, Count of Poitiers; Arnaut Daniel; and Bertran de Born.

Troubadour poetry, influential in the Renaissance, contributed to the development of the *dolce stil nuovo* (*q.v.*), which achieved its greatest expression in the poetry of Dante. See TROUVÈRE.

TROUVÈRE: One of a class of court poets of northern France who wrote at the same time as the troubadours of southern France and were much influenced by them. The *trouvères* wrote love lyrics, chivalric romances, and *chansons de gestes*. Among the latter are the Arthurian romances of Chrétien de Troyes.

TRUNCATED LINE: See ACATALECTIC.

TUMBLING VERSE: See SKELTONIC VERSE.
TYPE CHARACTER: See STOCK AND TYPE CHARACTERS.

U

UBI SUNT THEME: So called from the opening words *ubi sunt* (Latin: "where are") of a number of medieval Latin poems. The *ubi sunt* formula often appears within a poem as a repetend (*q.v.*), or refrain. One of the most famous examples of this theme, which expresses the mutability of things, is François Villon's *Ballade* (*des dames du temps jadis*), of which the most famous line is the refrain, *"Mais où sont les neiges d'antan"* ("Where are the snows of yesteryear?"). The poem has been translated into English by Dante Gabriel Rossetti as "The Ballad of Dead Ladies."

UNDERSTATEMENT: See MEIOSIS.

UNITIES: The three unities of the drama are action, time, and place. In the *Poetics,* Aristotle said that a play should be the imitation of a single action, the parts of which were to be so arranged that if any of them were removed, or shifted, the whole would suffer. He also indicated that the action of tragedy was limited to a day or slightly more. The Italian and French critics of the Renaissance made the unities strict laws, limiting the action to twenty-four hours and, with the introduction of unity of place, not mentioned by Aristotle, limited the scene to a single place or city. This interpretation of *les unités scaligeriennes* (so called although Scaliger had not insisted on them) often made for a crowded day in the life of the hero but the rule of the unities, despite protests from such writers as Lope de Vega and Molière, was not really broken till the time of Victor Hugo. In English drama, the unities have not usually been observed, although a writer will sometimes follow them for dramatic intensity. An example of a modern play composed strictly according to the unities is Tennessee Williams' *Cat on a Hot Tin Roof.*

UNITY: A unified work has a logical relationship of part to part within the whole. Although it has been maintained from the time of the Classical critics that the best works are coherent, self-contained, and free of episodes irrelevant to the work's purpose, the source of this element of unity has not always been agreed upon. The validity of the rules of dramatic construction called *the unities* (*q.v.*) has been much debated. The *Odyssey*, though episodic, is said to be unified by the presence of Odysseus. Similarly, unity of theme may bind together the disparate parts of such a work as *Henry IV, Part I*. However achieved, unity remains one of the criteria of literary judgment.

UNIVERSALITY: A quality which endows a literary work with significance not limited to a particular time and place. A work is regarded as having universality when, through its capacity to reveal human nature and the problems which face man, we recognize the truth contained within it. Sophocles' *Antigone*, for example, is not limited in significance to a specific culture because it is a Greek play based on ancient myth. Rather, by its dramatic skill, its magnitude and power of expression, it presents problems which involve all men as well as the individual characters of the play. Consequently, to call it a "Greek play" is only to describe its origins; its universality lies in its capacity to transcend the limitations of time and space within which the work was created.

UNIVERSITY WITS: A name applied to a number of young men who, arriving in London from Oxford and Cambridge in the 1580's, were influential in the development of Elizabethan literature. The wits included John Lyly, George Peele, Robert Greene, Thomas Lodge, Christopher Marlowe, and Thomas Kyd, the last considered one of the group though he had received his education at the excellent Merchant Taylor's School rather than at a university. Although the wits were not a literary school with common principles, among them they established or contributed to a number of the types of Elizabethan drama, such as the revenge tragedy (Kyd), the romantic comedy (Peele, Greene), and the history play (Marlowe, Peele), and did important work in other fields.

UPANISHADS: The major theological works of ancient Hinduism, consisting of mystical and philosophical writings in prose. Dated later than the *Vedas* (*q.v.*), the *Upanishads* (meaning "a sitting down at the feet of a master") emphasize Brahma as the supreme creating God. First made known in Europe in the eighteenth century, the *Upanishads* have influenced such writers as Schopenhauer, Carlyle, Emerson, and Yeats.

UTOPIAN LITERATURE: (*outopos*—Greek: "nowhere"). A type of literature in which an ideal society is depicted. The word *utopia* was first applied to this genre by Sir Thomas More in his work *Utopia* (1516). Like other writers who have envisioned perfect societies, he was influenced by Plato's *Republic,* which, in its emphasis on communism, established the pattern for many utopias to follow. During the Renaissance, not only More but also Rabelais, Campanella (*Civitas Solis,* 1623), and Bacon (*New Atlantis,* 1627) presented their visions of ideal societies. In modern times, Samuel Butler's *Erewhon* (1872), an anagram for *"nowhere,"* Bellamy's *Looking Backward* (1888), William Morris' *News from Nowhere* (1890), and H. G. Wells' *A Modern Utopia* (1905) have been contributions to the growing body of utopian literature.

V

VARIABLE SYLLABLE: One which may be stressed or unstressed in the scansion of a line of verse according to the demands of the metrical pattern.

VARIORUM EDITION: From Latin: *cum notis variorum,* "with notes of various persons." 1. An edition of a writer's work containing variant readings of the text and critical commentary and interpretation by prominent scholars and authors. *The New Variorum Shakespeare,* edited by Furness, is such an edition.

2. An edition presenting variant versions of an author's works, such as *The Variorum Edition of the Poems of W. B. Yeats,* edited by Alspach and Allt, in which a scholar may compare the changes which Yeats made in his poems.

VATES: Latin: "prophet." From earliest times, the poet has often been considered a seer or *vates,* divinely inspired, and his pronouncements have been accorded the status of prophecy. Virgil, for example, was believed to have predicted the future literally in his *Fourth Eclogue,* which celebrated the birth of a child who was to bring back the Age of Gold. For hundreds of years, the poem was read as a pagan prophecy of the birth of Christ and Virgil held to be a *vates.*

VAUDEVILLE: In modern American usage, a theatrical presentation consisting of a sequence of songs, dances, and other acts. Originally, the term, as used in France, referred to comic or satirical songs about well-known personalities. It later designated a light play with comic songs, or *vaudevilles,* interspersed. In this sense, the term has been used in English, but is no longer common.

VEDA: Sanskrit: "knowledge." The holy scripture of Hinduism, consisting of the four Books of Wisdom, each having the word *Veda* in its title: *Rig-Veda* (psalms or hymns) is the earliest and most important; containing over a thousand poems, the *Rig-Veda* is often allegorical and metaphysical. The others are the *Arthava-Veda* (spells, incantations); the *Yajur-Veda* (litanies and prayer-formulas); and the *Sama-Veda* (chants and hymns). It is believed that these writings date from between 1300-1000 B.C.

VEHICLE: See METAPHOR.

VERBAL IRONY: See IRONY.

VERISIMILITUDE: A quality possessed by a work the action and characters of which seem to the reader sufficiently probable to constitute an acceptable representation of reality. What degree of probability, or likeness to fact, is necessary to achieve verisimilitude has never been finally ascertained. For some, a close depiction of actuality, such as that found in Steinbeck's *Grapes of Wrath,* is required. For others, a degree of imaginative power sufficient to capture the reader's belief gives the work this quality however fantastic the events depicted. In this sense, even such a work as the *Rime of the Ancient Mariner* may be said to have verisimilitude.

VERISM: The doctrine that literature should represent unadorned reality even when it is sordid and ugly.

VERS DE SOCIETE: French: "society verse." A type of light verse which deals gracefully with polite society and its concerns. *Vers de société,* which often makes use of such French fixed forms as the rondeau and the villanelle (*qq.v.*), is usually witty, sometimes gently satiric, often elegantly amorous. An example is the mock epitaph suggested by the Earl of Rochester for Charles II:

> Here lies our sovereign lord the King,
> Whose word no man relies on;
> He never says a foolish thing,
> Nor ever does a wise one.

VERSE: 1. Lines arranged in metrical patterns; the term *verse* is sometimes distinguished from *poetry* (*q.v.*).

2. A single line of a poem.

VERSE PARAGRAPH: A group of lines, frequently in blank verse, arranged as a rhetorical unit similar to a paragraph in prose. Milton's *Paradise Lost* and Wordsworth's *The Prelude,* for example, are constructed of verse paragraphs.

VERS LIBRE· See FREE VERSE.

VERSO: See RECTO AND VERSO.

VIEWPOINT: See POINT OF VIEW.

VIGNETTE: A sketch or other brief literary work characterized by precision and delicacy of composition. A vignette may also be a section of a longer work.

VILLAIN: An evil character who acts in opposition to the hero. Sometimes, however, a writer centers his interest on a villain (*Macbeth,* Molière's *Don Juan*), and in other cases the villain comes dangerously close to seizing the major share of the attention in spite of the author (*Othello, Paradise Lost*).

VILLANELLE: One of the French fixed forms. Originally pastoral in subject matter (the name derives from *villa,* a farm or country house), it is often used for light verse. There are five tercets followed by a quatrain, all on two rhymes. The opening line is repeated at the ends of tercets two and four; the final line of the first tercet concludes the third and fifth. The two refrain lines are repeated at the end of the quatrain.

> A dainty thing's the Villanelle
>   Sly, musical, a jewel in rhyme,
> It serves its purpose passing well.
>
> A double-clappered silver bell
>   That must be made to clink in chime,
> A dainty thing's the Villanelle;

And if you wish to flute a spell,
  Or ask a meeting 'neath the lime,
It serves its purpose passing well.

You must not ask of it the swell
  Of organs grandiose and sublime—
A dainty thing's the Villanelle;

And, filled with sweetness, as a shell
  Is filled with sound, and launched in time,
It serves its purpose passing well.

Still fair to see and good to smell
  As in the quaintness of its prime,
A dainty thing's the Villanelle,
It serves its purpose passing well.

W. E. Henley, "Villanelle"

VIRELAY: (Also French, *virelai*). A name applied to either of two verse forms, neither of which is strictly fixed, derived from old French poetry. One, used for a poem of limited length, has only two rhymes; the first and second lines appear alternately as refrains. The other has an indefinite number of stanzas, each having two rhymes, one rhyme in long lines, the other in short. The short lines of one stanza provide the rhyme for the long lines of the next, the short lines of the last stanza rhyming with the long lines of the first. Neither form is common in English.

VIRGULE: A short, slanting line used in prosody to divide lines into feet, as in the following:

The Owl / and the Pus / sy-cat went / to sea
In a beau / tiful pea / green boat.

VOLTA: The turn in thought in a sonnet, usually at the end of the octet. An example is found in Shakespeare's Sonnet XXXIII, part of which appears below, in which he describes the sun first rising gloriously but then clouded over:

Anon permit the basest clouds to ride
With ugly rack on his celestial face,
And from the forlorn world his visage hide,
Stealing unseen to west with this disgrace:

(Volta) **Even so my sun** one early morn did shine,
        With all-triumphant splendour on my brow;
        But, out! alack! he was but one hour mine,
        The region cloud hath mask'd him from me now.

VORTICISM: A brief literary movement centering around the magazine *Blast, Review of the Great English Vortex,* which appeared
only twice, once in 1914 and again in 1915. Edited by Wyndham
Lewis, it printed some of the early work of T. S. Eliot and Ezra
Pound. These men, influenced by the English critic T. E.
Hulme, opposed the diffuse romanticism of English verse current at the time; they wished instead to establish a cool, precise
"classic" style. Though both Pound and Eliot did some of their
best work during the Vorticist period (Pound wrote the Mauber-
ley poems and Eliot those about Apeneck Sweeney) the magazine, something of a joke, was an extreme expression of their
views. After its early collapse, the members of the group pursued
their separate careers.

W

WARDOUR-STREET ENGLISH: A style which utilizes archaic diction
in an attempt to achieve elegance. The term, which is regularly
pejorative, refers to spurious expression; it is derived from
Wardour Street in London where there are many dealers in
imitation as well as genuine antiques.

WEAK ENDING: A syllable at the end of a line of verse which,
though stressed metrically, is unstressed in ordinary speech and
which calls for little or no pause before the next line, as in the
case of *and* in the following lines from Shakespeare's *The Tempest:*

> Thy mother was a piece of virtue, and
> She said thou wast my daughter.

WELL-MADE PLAY: (French: *pièce bien faite*) A type of play constructed according to a formula which originated in France in
the early nineteenth century and has remained influential. The
inventor and most prolific practitioner of the art of the well-

made play was Eugène Scribe (1791-1861), the seventy-six volumes of whose complete works contain some three hundred seventy-four plays, opera librettos and other theatrical pieces, many of them, however, collaborations. Scribe took the devices which had been part of comedy since the time of Menander and, with great technical skill, wove them into an unvarying formula.

The plot of a well-made play regularly revolves about a secret known only to some of the characters; revealed at the climax, it leads to the downfall of the villain and the triumph of the hero. The action, which centers on a conflict—especially a duel of wits—between the hero and his opponent builds with increasing intensity through a series of reversals which culminate in the climactic revelation scene. Misunderstandings, compromising letters, precisely timed entrances and exits, and other such devices contribute to the suspense. The *dénouement* is always carefully prepared and, within the framework of the manipulated action, believable.

Scribe's disciple was Victorien Sardou (1831-1908), from whose name Bernard Shaw coined the term *Sardoodledom* to describe this type of play-making. Scribe's *The Glass of Water* and Sardou's *A Scrap of Paper* (whose title suggests the sort of props with which well-made plays are replete) are among their best-known plays. The well-made play provided the form for the developing social drama of Augier and Dumas *fils* and influenced Ibsen, Wilde, Shaw, and innumerable others.

WIT: The term *wit* has, in critical and general usage, undergone periodic change so that its meanings, overlapping from period to period, have at any one time been numerous. In the Renaissance, the word *wit* meant "intelligence" or "wisdom," as in Spenser's sonnet which celebrates true beauty:

> Men call you fair, and you do credit it,
> For that your self ye daily such do see:
> But the true fair, that is the gentle wit,
> And virtuous mind, is much more praised of me.

During the seventeenth century, the term *wit* meant "fancy," (*q.v.*) implying such nimbleness of thought and such originality in figures of speech as was found in the Metaphysical poetry (*q.v.*)

of John Donne and others. In the latter half of the century, the meaning of *wit* changed. For Hobbes (in the *Leviathan*, 1651) judgment rather than fancy was the principal element of wit, and, in fact, he felt that wit could be achieved by judgment alone. The excess of fancy, he remarked later, resulted in a loss of delight in wit. As a poetic faculty, true wit was the poet's ability to see similarities in apparently dissimilar things. False wit, as later described by Addison, involved the association of words rather than of ideas; such linguistic devices as puns, anagrams, acrostics, etc., he listed as types of such wit.

In a famous passage from "An Essay on Criticism," Pope contrasts true wit, with its emphasis on judgment, with merely fanciful writing:

> Poets, like painters, thus, unskilled to trace
> The naked nature and the living grace,
> With gold and jewels cover every part,
> And hide with ornaments their want of art.
> True wit is Nature to advantage dressed,
> What oft was thought, but ne'er so well expressed.

In modern times, *wit* is limited to intellectually amusing utterances calculated to delight and surprise. See HUMOR.

WORD ACCENT: See ACCENT.

WRENCHED ACCENT: See ACCENT.

Z

ZEUGMA: A rhetorical figure in which a single word, standing in relationship to two others, is correctly related to only one. Unlike a syllepsis (*q.v.*), which is grammatically correct, a zeugma involves a failure of the single word to give meaning to one of the pair with which it is connected. In the commonly recognized zeugma from Shakespeare's *Henry V* "Kill the boys and the luggage!" the verb *kill* does not apply to *luggage;* instead, a word such as *destroy* must be supplied to complete the meaning of the statement.

A selected list of entries
arranged by subject

CHARACTER

Alazon
Antagonist
Braggadocio
Caricature
Confidant
Deuteragonist
Flat and round characters
Hero-heroine
Miles gloriosus
Protagonist
Raisonneur
Stock and type characters
Tritagonist
Villain

CRITICAL TERMS

Aesthetic distance
Affective fallacy
Ambiguity
Appollonian-Dionysian
Archetype
Concrete universal
Dissociation of sensibility
Four levels of meaning
Hebraism-Hellenism
Intentional fallacy
Objective correlative
Pathetic fallacy
Pseudo statement
Symbolic action

DRAMA

DRAMATIC ELEMENTS

Act
Agon
Aside
Catharsis

Chorus
Coup de théâtre
Deus ex machina
Hamartia
Hubris
Obligatory scene
Parabasis
Scene
Soliloquy
Stichomythia
Unities

DRAMATIC TYPES

Boulevard drama
Bourgeois drama
Burletta
Capa y espada
Cavalier drama
Chronicle play
Closet drama
Comédie larmoyante
Comedy of Humours
Comedy of Intrigue
Comedy of Manners
Commedia dell'arte
Domestic tragedy
Drama
Farce
Heroic drama
High comedy
History play
Interlude
Kabuki
Liturgical drama
Living Newspaper
Melodrama
Mime
Miracle

Morality
Mystery
New Comedy
Nō drama
Passion play
Restoration comedy
Revenge play
Satyr play
School play
Sentimental comedy
Thesis play
Tragedy
Tragicomedy
Well-made play

FIGURES OF SPEECH

Epic simile
Hyperbole
Metaphor
Metonymy
Oxymoron
Paradox
Personification
Pun
Simile
Synecdoche

LITERARY MOVEMENTS

Aestheticism
Classicism
Dadaism
Decadence
Expressionism
Georgian poetry
Graveyard School
Imagism

Impressionism
Irish Literary Renaissance
Naturalism
Neo-Classicism
Parnassianism
Pleiade
Pre-Raphaelites
Realism
Romanticism
Sturm und Drang
Surrealism
Symbolism
Transcendentalism
Vorticism

NARRATIVE TYPES

Allegory
Autobiography
Beast Epic
Bestiary
Bildungsroman
Biography
Detective story
Dream allegory
Epistolary novel
Exemplum
Fable
Fabliau
Gothic novel
Historical novel
Kunstlerroman
Novel
Picaresque novel
Psychological novel
Roman à clef
Saga
Sentimental novel

Tale
Thesis novel

PROSODY

PROSODIC ELEMENTS

Acatalectic
Accent
Alexandrine
Alliteration
Amphibrach
Amphimac
Anacrusis
Antistrophe
Assonance
Caesura
Consonance
Feminine rhyme
Foot
Incremental repetition
Leonine rhyme
Masculine rhyme
Meter
Quantity
Refrain
Repetend
Rhyme
Rhythm
Running rhythm
Run-on line
Slack
Sprung rhythm

PROSODIC FORMS

Aubade
Ballad

Ballade
Ballad stanza
Blank verse
Burns stanza
Canso
Canzone
Chanson de geste
Clerihew
Complaint
Couplet
Curtal sonnet
Eclogue
Elegy
Epic
Free verse
Heroic couplet
Idyll
Lay
Limerick
Mock epic
Ode
Ottava rima

Rhyme royal
Rondeau
Rondel
Roundel
Rubaiyat
Sestina
Skeltonic verse
Sonnet
Spenserian stanza
Tail-rhyme stanza
Terza rima
Villanelle
Virelay

RHETORICAL FIGURES

Apostrophe
Chiasmus
Invocation
Rhetorical Question
Zeugma

NOONDAY PAPERBACKS
available at your bookstore